SOCIAL CHANGE AT WORK

Social Change
at Work

The ICI
Weekly Staff Agreement

Joe Roeber

Duckworth

First published in 1975 by
Gerald Duckworth & Company Limited,
The Old Piano Factory,
43 Gloucester Crescent, London NW1

© 1975 Joe Roeber

ISBN 0 7156 0867 3

Typeset by
Specialised Offset Services Ltd, Liverpool
Printed by
Garden City Press, Letchworth

Contents

Acknowledgments

Too many people helped me in the writing of this book for it to be possible to thank them all adequately. I owe a special debt to Geoffrey Gilbertson, who sold me (not a hard job) on the idea of writing about WSA, and Jim Bell, who took over the role of helping the book forward. More generally, I want to thank the many managers, shop stewards and shopfloor workers in ICI and trade union officials who spent so much time with me. Most of those I would thank by name if I had the space are mentioned in the index. Some who are not are: Trevor Owen and Don Wilson in Central Personnel; Dugald Mitchell at Wilton; John Rousseau, who helped particularly with Chapter 13; Sarah Stewart, who provided the man-power figures; Nancy Taylor, who guided me through the dusty and cavernous files of Central Personnel; Maureen Coombes and Sheila Tracy, who typed and re-typed the manuscript; and Brian Delf, who drew the charts. I would also like to thank friends who forced their way through the rambling, tangled first draft and suggested ways of making it slightly less so: Bill Daniels of PEP; Charles Handy of the London Business School; Innis MacBeath, then of *The Times*; and people in ICI who checked particular parts for accuracy. (Needless to say, any mistakes are my own.) Colleagues at Imperial College, both in the Department of Management Science and the Industrial Sociology Unit, also provided valuable help.

Lastly, I want to thank two people whose help started even before the book was thought of: Bill Pounds, Dean of MIT's Sloan School, who gave me the chance to get away from *The Times* for a splendid year as a Sloan Fellow; and my wife, Anne, who has borne the whole lengthy business with angelic sweetness. To these are owed my very special thanks.

List of Illustrations

Introduction

There was a time, and it was not so long ago, when people were comfortably taken for granted in business organisations. This was not, or not altogether, because managers were indifferent to them but because the problem of reconciling the complex and diverse needs of individuals with the simple but stern requirements of the workplace was not urgent enough to claim management attention. The salient problems for managers were technical, financial, commercial . . . the hard, specific, finite problems of business which even now are regarded as the proper area of management interest. In times of high unemployment, or when — which comes to the same thing, as an influence on behaviour — there are lively expectations of unemployment, human problems were mediated away in the marketplace. But, as has been abundantly demonstrated in recent years, times have changed and human problems have moved to the·top of the pile. The name of the management game, which used to be called 'technical problem-solving' (or something similar), is changing. The change is resisted by the hard men of business — who include many successful managers — because human problems belong in a soft, low-status area traditionally occupied by ex-officers and other marginal men. But when the very existence of companies, and even of Britain, can be threatened by labour problems there is no denying the importance of solving them.

Some would argue that this change reflects a loosening of the essential disciplines of a healthy society; that it is all of a piece with the decline of religion, long hair, drug-taking and Women's Lib. And so it is, but not in the sense that is usually meant of a decline from fixed standards. Such changes have it in common with strikes, Monday morning absenteeism, high labour turnover and restrictive practices that they represent the assertion by individuals or groups of their own self-interest in the face of the traditional values — and, by some standards, against the best interests — of society as a whole. If assumptions about what a management can demand of a workforce have been challenged, so have assumptions about the rule of law, the place of authority, the duty that a citizen owes to his state. Such ideas used to be contained in the phrase 'the social contract', invented by political philosophers to explain the otherwise puzzling willingness of citizens to subordinate their individual self-interest to that of the State, even to laying down their lives for it. It involved the whole people and its rulers, and was held together, defined almost, by the willing acceptance of laws designed to secure the common good. But no contract is eternal. At any point of time, the terms of the social contract reflect the balance of power within society. When the balance shifts so must the contract, or lose its force. (Indeed, before Mr Harold Wilson cleverly appropriated the term for his voluntary incomes policy, this book was to have been called "Steps to a New Social Contract".) Hobbes described the lot of man alone, without society, in a famous passage: 'No arts; no letters; no society; and which is worst of all, continual fear and danger of violent death; and the life of man, solitary, brutish and short . . .' We are not yet there. But it seems to me that the old industrial order has not so much changed as broken down. And this breakdown has contributed as much as anything to an industrial performance which is so abysmal that it has raised questions about Britain's ability to retain a place among major industrial powers of the world.

It is an extraordinary situation to be facing the very country in which the industrial revolution started; one which was, not so long ago, the richest and most powerful country in the world. And it is tempting to look back into the golden past for solutions. After all, they managed things better in those days. 'The right to manage . . .' 'A fair day's work . . .', 'People knew their place . . .': the phrases come easily. The prescriptions follow: bring back the Rule of Law, make contracts enforceable, outlaw unofficial strikes.

If the old industrial order of Britain had had anything to do with the Rule of Law, there would be more point in attempting to revive it. But the old order had more to do with the Rule of Privation: the high unemployment and low wages that put great power into the hands of people who could offer employment. There was no 'right to manage', only (and far more effective than such a diffuse moral injunction) the crude power to enforce managerial will; none of the detached and equal relationship suggested in 'a fair day's work' when what constituted fairness was unilaterally defined; none of the willing compliance implied in 'knowing one's place', when there was no choice for the individual to do otherwise.

Moreover, there is a moral tone to the old order which, when it comes to looking for the way ahead, is positively dangerous. Perhaps it is just that naked power is uncomfortable, even embarrassing, to live with, so that society has preferred to cover it with a scrap from the cloak of a larger morality — which serves to rationalise and domesticate some pretty stark facts about the unequal distribution of power in society. It is the frustration of a thwarted sense of moral order that has generated the high pressure of indignation over the unions' recent use of their power. But it *is* misleading in the context of industry, because to apply the measure of a by now antique (and in any terms highly suspect) social morality can tell us very little about the underlying shifts which have brought about the changes in behaviour at the surface. Still less can such an analysis help us to respond imaginatively and constructively to the changes. The moral order is unchangeable and a moral view can only lead back.

I do not mean to suggest that a moral view of social order is out of place; on the contrary. But if the social contract is being 'broken' at the workplace, we ought to ask on what basis it had been agreed before attempting to remake it in the old image. Inasmuch as there was a social contract implied in the wage/work bargain, it was very far from the voluntary abnegation of personal desires in the broader social interest that is implied by that term. It does not require much imagination to see how very far from voluntary has been that self-abnegation, how coercive has been the economic system which enforced it and how far it served the interests of the dominant economic groups. The coercive power of the economic system, direct and referred, has greatly declined in the recent years of relative affluence and full employment. People are no longer so easily forced to abnegate individual desires by the threat of privation (or the promise of salvation). But the existence of society requires, is defined by, some degree of self-abnegation, whether it be willing — as political philosophers would have — or coerced.

People are inconveniently stubborn, for their rulers: given choice, they will exercise it in what they see to be their own interest. I have suggested elsewhere* that, as individual choice — which is to say discretion, or power in decision-making — becomes increasingly available, industrialised society must move towards a "voluntary society". The defining characteristic of such a society would be the ownership by an individual of the decisions affecting his life, and therefore his commitment to them. Commitment was assumed in the social contract of political philosophers, but not power over the decisions. So it is in the workplace. It seems obvious that the industrial troubles we are experiencing in some form throughout the Western world derive, as much as anything else, from the fact that the new realities of power have not been reflected in the terms of the social contract at work. The worker may now have the power but he is not being given the opportunity to exercise choice within the system. It is not surprising that he should therefore choose to exercise it, disruptively, outside. It is no longer possible to assume the participation of people in an older social contract, yet this is the assumption on which industry is still run — and on which governments still govern. A new contract is needed, based on the principle of an individual's owning the decisions affecting his life. It is my view that the development of productivity bargaining has comprised a step towards that new contract. Before looking at the attempts of one particular company to work out its new social contract, I want first to discuss how the redistribution of power has manifested itself inside industry as a whole.

The force for change

There is rage because the unions are perceived to be acting against the economic interests of the country. But as far as they are concerned, they are merely acting in the interests of their own members. I think we can assume that their interest can be defined in terms that are not much different today

---

* In the first part of my book, *Organisations in a Changing Environment.*

from what they were for their fathers — or for nearly anybody. Most people want a better life (however one defines it); they want secure work; perhaps they want commitment and satisfaction in their work, though this is more debatable (projection of a middle-class value?); they want the freedom to choose what they will do. What has changed is the power that is now in the hands of the unions, and of industrial workers generally, to enforce these wishes. And where a government, acting to restrain pay or to limit the power of unions, is seen to be threatening those interests, it can expect to be resisted.

The power has two sources: economic and political. I spoke earlier about the Rule of Privation, the environment within which the old industrial order operated and in which were formed its characteristic assumptions. Where there is affluence, the old sanctions have much reduced force: sack a man in a time of full employment and he will walk down the road to more money. Thus affluence works two ways. First: by diminishing the 'rights' of managers. (There still remains a managerial task but the exercise of arbitrary authority is not the only way to perform it, although traditional.) Secondly, affluence gives to the worker, through more money and multiple job opportunities, the chance to exercise choice in his own interest. And better education, television and travel give him a wider range of 'life models' to choose between. In these ways affluence, even limited British affluence, has shifted the balance of power between labour and capital towards labour, and for this reason alone man-management issues have become salient features in decision-making — where they had previously been taken care of by the environment.

At a 'political' or non-market, level, the unions have acquired considerable monopoly power, buttressed by special privileges, which has enabled them successfully to apply pressure to companies on behalf of their members. Obviously this shift is closely connected with the changes in the labour market. That the political power can be used independently, however, is demonstrated by the ability of unions to hold wages, and even demand increases, in times of increasing unemployment. The strength gained by unions through grouping men into large bargaining units — a process that goes back much further than the onset of affluence —

represents another element in the shift of power towards labour.

Lastly, with the development of technically more complex industrial processes, the jobs are becoming increasingly skilled and responsible.* This is a change which is more specific to a company like ICI, where technological progress is rapid, and results in ever larger and more costly plants with more complex instrumentation. Mistakes are becoming intolerably expensive, and the training the worker receives and the care he takes at his job become increasingly important. Again, this represents a shift of power toward labour — certainly in relation to times when manual workers were 'hands', interchangeable for the convenience of the process at the will of management.

The net result has been greatly to increase the power of shopfloor workers to make their wishes felt. But neither the wishes nor the machinery through which they become influential have adapted to this new reality. A perfectly responsive system adapts to change without lag; social systems are not like that. The changes in the power structure have, as a result, taken place beneath an undisturbed surface of inherited assumptions and institutional arrangements. This should not surprise us: values and institutions, because serving a wider range of needs than the ones that brought them into being, have a vitality which enables them long to outlive their initial purposes. More broadly, even if complex systems did not have the property (essential to survival) of resisting change in the interests of internal stability, the individuals of which they are made up have their own personal investments in existing relationships. As a result, the new realities manifest themselves within the old forms, usurping them, an unsuspected new hand within an old glove. But the old forms are also subtly influential, shaping and guiding — and limiting — the new power as it emerges.

A number of closely-related changes in Britain's industrial relations have resulted from this shift in power. I shall mention only three that are notably at odds with inherited

---

* Although the opposite has been notoriously true of the kind of assembly-line operations found in the motor industry.

assumptions and formal systems of control.

First, there has been a progressive diminution of the area of management discretion in postwar years. In times of high unemployment and low wages, that discretion was once almost complete. The balance has now swung so that workers, shop stewards and the official union organisation have been able to claim progressively more of the intervening decision-making territory. The ability of managers to make decisions without reference to any of these groups is now limited. It is impossible to generalise across industries or between different parts of the country, but it is probably fair to say that technical problem-solving is the last remaining bastion of management discretion, and even there it is limited when decisions lead to significant changes in the workforce. But the assumption of managerial prerogatives — which has, as I have said, acquired almost moral overtones (a sure sign that it has lost its real force) — remains in the traditional managerial consciousness, to shape management responses. Even now, as witness the values that were implicit in the 1972 Industrial Relations Act, there appears to be a widespread belief that present conditions are a temporary lapse from normality: given time, a touch of unemployment and the reassertion of ancient disciplines, everyone will come to their senses and the good old days will return. But redundancy and discipline have been firmly taken into the negotiating region. They are not likely to be returned to the managers. One of the problems we shall come to arises from managers' unwillingness to accept that their immemorial rights and privileges are no longer absolute but contingent on the approval of the managed.

Secondly, the unions no less than management pursue goals that belong to the past and within a framework of assumptions that have little relevance to the present. From the inherited need to preserve their members' jobs (and jobs for their members) arise the battles with management over redundancy and manning and with each other over demarcations. These comprise a powerfully conservative force when single-mindedly pursued with the strength that the unions now have — a rational enough course if companies are narrowly defined as justifying themselves only by the employment they provide. But it has severely limited both the

companies' capacity to adapt to changing competitive conditions and the range of opportunities available to their
members. Following this logic, it seems to me that unions are
as responsible for the generally low level of wages in Britain
as incompetent managers. The offensive strategies of unions,
pursuing higher wages, are arguably beneficent because more
dynamic. But even here — as was seen with the 1974 strike of
coal miners (or, in another context, with Middle East oil
producers) — the pursuit of old, short-term goals with virtually unrestrained power can lead at best to instability, at
worst to the replacement of one tyranny with another. The
assumptions that the goals are relevant and that negotiating
power is more or less in balance do not hold when the
underlying balance of power has shifted so radically.

Thirdly — and closely related to the above — power within
the unions has shifted quite as radically as between unions
and employers. The growth of shopfloor power has been
exhaustively studied, not least by the Donovan Commission.
For the purposes of this argument, it will suffice that the
form of much company-union negotiation (and indeed of the
involvement of the TUC in government policymaking)
assumes a power to enforce central decisions that does not in
fact exist. National agreements are repudiated, solemn and
binding promises are ignored but the business of making them
goes on, perhaps because it is better than nothing and at least
gives a comforting illusion of control. Meanwhile, of course,
the power continues to seep down the structure, to shop
stewards whose place in the official scheme of things is, to say
the least, ambiguous.

Productivity bargaining

A fourth item could have been added to the list. It is not a
change, but it is a restriction placed by ritual on the freedom
to adjust to reality: the range of issues over which management and unions have chosen to bargain, and the assumptions
behind that choice. That negotiations have been restricted to
pay and conditions has largely been a management choice,
originating in management's view about those decisions that
'properly' belong there. But since the late fifties the reality of
power has locked management into a position from which

such negotiations provided no escape. The unions — unofficially, at shop steward level — acquired power over issues like redundancy and discipline which had become matters for informal negotiation. The decision of Esso at its Fawley refinery to bring questions of working practice formally into the negotiating arena amounted to the institutionalisation of an informal power reality. This, together with the productivity agreements that followed, has been extensively studied; I do not propose to go further into the question except insofar as it is necessary to put the ICI agreements into context.

Esso brought consultants into its Fawley refinery in 1958. Performance, specifically labour costs, compared unfavourably with performance at other Esso refineries. But change was blocked by the realities of union power — restrictive practices, demarcations and manning agreements — and by the practice of offering systematic overtime to make up earnings. With the assistance of shop stewards, who played a major part in questioning established practices and testing out alternatives, a detailed catalogue of proposals, the Blue Book, was drawn up in 1960. The main aim was to reduce overtime drastically — from 18% to between 2 and 6% — and to make a number of other changes (abolishing craftsmen's mates, cutting teabreaks and so on). In exchange for these changes, pay would be increased by a total of 40%. 'Buying the rule book' was the phrase coined for this operation.

What is important to us is that most of these items were matters that nominally lay within the power of management to dispose but were, in practice, untouchable. By negotiating their removal with the unions, the management was conceding a large area of management prerogative; by including the shop stewards as central figures in the process, it was recognising the reality of the stewards' power.

A number of other agreements followed. McKersie and Hunter* say that the number of agreements made in the next years were:

$$
\begin{array}{rcl}
1963 & - & 4 \\
1964 & - & 14 \\
1965 & - & 28 \\
1966 & - & 27 \\
\end{array}
$$

*References to this, and other books mentioned (and some that are not) will be found in the Bibliography.

This they call the first phase. For it was followed by an
enthusiasm of a different order. What happened in between
was the arrival, in 1965, of the Labour Government's Prices
and Incomes Policy. The White Paper laid down the
productivity criterion under which pay increases above the
norm were to be allowed — 'where the employees concerned,
for example by accepting more exacting work or a major
change in working practices, make a direct contribution
towards increasing productivity in the particular firm or
industry.' But this was not by itself sufficient inducement
until the statutory incomes policy of 1967, under which
productivity increases provided the main justification for pay
increases. Ulysses-like, the managements of beleaguered companies lashed their pay increases under the fleecy bellies of
productivity agreements to get them past the Cyclopean eye
of the NBPI, in order to meet the unabated demands of their
workers. McKersie and Hunter report that the second phase
of productivity agreements went like this:

Jan. 1967	— June 1968	761
July 1968	— Dec. 1968	1,107
Jan. 1969	— June 1969	977
July 1969	— Dec. 1969	874

Thereafter, there was a sharp decline, which was widely
attributed to disillusion with empty agreements but on which
Alan Flanders commented in the introduction to Towers and
Whittingham: ' . . . I prefer the simpler explanation that
productivity bargaining's loss of favour is largely due to the
decline of income policy and the growth of unemployment.'
(I shall return to this at the end of the book.) Flanders goes
on to suggest that disillusion occurred mainly because the
distinction was not drawn between the two types of
agreement, partial and comprehensive. 'The silent implication
was that they were similarly beneficial and differed only in
degree, not in kind. This was a fatal error. Most of the
productivity bargaining that incomes policy helped to promote (where it was not entirely notional) was of the partial
variety and consisted either of simple effort bargains or of
buying out one or more restrictive practices of particular
groups. As it rarely failed to sanction any of the cases

submitted to it, vetting [by the Department of Employment and Productivity] increasingly became a mere formality.'

None the less, according to a study of the productivity criterion cases by Daniel and McIntosh, the achievement was greater than this suggests. For a start, only 30% of the agreements were irremediably 'partial'; the rest were, if only by piecing together a series of smaller agreements, 'comprehensive'. The ground covered by the agreements was extensive, and included changes in working methods, technology, manning levels, break times, overtime, payments systems, workload, shift working and a number of other categories. More than three-quarters of the managers the authors interviewed thought the agreements worthwhile; a smaller proportion – but still a majority, two-thirds – of union representatives concurred. However, it is worth remembering in all this complexity (since many things were being attempted at one time) that the single most important feature of the agreements for the workers was their increased pay.

The productivity bargaining movement – for such it was – left a durable legacy. Nationally, the fact that pay increases could only be justified by higher productivity, however spurious the arguments, was a powerful agent of change in management and union attitudes. The old idea of bargaining for pay increases was challenged by a more rational process of agreeing changes that were beneficial to both sides. It marked a move away from traditional distributive bargaining – 'zero sum game' bargaining over a fixed amount of some resource, so that one party's benefit has to be to the other's detriment. And it marked the arrival of cooperative bargaining – from which both parties may hope to gain. The first was (and is) a brutal confrontation between two separate systems of logic which can only be resolved by displays of power. The second is a situation where both the management's production needs and the unions' employment needs are achieved, with both being conscious of improving their positions.

The ICI agreements

ICI was among the first companies to negotiate change with

the unions. Its first agreement was made in 1965, at a time
when a number of other pioneering companies were explor-
ing the route opened up by Fawley: including Mobil at
Coryton, Shell at Stanlow, the electricity agreements, British
Oxygen, Steel Company of Wales and Alcan. It is worth
noting that these early agreements were more complex and
complete than many of the later agreements made in the
flush of the Incomes Policy. None the less, the policy created
a favourable political environment, making it easier for the
unions to accept in the later phases of the programme
(1968-9) when ICI was able to present itself as the champion
of its workers' cause to the government.

There were two agreements, the first for trials and the
second covering the whole company in 1969. They were
comprehensive — covering all ICI's workforce with one
agreement, jointly negotiated with all the unions at once.
Within that framework, they were locally agreed in their final
detail. This was a fairly common pattern, but it had never
before (or has since) been attempted on the enormous scale
of ICI. Indeed, the size and scope of the agreements, the
amount of change and the enormous effort required to bring
it about are outstanding features of the exercise.

Other features will emerge from the narrative. I shall
mention only two at this stage. First, the agreements, the
negotiations leading into them and the detailed work that
emerged from them comprised a programme of total change
which was open-ended. The weakness of partial agreements
— and the reason Flanders makes his point about the dangers
of confusing them with comprehensive agreements — is that
they cannot be more than wage-work bargains of the most
traditional sort, whatever the intentions of the designers.
Organisations are complex systems and exert manifold
influences on the subsystems which comprise them. Take one
of these pieces away — a group of skilled workers, for
example, or even a self-contained group of workers on a plant
in a larger factory — and it may be possible to change their
methods of working in limited ways. But they will return to
an unchanged environment of hostile, or merely indifferent,
workmates and, almost more important, managers. Small,
formal changes may be achieved, but larger changes in
attitudes and working relationships are impossible. However,

once the logic of organisational change is accepted, there is no stopping short of changing the total system; hence the importance of their being comprehensive. And ICI found that, having started with a limited programme which had some behavioural overtones (not as strong as enthusiasts would like to believe), it was engaged in a massive programme* of management education and change at all levels. For the aim of the programme was not just to buy out a number of unproductive practices, but to bring about fundamental changes in the way work was done and defined.

It was in this respect that ICI's agreement differs most from early agreements like Fawley, whose importance is more in what it has led to than in its specific achievements. That was a closed-ended, one-off agreement; further advances could only be bought by repeating the process; there would always be more issues to bargain over, but the basic structure of relationships and bargaining was unchanged. Later agreements were able to build on this beginning. And ICI's agreements were not designed to bring about specific changes, but to introduce a new process of change, a way of looking at work and continuously thinking about it that was open-ended. This has not been an unqualified benefit – the process is too diffuse – nor has it been an unqualified success – the size of the company makes the achievement of any sort of homogeneity a pipe dream. But it is by orders of magnitude more powerful as a method of changing than agreements with more satisfactorily finite and limited aims.

The second feature worth mentioning at this stage is the approach chosen: through trials. These were, in some senses, experiments, allowing the company and unions to test out their early ideas on the ground with the intention of refining them. They also served an important psychological function, of allowing both sides to see what might happen while remaining uncommitted to a larger change. But the trials were themselves a cause of considerable trouble, being effectively partial agreements taking place within a larger, unaffected (and often hostile) management and union environment. As a result, problems were encountered which

---

*However, to call it a 'programme' implies a good deal more conscious planning and control than there was or, in such a complex system, could have been.

nearly caused the whole enterprise to founder, problems which required heroic determination to overcome.

The process is by no means over, but ICI is now far better placed to coexist with the power realities of the present day than it has been. It is possible to see such programmes as basically humanistic in intention, as many managers and behavioural scientists would see them, or as calculated attempts by management to regain control at a time when the growth of workers' power brings the disruption of the system within reach, as Marxists do. I see it, much more fundamentally, as an attempt — although not consciously contrived as such — to respond to, and release strains set up by, the shift in power within the organisation. That the net result of the programme, humanistic or Machiavellian in intent, has been to push the centre of gravity of decision-making down into the structure of the company is no accident: it accords with unacknowledged reality.

About this book

Two sorts of bias will be apparent in my account: derived from my sources and from personal inclination. Although I travelled over the company, visited scores of works and spoke to hundreds of people, much the most coherent and comprehensive accounts were available from management, and in particular from management files (which I have used extensively). These are bound to colour my account — which is not quite so sinful as it sounds, since Roberts and Wedderburn, in a very different report on WSA for the TUC, admit to a similar bias, and for much the same reasons. In addition, and for the reasons I have just described, I start from a firm conviction that agreements like ICI's WSA are a Good Thing. It would be a mistake to read this as another bias towards the management view, simply because the agreement originated from and became identified with management. It is inherent in the structure of complex organisations that innovation tends to result from management initiatives. And it is part of the historical role of unions that they should resist change. More basically, the identification of management with any move, in whatever direction, marks it as a bargaining issue: 'If management wants it, they

must be made to pay for it.' But that tells us nothing about
the benefits, for the organisation and for the people working
in it, of a particular change. It seems to me, as a result, that
the benefits from WSA are potentially considerable and the
ritualistic opposition to them in some parts of the company
was unfortunate.

But this view belongs to the cooperative, or integrative,
world of WSA itself. If the 'zero sum game' view is taken, it
would be necessary to agree with Tony Topham: 'Productivity bargains are an attempt to achieve a predictable,
controllable movement of incomes . . . closely related to
changes in productivity . . . preliminary reforms in institutional practice to lay the foundations for a national incomes
policy conceived as a defence of the profit-making system. It
must seem to establishment opinion that the mirage of an
effective incomes policy is real after all, that they are near to
a breakthrough . . .' For the conclusion that this sort of
reasoning leads to is the one for which Mr Topham is
best-known: workers' control. Any accommodation with
management is a betrayal of the movement, leaking away the
potentially fruitful pressure of conflict into areas that lie
within management control. I see the logic of this, but I do
not accept its necessary nature. Destroy the system and the
problems remain of how to run whatever will replace it. But
if the systems are somehow immortal, the only point at issue
is how to introduce the workers' interest to a decision-
making process that must also take account of many other
competing interests. It seems to me that productivity
bargaining offers this possibility. However, if it is assumed
that conflict can be resolved only by confrontation between
powerful groups, any battle will be viewed in purely sectarian
terms — and the issues at stake become irrelevant. I hope that
a larger view may be closer to reality.

A third sort of bias arises from the retrospective view of
events. The outsider, visiting the scene of a great battle, can
recapture some important features: he can describe the
strategy and, minute-by-minute, he may be able to recon-
struct the tactical moves; he can assess the result in terms of
the numbers dead, territory won and governments over-
thrown. But he cannot describe what the battle was like any
more than a researcher can objectively describe a love affair

in terms that convey any of the sensations of love. In a change of the sort I am attempting to describe, the process is quite as important as the change; indeed, the process *is* the change. But it is difficult to capture the essence after the event.

Memory becomes adjusted to the present state of affairs; sworn enemies of the agreements were turned by the patient alchemy of time into lifelong supporters – of what had become, let us remember, a success. (Memories might have been differently arranged had the whole project failed.) It is not surprising that the files, with their contemporary records of disputed events, should become progressively more important to me in my search for facts, nor that the files should, in turn, exercise their own distorting effects. What remains in the files are the ashes of dead disputes: strikes, arguments, crises of all sorts . . . conflicts that were the distracting surface under which change was taking place, although it is tempting to see them as change itself. However, to look behind the conflicts raises the more dangerous temptation of assuming purpose and rationality in decisions that were more often the attempts to catch up with, rather than master, events. We know where ICI's WSA ended: it is tempting to assume that it was always intended to get there. But the whole process was very much a question of trial-and-error, and had to be since the real problems could not be known until they were encountered.

It ought to be evident by now that a retrospective reconstruction of this sort raises questions, of fact as much as of interpretation, that cannot be satisfactorily answered. However, it is necessary to ask them. ICI's agreements are among the most ambitious attempts that have yet been made to change a company's culture. (If scale is the measure, they are the most ambitious.) It is my view that the attempt will have to be made in some – almost certainly quite different – form, within the next decade or two, by every major employer in the country. It is part of changes that are transforming our society. We must understand them if we are to anticipate them constructively and not passively to allow ourselves to be overwhelmed by them.

PART I

Some Background

1
ICI : A Thumbnail Portrait

Before we consider what led up to ICI's new labour agreement, we need to know about the company itself. The company is the setting for the agreement and it also, obviously enough, shaped it.

The setting is exclusively British. Labour agreements do not travel well. Indeed, they do not travel at all between different labour markets and national cultures. But the national focus hardly simplifies the picture for us. ICI is the biggest industrial company in Britain and, hiding under the deceptively simple description of a 'chemical company', it is really a conglomerate which spans most of the industrial conditions encountered in Britain. Any portrait of the company must reflect these salient characteristics, some of them peculiar to the company and some common to the chemical industry: its great size; the wide range of products made (and markets served); the nature and variety of the technology; the skills; the geographical spread; the rapid rate of change; and the organisation which has evolved to manage the twin problems of size and diversity.

The company that emerges is bewilderingly complex; one's mind reels at the prospects of accommodating such diversity within the frame of a single agreement. Yet this is what ICI has attempted.

After all, what has the manufacture of explosives to do with naphtha-cracking? What has either to do with nylon spinning or paint manufacture? The first, naphtha-cracking, is carried out in huts tucked into the sand dunes of the remote Ayreshire coast. Naphtha crackers are those towering, steaming complexes of silver columns, pumps, pipes and tanks — the industry's modern face. Nylon spinning is not even a chemical process. ICI spins the fibre at Gloucester and

Pontypool; the works are swarming with people doing small, repetitive, almost assembly-line jobs — whereas chemical plants can often seem empty. ICI makes its paint in, among other places, a remote and charming country town. And why not? for paint manufacture is another physical job of mixing and packing — a relatively simple one — and marketing it is more crucial to success than making it.

Each of these processes requires it own characteristic workforce, ranging from the highly sophisticated skills and teamwork needed to run the large, expensive single units of the petrochemical plants to the relatively rudimentary skills, though with great if infrequent dangers of explosives manufacture. The 80-odd ICI works in Britain are potentially all separate industries under the umbrella of a common financial parentage.

Difference is piled on difference. These very different works operate in unique local environments whose effects permeate, and indeed determine, the web of human relationships. A third of ICI's workforce is employed on Teesside, in the Northeast, where the company has the huge petrochemical site of Wilton and the fertiliser factory of Billingham. It is a region of long-established heavy industry — much of it declining — with high unemployment, a history of privation, and well-organised, militant unions. Management in these conditions has little to do with man management at, for example, Stowmarket. There ICI's paint works is one of two large employers in a rural area in which the nearest industrial concentration is twenty miles away, at Ipswich. At Gloucester, the nylon factory draws from a workforce that includes men from the virtually defunct but once glamorous and high-paying aircraft industry and dispossessed miners from the Forest of Dean.

In each of its locations, more differences still can be traced to the company's local history. At Ardeer in Scotland, where ICI make explosives, the company and its predecessor have been the only substantial local employers for more than a century, as in the salt-based industries of Cheshire. At Billingham, a brand-new chemical plant was set up in 1919 and was extended to become one of the technological marvels of the 1930s — when it also provided secure employment in a region of high unemployment. In these places,

Fig.1 **ICI locations and manpower distribution**

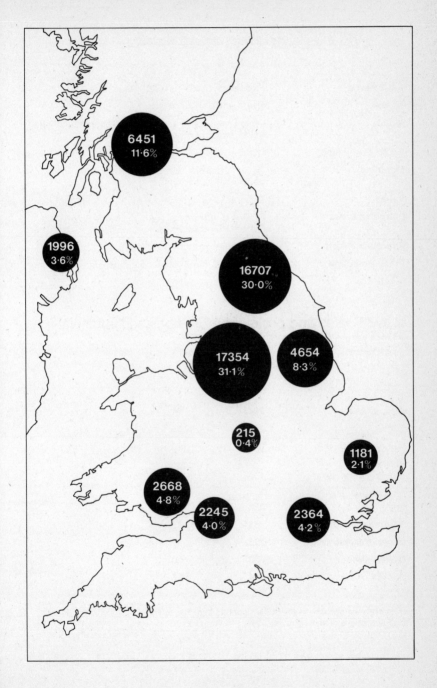

Fig. 2 **a. ICI's Divisions and main products**

Agricultural	Fertilisers, industrial chemicals, catalysts
Fibres	Nylon and polyester fibres
Mond	Plastics monomers, chlorinated solvents, alkalis, acids, salt, chlorine, lime, titanium
Nobel Explosives	Blasting explosives, detonators, propellants
Organics	Dyes, pigments, rubber chemicals, urethanes, detergents, silicones
Paints	Decorative and industrial paints, wallpapers
Petrochemicals	Olefines, aromatics, glycols, phenol, Dimethylterephthalate, nylon 6:6 salt
Pharmaceuticals	Medical and veterinary drugs
Plant Protection	Herbicides, fungicides, pesticides, seed dressing
Plastics	Plastic resins and products

b. 1973 sales and profit of ICI divisions and subsidiaries in Western Europe.*

	Sales (£m)	Trading Profit (£m)
Agricultural	208	34
Fibres	197	18
General chemicals	376	65
Paints and building services	100	9
Petrochemicals and Plastics	384	41
Pharmaceuticals	51	15
Imperial Metal	275	31
Miscellaneous	22	2
Europa	251	15

*ICI does not publish details of divisional trading. The figures given above are no more than indications of trading areas.

there was (and is) a strong ICI tradition — ICI families with
generations of employment; ICI representatives on the
council; and often the very palpable presence of an ICI
factory to remind people where their money came from. But
a site like Wilton — now the biggest concentration of investment in the company — was started after the Second World
War. It can draw on no ICI tradition; the workforce is
younger; the shop stewards are more union, less ICI, men.

Let us take a more analytical look at some of these
differences.

1. *Size*

ICI is not only Britain's biggest industrial company: it has
been — according to the prevailing rates of exchange — the
biggest chemical company in the world. Sales in 1972* were
£1,693m and assets £1,869m. ICI has 350 subsidiaries and is
active in all major industrial and most non-industrial
countries. However, in spite of this international spread, ICI
is in tone and management almost entirely British. And the
British factories are by far the most important part of ICI's
manufacturing interests. £291m of ICI's overseas sales of
£918m in 1972 was exported from the UK, which accounted
for 63% of total sales. Counting subsidiaries, ICI employs
132,000 people — about two-thirds of the total workforce —
in Britain.

2. *Organisation*

The company is divided into nine divisions, largely autonomous and profit-accountable, answering to the Main Board
and monitored through a system of central planning and
budget controls. Some of the divisions are substantial
businesses in their own right. Mond, for example, employed
17,000 people and had sales of £340m in 1972 — ranking it
32nd among Britain's largest companies. With the power that
size confers and the independence of separate accountability,
the divisions tend to be somewhat prickly about interference

*I shall use 1972 information in this chapter except where indicated. Although
the figures were different in 1969, when the agreement was finally signed, the
differences are marginal in terms of their effects on the setting ICI provided.

in their internal affairs. And for the most part they are left to get on with their business.

Two main elements of power ('reserve powers') remain at the centre: the Board has final say over the investment decisions that determine ICI's future shape; and labour policy is centrally determined (see next chapter). Although limited, these powers give strategic effective control to the centre. The problem is a familiar one in large companies: striking a balance between the conditions within which individual managers can act independently and the need to maintain control and pursue unified company policies. In a chemical company it is further complicated by the high degree of interdependence between the divisions. The chart (Fig. 3) shows some of these trading links and may make clearer the rationale of having a large, integrated chemical company.

3. *Products and markets*

ICI sells 12,000 different products in packages that range from less than an ounce (e.g. dyes and pharmaceuticals) to lots of tens of thousands of tons (heavy chemicals like caustic soda and ethylene). They cover a wide range of uses and markets, roughly divided between consumer goods and industrial goods. The first, usually bearing an ICI brand name, are sold direct to the consumer: e.g. 'Dulux' paints. 'Terylene' fibres, 'Savlon' antiseptic. The second are sold to manufacturers for use in their own processes: acid and salts for metal treatment; soda ash for glass manufacture; plastics for fabrication into buckets or fishing nets.

By far the greatest part of ICI's goods are sold to industrial users. The consumer never knows how many of the things he buys have ICI's products involved somewhere along the chain of manufacture.

4. *Technology*

It will easily be imagined from the range of goods that, even though they are all made by chemical processes, the range of technologies involved is almost as wide: there can be little in common between the manufacture of dyes and of sulphuric acid. The differences can be defined along a number of

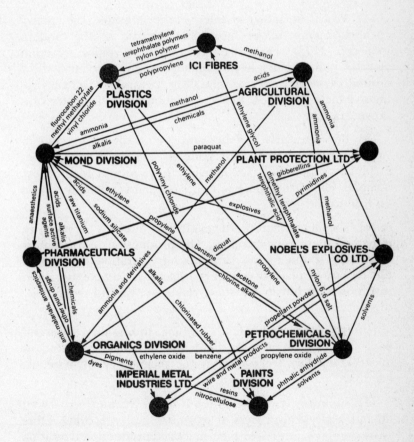

Fig 3 Interdependency

dimensions: scale; continuous or batch-process; requiring mental or physical effort; repetitive or non-routine; labour or capital intensive.

The sharpest difference is illustrated by the range of capital-intensity — the measure of the amount of capital plant a worker has at his disposal. In ICI the range is wide: from £30,200 per employee in Petrochemicals Division to £8,500 per employee in Paints Division. But this does not by itself tell us much about the nature of the work. Let us look at some examples:

(*a*) Probably most people would consider the petrochemicals plant to be most characteristic of the modern industry. Huge, expensive collections of pipes, reaction vessels, pumps and heat exchangers, the products flow around them invisibly, continuously, controlled from instrument panels that look like the communications centre of a power station.

(*b*) But dyestuffs can be, and are, made in batches in wooden tubs, stirred with paddles. The processes are individually simple but cumulatively they amount to the most complex chemical processes in the company: some dyes have 40 reaction stages.

(*c*) The manufacture of explosives has no relation to either of these two extremes. The production technology is extremely simple: a physical mixing operation that would not be out of place in a marzipan factory. Complexity is not in production but in the slow, elaborate, careful technology of safety.

(*d*) ICI also makes calcium carbide, in big, dirty, hot and dangerous electric furnaces that belong in a steel mill. And, as in steel, the key technology is the technology of materials handling.

(*e*) Spinning synthetic fibres is not a chemical process at all but a physical process of extruding and stretching. Fibre works employ armies of men in a mass production operation that is highly scheduled and rigorous — more like the assembly line of a motor factory.

(*f*) ICI even has small assembly-line operations: assembling detonators and packing drugs. These two operations employ hundreds of girls in conditions that could be reproduced in electronics factories.

Each creates its own working environment, its values, social organisation and local tradition. The work of a man on a carbide furnace is extremely demanding physically. How can it be compared with the job of a process worker watching the instrument panel of a large plant? How can the methods of working in a process unit — a small group whose work centres on the control room of one plant — be compared with men tending hundreds of small units in a spinning factory? The problems of covering such technical diversity with a single agreement were bound to be considerable.

5. *Engineering*

A special case of technological difference, extremely important as a factor in the WSA experience, derives from the fact that a modern chemical factory is in not one but two quite different industries. Each chemical factory also contains a sizeable engineering works, bending, welding and cutting metal as in any Midlands job shop. They exist to maintain (and, in the bigger factories, to construct) chemical plant.

6. *Skills*

The workforce employed to run these plants and manage the company has a structure defined by skills. Management is predominantly composed of graduates, who account for 8% of the employees. More generally, the workforce is (or was, at the time of WSA) divided into payroll and staff: 62,000 hourly-paid and 38,000 monthly-paid employees respectively. Payroll splits further into members of craft unions and non-craft — about 1:2. These distinctions are important since they define communities with different values and needs — and still greater differences in their response to any initiative from the centre. Each division has a special 'flavour', derived initially from the technology and manifested in the special skills (or lack of them) required. The difference in grades structures that emerged from the ICI agreements (Fig. 11, p. 261) illustrates well how different the divisions are.

The main point is that the workforce contains a high level of skills and that the level is continually rising as the technology of the industry is developed.

7. *Geography*

ICI manufacture at 70 locations in Britain. About half the workforce is divided equally between the Northeast, around the Tees, and Northwest, the other side of the Pennines.

The areas where ICI has its works range from regions like the Northeast with an industrial history that goes back nearly two centuries to an isolated, semi-rural community like Stowmarket in Suffolk. Each site combines local factors — industrial history, local union tradition, employment record, competing industries — which creates sharp differences between them. Some of the problems encountered in introducing WSA were only to be explained by consideration of these factors.

8. *Change*

The chemical industry grows at twice the rate of manufacturing industry as a whole: due to a combination of the growth of existing markets and the creation of new markets by the invention of new products. More than a half of ICI's sales are accounted for by products that were not on the market 15 years ago.

The rate of change is characteristic of a technology-intensive industry. But it is the result too of hard work. In the five years to 1972, ICI spent more than £250m on research and development. Even more must be invested if the ideas the laboratories develop are to be turned into sales: ICI's capital investment in the same period amounted to £777m, of which something like two-thirds was spent in Britain.

The importance of this for us is in the creation of a fluid and rapidly-changing work environment. In some places — at the petrochemicals complex of Wilton in the Northeast, for example — this had an unsettling effect. The stability of the

workforce suffered. More generally, however, it has marked
the company as one used to change, with the capacity to
change built into its structure. However, even such structures
can be inefficient and the beginning of our story is ICI's
discovery that parts of the environment had evolved away
from it, that it may be good at technological adoption but
more than technology changes.

This, briefly, is ICI. A gigantic company with a wide range
of activities and geographical spread. That WSA emerged in
the form of a 'framework' agreement was natural. Only
within the commodious embrace of a loose agreement could
the wide diversity of local conditions be accommodated. The
particular balance between the specific (laying down wage
rates) and more diffuse matters of general principle (methods
of working) was struck for reasons that will become more
apparent in the next chapters.

2

Relations with the Unions: History

ICI's agreements — the Weekly Staff Agreement and the trials that preceded it — had to be worked out in closest concord with the unions. It would have been pointless to have tried to impose changes so radical without the unions' full participation. Perhaps more to the point, the company was bound by the terms of its agreements with the unions to seek their approval of the changes. It is therefore appropriate to start with a description of the relationship between ICI and the unions, a relationship which always provided the background — and often the foreground — of the story that follows.

1. *Negotiating structure*

One of the first executive acts of Sir Alfred Mond, on becoming Chairman of ICI at its formation, was to import the whole of Brunner-Mond's labour relations system and policies.

Readers interested in the circumstances surrounding the formulation of these early ICI policies should refer to the ICI *History** where these matters are dealt with in detail. We are concerned with the resulting form of ICI's relations with its unions and the management within the Company of its labour relations policies.

The main effect was the centralisation of labour policy and the formation of a strong central Labour Department — which ran parallel with a Central Staff Department. The reasons were clear: the company was young, formed of disparate parts; it was important to achieve consistency in

*W.J. Reader, *Imperial Chemical Industries, A History*, vol. II, Chapter 4.

treatment of employees and in company policy in matters of wages and relations with the unions. However, the salience of these advantages changed with time. By the time the new pay agreement was being worked out, in 1965, the early transitional arguments for integration were fully worked through. But the policy remained. And since the fact of centralisation was to be influential in the changes we are considering, the reasons for its survival deserve some discussion. On the face of it, the main reasons were power-political. The benefits from maintaining ICI's bargaining strength as a unit outweighed the industrial relations and management costs of centralised rigidity; the threat of being 'leap-frogged to buggery' — the works being picked off one by one, advances gained at works with strong unions or weak management (or both) being used as precedents elsewhere — was thought to outweigh the benefits from a flexible response to local conditions. However, although substantial, these were not the overt reasons for continuing with the status quo and they remained in the background. Indeed, it would not have been in the ICI culture to have taken such a hard-nosed line on personnel policy.

It was a live subject of debate, and there were always managers in the divisions who were pressing for greater control over their relations with the unions. Yet, surprisingly, in the latest report to consider the matter officially a consensus emerged in favour of maintaining a reserve power for personnel matters at the centre. Perhaps it is not so surprising when one considers the comfort to be derived from having Central Personnel standing between the Divisions and any direct confrontation with the unions over the major issues of pay and conditions. It was the way things had always been done; Central Personnel Department (known as CPD) had developed a formidable expertise in negotiating with the unions. The divisions may well have felt, privately, that they were less likely to succeed. CPD had also been a source of innovation; it had been responsible for the development of the techniques of work measurement and job appraisal in the company. The competence of its industrial relations experts was most efficiently used by pooling them at the centre. The logic behind CPD had been tested by the divisions over a long period and had been found successful.

There was a more fundamental reason. There is a massive inertia in large systems that makes it likely that almost anything will continue to be done in the existing way until the benefits of making a change (if any) can be neither disguised nor ignored. Without large potential benefits, there is no energy to push the system into new ways. On the contrary, everything acts to maintain the status quo: a great and easy familiarity with the old ways; the investment in them of too many people's experience and attitudes; the swarming details of routine; the convenience of the well-understood and the comfort of predictability. Change takes people into the realms of the new, the unfamiliar and the suspect — all to be resisted.

At a more specific level, and without suggesting anything more sinister than the will to individual and organisational survival, nobody who benefited from centralisation was likely to encourage a move toward devolution of power. Because of the reserve power which it administers, CPD is one of only two departments at Millbank with real power within the company. (The other reserve power is financial.) Similarly, in a period when power has been seeping into the unions' grassroots, the central negotiation of pay agreements is one of the few elements of real power left to the national offices. In neither case was it likely to be lightly relinquished. Yet, if there are good power-political reasons for centralising, there were also good organisational reasons for pushing the freedom to negotiate with the unions down the structure to the managers most directly involved.

These factors have institutional form in the system of central negotiations which provide the main official contact between company and unions. Eleven unions, or groups of smaller unions, are signatories to the agreements which comprise the contract of work between ICI and its payroll. (The signatory unions are listed on page 21.) The agreements themselves are relatively unchanging and cover two main areas: working conditions and negotiating procedures. Pay rates are not in the agreements and have come to be subject to annual negotiation. The old pay structure is described in the next section: it provides the structure of base rates, differentials and special payments which are uniformly applied throughout the company's UK locations.

The working conditions schedules need little explanation. They comprise the rules of the wage/work bargain: the number of hours worked, mealtimes, overtime, shiftwork and holidays – all in schedules covering different kinds of workers (daywork, nightwork etc). 'Procedure' is more complex, since these are the rules of the political contract between company and unions. At the top of the structure are the contacts between company representatives and national union officers; at the bottom are the contacts between management – which includes supervisors – and the groups of men on the shopfloor and their elected representatives, the shop stewards.

The system of labour relations which has been worked out within the limits of the agreement has been, for the most part, highly successful. The powerful central Labour Department devised and managed policies; it negotiated with the unions; and it ensured that the policies were uniformly applied. The Divisions worked within this framework (sometimes under protest) to apply the policy at local level using an analogous structure of Central Division Labour Office with satellite labour managers at works levels. And this system delivered to ICI a strike record that was second to none in British industry. This, the conventional view, is not universally accepted. One Main Board director said, refreshingly enough: 'No strikes at all is seldom a sign that the business is being effectively managed. It is usually a sign that management has given up.' It is not that strikes are a sign of a desirable toughness but rather that, since conflict is an inescapable part of the relationship between management and unions, strikes cannot be avoided if a management does its job properly. However, while this view has the appeal of a robust simplification, it is not commended by logic: the occasional strike may demonstrate that a manager hews close to the line of the possible; but strikes are disruptive and costly; the optimal strategy would be the (far harder) one of staying close to the line without straying across it.

ICI's good record did, however, carry a cost. A company in a capital-intensive industry, like chemicals, where labour costs can be a small part of final costs, has less reason to resist the expensive demands of a workforce than a more labour-intensive company. It is also the prisoner of its heavy investment, in which the high level of fixed costs makes it imperative to keep up production. All the pressures, therefore, are towards buying off trouble that might threaten production.

2. *Disputes procedure*

An important part of ICI's long labour peace was the generally accepted Rule of Law. The schedules in the labour agreement laid down rules for dealing with disputes which could not be settled locally. The rules ('procedure') are common to many British companies and provide for a series of meetings at a number of levels, successively drawing in people higher up the company and union structures. Thus, a dispute may proceed from the shopfloor, through meetings with the manager directly responsible to the works manager. If there is no settlement (or if the issue touches on questions of union or company policy and cannot be locally dealt with) official representatives become involved in 'procedure', which allows for a 'local conference', involving local officers of the union; an 'intermediate conference', at which a representative from the national office will attend; and a 'headquarters conference', held between the headquarters authority of the union and the Central Personnel Department. A timetable is intended to ensure that the meetings take place within eight weeks of the first request.

This structure is a safety net to catch the exceptional cases that escape less formal procedures. Its formality is part of the objectivity needed if it is to satisfy the requirement for visible justice – and provide a credible alternative to more direct, and disruptive action. But how few the cases are that go to 'procedure' is shown by the Table below:

Conferences	1970	1971	1972
Local	197	214	208
Intermediate	65	85	55
Headquarters	25	30	16

The last step, which has rarely been taken, is arbitration, if a headquarters conference cannot reach agreement.

By far the greatest part of disputes, more generally

defined — the fine detail of the political relationship between employees and the company — takes place at the local level. There is a schedule of 'factory procedure' which provides for an escalating series of meetings, starting with the supervisor and ending with the works manager. The people involved are the managers, workers, supervisors and shop stewards. More important, in terms of volume, are the problems which are informally handled between shop stewards and supervisors or managers.

3. *Shop stewards*

To set the 200 or so disputes that go through 'procedure' annually against the tens of thousands handled informally at a local level (my guess) is misleading, since the two processes are not strictly comparable nor are the issues handled similar. But the comparison does demonstrate that the huge bulk of the unions' interaction with the company is handled in the course of the detailed, day-by-day activities of the shop stewards, a fact which became highly significant in the introduction of the productivity agreements. This is a situation that has come about gradually and represents a massive shift of power within the unions towards the local organisations. Given the democratic constitution of most unions — and particularly of the powerful engineers' union, the AUEW — it means that there is no machinery for *enforcing* nationally-made agreements at the local level.

Shop stewards were recognised within ICI as workers' representatives at the signing of the principal labour agreement, in 1947. The company had seen, quite accurately, that it would be dangerous to allow a political structure of negotiations by workers' representatives to become a framework of national negotiation. (For the alternative structure of consultation provided by the company within the works council system, see Section 5 of this chapter.) None the less, as part of the agreement provision was made for the recognition of representatives. The threat, if threat it was, was limited by the low level of union membership at the time — perhaps as low as 40%. But this has changed.

Stewards are elected by their union workmates. There are now 1,800, representing the 56,000 weekly staff. The size of constituency varies, from more than 50 people for general worker unions in some places to much smaller groups for craft unions. (There are isolated cases where the shop steward is the only member of his union in a works.) Their function is to represent the worker's case where there is a disagreement with management, more specifically with the supervisor who stands at the place where the management structure impinges directly on the workforce — in the jargon, the 'interface'. We should note in passing that, although the steward-supervisor relationship can be a source of strength ('We fix things together'), this automatically sets the steward up in opposition to the supervisor ('I shall by-pass him if I can get to an answer I like better') and the growth in the stewards' power has been accompanied by, although it has not caused, a loss of supervisory prerogatives. Where the power situation (and, willy-nilly, the management) permitted, the unions felt able to assert themselves to the point where, as at Wilton, they controlled management access to the workforce: at one stage in the Wilton negotiations, they were able to insist that assistant foremen should be excluded from work-group discussions on job descriptions; in the Terylene Works, managers were not allowed into the notoriously over-staffed packing room on the grounds that they might carry out covert work measurement. ('I suppose they thought we'd have stop watches in our pockets', a manager laconically observed.) Such bizarre reversals of the normal order are more easily understood if seen as the use of power defensively.

Strictly speaking, the steward's powers are limited to representing his constituents' interests to the management. In practice, the stewards are the first line of defence of their union's privilege and demarcations, watching for any move by management that might threaten their ownership of work at the factory. It was in this role, rather than as representatives for individual grievances, that they were to be so closely involved in the introduction of the agreements.

The leading part taken by the stewards in this process as a result of the company's real need for their participation has consolidated their position more effectively than any amount of agitation. By 1965, they had become powerful — and, when management was sufficiently enlightened, useful —

figures in some parts of the company; elsewhere, management did its best to limit contact, in the hope of limiting power. But the long involvement in detailed negotiation over the agreements enforced a change in management (and steward) attitudes. ICI was reluctant enough to recognise stewards in 1947; there was never any question of officially recognising another step in the representative hierarchy — the senior shop stewards, representatives for groups of stewards belonging to particular unions — although they were recognised *de facto* at Billingham from the late 1940s. And it is easy to see why the company adopted this obstructive policy. Hard as it is to contain the influence of the stewards, it would be far more so for representatives working across the whole factory. The system was aimed at tethering the steward to his constituency, to a part of the factory, limiting his freedom of operation in time and space. No such limits could be placed on a man who represented several parts of a factory and several hundred men. Yet, for the practical purposes of introducing the agreement, the company had to deal with limited numbers of representatives rather than large groups and senior shop stewards were allowed into existence.

4. *The unions*

So far I have talked about the unions as though they were a monolithic entity. Nothing could be further from the truth. They are a collection of bodies whose great pride and individuality is rooted in very different histories and purposes. Although there is an abstraction of 'trade unionism' which they have in common, their definitions of their own collective and their members' individual self-interest is more often than not in conflict and they themselves are more often than not in competition.

The following is the list of unions from the blue booklet:

General and Municipal Workers' Union
Transport and General Workers' Union
Process and General Workers' Union
Union of Salt, Chemical and Industrial General Workers
Amalgamated Union of Engineering and Foundry Workers

Electrical, Electronics, Telecommunications Union —
    Plumbing Trades Union
Amalgamated Society of Boilermakers, Shipwrights, Black-
    smiths and Structural Workers
Association of Patternmakers and Allied Craftsmen
National Federation of Building Trades Operatives
National Union of Vehicle Builders
National Union of Sheet Metal Workers, Coppersmiths,
    Heating and Domestic Engineers

ICI's attitude to the unions was from the start at least
permissive and at best positively helpful. The company was
formed at a time when the unions were, in the aftermath of
the General Strike, at their most demoralised. In the early
days of the company's history, the union membership was
actually dropping. By the time of the 1947 agreement,
probably less than half of the total payroll were unionised
and most of those (particularly in the Northeast). were
craftsmen. The company could easily have taken advantage
of the unions' enfeeblement but didn't. Perhaps it didn't have
to. The policy of leading the industry in pay and conditions
(of which more in Section 3 of the next chapter), the staff
grade scheme, the works councils and a history of being a
steady employer had achieved the intended objective of
focussing employees' primary loyalties on to the company.
But the growth in union membership after the war gave them
more real strength in negotiations with the company at local
and national level. And when the WSA was finally agreed, in
1969, ICI in effect conceded the principle of 100% union
membership which the unions had been pressing for.

The main unions, which took a leading part in local
negotiations throughout the company, are the two large
general worker unions, the T&GWU and G&MWU (which
alternated, depending on the region), and the two largest
craft unions, the AUEW and ETU. Other main groups of
unions are the 'black trades' (Boilermakers, etc.) and the
building workers. Union membership through the company
varies with the demands of the processes — or more precisely,
with the balance struck between process and maintenance
(predominantly skilled) work — which depends on the type
of plant. It also varies with local pressures: for example, the

militancy and strength of the AUEW in the Northeast has enabled it successfully to lay claim to jobs in the Terylene Works at Wilton which are done by unskilled men at Kilroot in Northern Ireland.

The main point of difference to establish at this stage is the division – almost a class distinction – between skilled and unskilled workers. The skilled worker bears the same relation to his unskilled brother as a professional man does to the rest of the labouring middle classes. As with the professional man, the craftsman is set apart by his training in early life (which was 5 but is now 4 and could come down to 3 years' apprenticeship between the ages of 16 and 21), by the access this gives him to more complex and demanding work for which his skills uniquely equip him and by the higher pay he receives in recognition of his skills. And, as in the professions, he carries – and is conceded – a consciousness of superiority which amounts to one of those class distinctions so dear to the British heart.

The division goes back to the beginnings of the trade union movement. The threat posed to it by the 'flexibility' provisions of the weekly staff agreement lay at the root of much of the opposition from craft unions. More important, however, was the threat posed to ownership of jobs. The craft unions could lay unique claim to categories of work, defined by the skills necessary to carry them out. About these there was no argument. Less clearly defined were jobs that lay between the unions, or where several skills might be needed for a given job. The conflict would mostly be resolved in the first case by habit rather than by logic; although most instruments are electrical, for example, most instrument artificers (one of the more elaborate and highly-paid skills in the industry) are members of the AUEW which had laid claim to instrument work in earlier days, when instruments were not electrical. In the second case, the issue would be resolved by demanding that the relevant craftsmen should be present to do their bit: a simple job such as changing a pump might require the presence of an engineer (to remove a guard), an electrician (to isolate some electrical mechanism) and a plumber – while the process worker would stand around.

More difficult problems were created by the development of new jobs in new technologies. Electronics play an increasingly important part in the running of complex process plants. New gadgets may be considered part of the instrumentation, in which case they will be fought over by ETU or AUEW instrument artificers. Or they may be part of the control equipment, when they fall into the general workers' domain. (On some plants, process workers can interrogate the computer 'on line' through terminals in the control room for information needed to run the plant.) More prosaically, the increasing use of plastic components raises problems between even more unions. These problems are not trivial. They are life and blood to the unions concerned: one of the most damaging strikes ever suffered by the shipbuilding industry was the result of a dispute between joiners who built the traditional wooden superstructure of ships and boilermakers who weld and drill metal plate, over who should drill holes in the new aluminium superstructures.

This is not a parody of the problems which union 'ownership' of work gave rise to; it can be repeated many times. The costs to the company were revealed in the inter-firm comparisons discussed in Section 1 of the next chapter; the possible saving that could be achieved by dismantling the whole apparatus was hinted at in the manning studies described in Chapter 5. But neither of these pieces of information — so influential in managerial logic — could touch the logic of the union's position, based by long habit and deeply-held conviction in the overriding importance of defending their members' jobs and, in their own interests as unions, of maintaining the level of their membership. To destroy the old patterns of ownership, the accretion of years of struggle, was to pose a threat to the accepted meaning of the unions themselves.

Moreover, it was a threat which did not affect the unions equally. Any re-distribution of work would favour some unions — specifically the general workers — at the expense of others. (Or would seem to. In fact, the threat to jobs was more evenly spread. The more fundamental threat came from loosening comfortable old structures, restoring to management some freedom to act when restricting management freedom had been the main objective of union policy for more than a century.) As a result the process of introducing the agreements was characterised by tension between unions as much as between unions and management; stiff opposition from the local AUEW organisation, backed up by the Black Trades, and a more welcoming attitude from the general workers with the ETU standing to one side, confident that its members could only gain from increasing automation and instrumentation.

5. *Works councils*

Although they did not play an active part in the formation and introduction of ICI's productivity agreements, this chapter would not be complete without a brief description of the works councils, a structure of worker representation set up by the company to run in parallel with the union/company negotiating structure. It did not exist to negotiate, nor indeed to decide anything, but to promote communication between management and workforce by providing a procedure for consultation. A number of non-trivial areas were reserved to the councils — pensions, profit-sharing and the old staff grade scheme, as well as welfare issues. But, even here, they had no power to decide. The unions thought councils sinister from the start; and there may have been an element of an attempt to pre-empt — or at least to compete away — some union functions. But announcing their founding in 1927, Alfred Mond advanced a more innocent reason:

'One of the problems which troubled me a good deal before I decided on the merger . . . was how would it be possible to maintain personal contact between those directing the industry and those employed?'

The councils were therefore devised as a means of persuading the worker that he was 'part of a living human organism and not part of a machine . . .' They also had a more calculating — and still unsinister — purpose: to encourage the workers to feel a primary loyalty to their company — a company which paid them better than others in the industry, provided all sorts of fringe benefits and was concerned enough about their welfare to provide a channel through which their worries and problems could be discussed. A model propaganda speech circulated to works managers at

the time of the first election for works councillors in 1929
says:

> '. . . if a worker has a complaint to make or feels he has
> some grievance, he will be able to make his voice
> heard . . .'

Subjects before the council would be:

> '. . . the comfort, safety, health and well-being of all
> employees in these works . . .; sport and recreation; the
> ways in which time, material or expense could be saved;
> the administration of the Sick Benefit, Benevolent and
> Hospital Fund scheme. . . .'

Matters of importance to the company were left with the
management.

John Rhodes, for some years the Secretary of Central
Council, said that 'it would be a mistake to look for the
achievement of the works council scheme in concrete
decisions. It was most useful at the human level . . .' The
councils, at their different levels, were forums where management and payroll could meet and talk about things informally. None the less, there were some achievements — or rather
decisions which the councils had decisively influenced; for
example, the idea for profit-sharing originated in a works
council. But these were, while useful, on the margin of the
company's affairs.

As a result, although it was unquestionably important for
there to be direct contact between senior management and
the shopfloor, however token, this purpose was not enough
by itself to keep the scheme constructively alive. It had a
fatal weakness. By reserving all substantive issues for discussion with the unions — largely at their insistence — it was
inevitable that the council system would come to seem
increasingly irrelevant.

It is important to remember that this was not the case
when works councils were set up. Those were the days
following the General Strike, and the far more damaging coal
strike, when a confrontation between capital and labour
seemed inevitable and civil war was being nervously talked
about. Mond was active in trying to bridge that gap.
Moreover, there was a real communications need in the

company. Union membership was low; shop stewards did not exist officially as representatives for discussing grievances. The works council scheme served a useful purpose in those conditions, but it did not have the vitality to survive purposefully into different ones. The experience of the war changed — as wars usually do — the perceptions of the men who had gone to fight in it. Displaced from the home environment, their ideas changed; they returned with more independent attitudes, voted the Labour Party into office and joined their unions. Flexing their new membership muscles, the unions used this strength to usurp or constrain the competitive works council structure for discussion and negotiation. By the end of the 1950s the councils were about as meaningful as the British Commonwealth and increasingly acquired the same embarrassing aura of good intentions and impotence. Like that consoling remnant of an imperial past, their functions became increasingly honorific and lacking in content.

It is a curious chapter of ICI's paternalism. The councils could not survive unchanged into a world of high wages, low unemployment and television-broadened minds. They were, however, appropriate to an earlier set of conditions which, in 1972, they re-joined. More than anything else, they could not survive the growing division between the consulting processes they represented and the negotiating powers of the unions. The joint consultation system which was introduced then in an attempt to integrate the works council idea with the political system of local union representation, is described in Chapter 12.

PART II

The Roots of Change

3

Response to Economic Change

The Weekly Staff Agreement did not spring fully-armed into the world in 1969 but was the result of a long and complicated gestation and birth. Behind WSA lay more than three years of trials — tortuous, frustrating and successful in equal parts. And behind the trials lay decades of evolution in ICI's management policies which, in retrospect anyway, led logically and consistently towards WSA.

For the purpose of this book, the starting-point was the report in January 1965 of a management committee — the 1964 Wages Structure Panel — which started off the chain of events leading to WSA. It should not be considered in isolation, but should be set in the context of changes that have taken place, more or less continuously, through the company's history. The Panel drew together four major strands of change or tradition which were:

1. The company's changing position in the chemical markets of the world. More accurately, the fact that its commercial environment had changed and ICI had not changed with it.

2. The methodical review, analysis and change of the wages structure which had always been an important part of ICI's policy.

3. The growing feeling that certain aspects of ICI's traditionally paternalistic management culture, if not most, were out of keeping with modern social conditions.

4. Changing expectations of employees.

If these are seen as yielding answers to the question
What? — indicating the need for change and some likely
directions — they could not answer the question *How?* This
was to be found in a fifth, more recent, development — of
the techniques for changing organisations and theories about
work and job satisfaction that were being developed in the
USA by behavioural scientists.

1. *ICI's commercial future*

While the other strands mentioned — the ethical and wages
structure developments — represent continuing and evolutionary changes within the company which led towards
WSA, it is probable that the actions taken in 1965 would
have remained within the limits of existing policy unless a
crisis had threatened in the company's commercial environment. The need for a commercial re-think within the
company had gathered force from 1960 onwards until it
created a situation of crisis. Also the arrival on the company's
Main Board of Peter Allen, as Deputy Chairman, after he had
spent some years as Chairman of ICI's Canadian subsidiary,
brought into the board room a man with experience of a
different working environment, who knew that different
ways of working were possible, and that the assumptions
which ruled ICI's management were not necessarily unchangeable. As with the other strands we shall discuss, ICI's
commercial situation is inextricably bound up with, and
provides the setting for, its managerial culture. It is therefore
necessary to go back in history for a better understanding of
the situation in which the company found itself in the early
1960s.

From the company's formation, it dominated its markets.
Indeed, the moving force of the merger, Harry McGowan,
had articulated quite explicit 'imperial' ambitions for the
company. Under the pre-war cartel arrangement with DuPont
and I.G. Farben, each company was allowed dominance in its
home market and allocated parts of the world. ICI's share
was the British Empire and, jointly with DuPont, parts of
South and North America. The arrangement came to an end
after the war — when I.G. Farben was split into three, more
manageable, companies and DuPont was successfully taken to

court by the anti-trust division of the US Department of Justice. But some of the old attitudes remained. This had effects on the company's management which lasted long after the imperial reality had departed: specifically, marketing and financial functions had no reasons to develop strongly in a company which was not under great pressure on either front. There were other effects, notably in the management view of the world.

In the 1950s, the world was still picking itself up after the war; demand far exceeded supply; every company was hard at work making as much as it could with existing plant. There was, in short, no inducement to break new ground either technically or commercially — any more than there was pressure on managers to impose tight controls on their use of labour. But this situation of surplus demand could not continue for ever; nor were the old barriers and assumptions of the pre-war chemical industry to remain. By the end of the fifties, the old assumptions of the industry were visibly eroding. The following are some examples:

(*a*) Use of petroleum feedstocks for making organic chemicals had been growing rapidly in America before the war, and after the war throughout the world. The seemingly inexhaustible demand for plastics and synthetic fibres led to heavy investment in the plants for making the basic building blocks. This situation was confirmed by the arrival in the chemical industry of major US oil companies seeking new areas of investment for their immense cash flows. By the end of the 1950s, there was surplus capacity which could only be justified by continuing rapid growth. The US recession in 1958 sent many of these new entrants in the chemical industry to look for markets elsewhere. Their products soon arrived on a European market which was already over-supplied. Prices of plastics collapsed, and in the early 1960s there were numbers of anti-dumping applications by European chemical producers in an effort to stem the flow. However, by then prices had been brought to levels at which existing operations were unprofitable. (The same sequence of events — optimistic investment leading to surplus capacity — led to a similar crisis in synthetic fibres 10 years later when a downturn in demand hit the world textile industry.)

(*b*) Among ICI's most important products were bulk fertilisers. ICI, with its Billingham complex, was among the world's leading producers of nitrogenous fertilisers. Hydrogen for the process came from coal. But, in many parts of the world, this was being replaced progressively during the 1950s by natural gas, based on new processes. In common with other European producers with an enormous investment in the old technology, ICI was reluctant to move away from its traditional raw material base. Moreover, natural gas was not then available in Britain. (It was available in Trinidad — but that is another story.) The problem of using petroleum as a feedstock was solved by the engineers at Billingham in a major technical feat, and huge investments were made in the new process in the mid-sixties. The new plants were troublesome and, by then, nitrogenous fertilisers from similar plants elsewhere in the world were seriously threatening the position of ICI and other European producers.

(*c*) ICI had always been among the world's leading dyestuffs manufacturers but, although there was extensive export of dyes, the profitability of Dyestuffs Division was intimately bound up with the UK domestic textile industry. However efficient and cost-conscious the Dyestuffs management tried to be, there was little it could do about the seemingly unstoppable decline of UK textiles as imports from low-cost-labour countries rose.

(*d*) The fate of ICI's explosives division was similarly settled outside the company. The main markets of this once highly profitable activity had been the British coal-mining industry and exports. But, from 1957 onward, the coal industry in Britain went into a sharp decline; overseas markets were increasingly pre-empted by local manufacture; and explosives in mining generally gave way to the use of ammonia nitrate slurries.

More generally, technological changes in the chemical industry were leading inexorably towards fewer and larger units, each serving a wider area. National boundaries were beginning to mean less as the level of import duties became comparable with the economies of large-scale production.

Many of the new entrants to the industries had no investment in — and even less patience with — the old boundaries and protected markets. The result was that the company came under increasing pressure on a number of fronts.

The increasing competition in the chemical market was reflected in the level of prices. The price index for ICI's chemicals dropped by more than 20% between 1958 and 1967. (It was hailed as an achievement in the Annual Reports of the time.) The UK index for manufactured goods rose 21% in the same period and the average pay of ICI's UK employees increased from £770 per head to £1,220 per head. ICI moved to contain this massive inflation in its costs by investing heavily in new capital plant. However, the company's results are very sensitive to the trade cycle, and return on capital fluctuated between 13% in the good years (e.g. 1960) and 8% in the bad (e.g. 1966). This instability in the earnings line had an adverse effect on ICI's stock market rating. More to the point, the return on capital showed no signs of keeping up with the cost of new borrowing. By the mid to late sixties, ICI was therefore in a position of earning less on funds employed than it was paying out to long-term lenders of fixed interest capital.

A number of actions were taken at the level of economic rationality. With the arrival of Sir Paul Chambers as Chairman in 1960 — the first non-technical Chairman for some years — there was a change of emphasis in managerial skills. Financial and commercial ability were to become important attributes in managers; the old technical dominance was threatened. Sir Paul also initiated a massive investment programme, designed to equip ICI with the best capital plant available. (The programme was inevitable but had mixed blessings: plants were erected which were designed at the limits of what was technically possible and took several years to commission fully; the programme so over-stretched ICI's resources — and those of the UK engineering industry — that it twice went to the market for expensive capital, in 1966.) The main lesson of the 1960-2 crisis was that ICI was operating in a truly international market. The old geographical structure had disappeared. The only standard of judgment would have to be the performance of its competitors. A series of comparative studies was set in motion.

The first look at other companies showed that European companies in general performed far less well than their American competitors. But, as far as it was possible to judge (and the nature of disclosures made this extremely difficult), ICI performed less well than any other major chemical company. For example, in terms of sales per employee, ICI performed between one-half and one-third as well as the six major American companies and did less well too, though by a smaller margin, than the three major German companies. In terms of gross trading profit per employee, the Americans did between twice and five times as well as ICI. In terms of added value per employee the ratios were similar. Part of the explanation for this discrepancy was to be found in the different environments within which the companies operated. As the relationship between the costs of labour and capital alter, so will the benefits of adopting a more or less capital-intensive mode of operation. The British employees of ICI received as little as a third of the pay of employees of the American companies and, in compensation, the gross fixed assets per employee of the American companies were far higher than that of ICI. As a result, by other measures of performance, the company showed up far less badly.

It seemed evident that the difference in performance between these competing companies lay in their use of manpower, and, in 1964, ICI carried out a very detailed reciprocal survey with an American company, chosen as the best match in terms of size and product mix. A number of differences in practice and policy — also in attitudes toward costs and profits — were identified. Most important, it was found for a selected group of comparable activities that ICI employed three times as many people per unit of sales and more than twice as many people per unit of assets as the comparison company. And in terms of sales per unit of assets, ICI did three-quarters as well as the other company — which would not have been expected as a result of the adjustments described above.

Many senior managers in ICI, particularly those with experience of overseas companies, may have suspected the situation; but the detailed survey came as a shock. It did, however, provide ammunition for those on the Main Board interested in change, of whom the leader was Sir Peter Allen.

As we have seen, a large part of the differences represent the effects of operating in different environments. However, where, in an industry like the chemical industry, the competition is international and based in technology which is freely available, these fine distinctions may not be so important. What matters is final costs. Moreover, a company with the more labour-intensive operation is going to be vulnerable to increases in wages. This was the crucial point for ICI since any estimate of future trends showed increasing wages that would render the company vulnerable to international competition.

The result of these studies and discussions was to focus Board attention on the issue of *labour productivity*. The conclusion could not be escaped: ICI was weakest in its use of manpower. And if the commercial crisis that lurked on the horizon was to be avoided, a major effort must be made to increase output per man. This awareness at Board level was an important enabling condition for approving recommendations of the Rutherford Panel (the 1964 Wages Structure Panel) that were so radical as to be almost revolutionary. It is worth noting, as it were parenthetically, that they were unlikely to have been approved in the absence of such an energising crisis. Presenting itself in that way, the need for action was legitimised, a subject for serious consideration which it would not have been (one may hazard the guess) had it been presented overtly as — what it was later revealed as — a problem with its roots in the traditionally 'soft' area of labour and social policy.

2. *Evolution in the wages structure*

ICI has had a long history of innovative interest in methods of controlling and rewarding work. The tradition of management inherited from Brunner-Mond (of which more in the next section) was as sensitive as the times permitted — or required — to the human needs of the workforce; it was part of this emphasis that the control and motivational aspects of the reward system should receive high priority. ICI had developed formidable expertise in the area of work study, work measurement and bonus incentive schemes. The system was under continual study and was periodically reviewed: the management committee already referred to was set up for such a review. Before we consider the evolution of the system in more detail, we should look at the production function of the industry which determined the structure of work and so, to a large extent, of wages. The 1969 *Report** of the National Board for Prices and Incomes on ICI's proposal to increase wages says:

'The industry is in a state of continuous technological advance with constant effort to improve performance. Thus at any one chemical factory it is fairly common to see some completely new plants being constructed, some substantial modifications being carried out to existing plants, as well as production proceeding at the remainder of the plants. [In the chemical industry a "plant" is the assembly of equipment necessary to carry out a process or group of processes; there may be many "plants" within a "works" or "factory" and there may well be more than one works or factory on a "site".] Most chemical processes are concerned with the handling and processing of "aggressive" substances. By "aggressive" in this sense is meant that the material will attack in various ways, by chemical reaction or by corrosion or abrasion, the materials of which the plant is constructed. The selection of materials of construction for any particular process is usually one of compromise. The more commonplace materials may well be fairly rapidly attacked and require frequent replacement, but the cost of this must be balanced against possibly much higher costs which may be involved if less commonplace materials are used. But in the general run of chemical processes the penalty of a high maintenance requirement is accepted. Substantial maintenance is involved, particularly of specialised components of the plant such as motors, pumps, valves and particularly sensing devices and instruments.

'This has led in the conventional chemical factory to a division of responsibility between process operation and maintenance. This is reflected not only in the "shop floor"

---

*Report No. 105, Pay of General Workers and Craftsmen in Imperial Chemical Industries Ltd. Cmnd. 3941, p.20.

workers but also in the management structure. Traditionally the process operators have been recruited from general rather than craftsmen workers and training has been given within the works, although latterly more formalised training schemes have been developed. Thus the chemical operator, although skilled, is not regarded as a craftsman. The plants are, however, maintained by a number of skilled trades who belong to craft unions. The most ubiquitous craftsman found on the chemical works is the fitter who is generally required to dismantle, erect and repair the plant. Other specialised skills are also demanded, such as welding and plumbing, sheet metal working, and boiler-making. Another important group of craftsmen is concerned with electrical installations and in the maintenance of sensing devices and instruments.

'As technology has developed new skills have been demanded from both the maintenance crew and the process operators, but until very recently the clear distinction between the two has been maintained. This distinction has been reflected in the management structure, the usual form being for a works manager to control a production manager and a chief engineer who is generally responsible for the engineering and maintenance functions of the factory.'

The first consequence is that ICI is really two different, if not entirely separate, industries: the chemical industry, concerned with operating the plant, carrying out chemical processes and making the products; and a sizeable engineering industry whose involvement with the process industry ranged from the very close one of shift maintenance — carrying out the running minor repairs needed to keep a plant on stream — to the more arms-length relationship with the engineering workshops, carrying out major overhauls and even design and construction of complete plants. On large sites like Wilton and Billingham, the Engineering Works employed 2,000 men each; at Wilton the works was hived off as a wholly owned subsidiary — Engineering Services Wilton Ltd — which can also take on outside contracts. The process side was managed by graduate chemists and operated by general workers — members predominantly of the large general workers unions, the T&GWU and G&MWU. The maintenance side was managed by engineers and operated by craftsmen — members of many craft unions, of which the two largest were the AUEW (engineers) and ETU (electricians). I say 'was' because one of the first recommendations of the Panel, and one which affected management more than the payroll, was to merge the two functions.

The earnings of an ICI worker had four main components: base rate, job rate, overtime and incentive bonus. (There was also a profit-sharing scheme which does not concern us.) The first two comprised the reward for the job done; the third for extra time worked; and the last for effort. The *base rate* was negotiated separately for three main groups of workers: general workers, predominantly members of the T&GWU and G&MWU; building trades, and other crafts, of which the engineers' union, AUEW, and electricians, ETU, were by far the biggest. In addition, the workers had a *job rate*. For the general workers it was arrived at by job appraisement. Jobs were given points by work study officers under four headings: mental requirements, physical requirements, acquired skill and knowledge, and working conditions. The points were weighted and summed, the total defining which of the 22 job categories, going up in steps of ten points, the job fell into. Craft jobs were differently appraised, craftsmen being put into four grades on their managers' recommendation. It was an unsatisfactory compromise, giving rise to bitter talk of 'blue-eyed boys', but enforced by the unions' refusal to be appraised on grounds of principle — they were paid for their skills as time-served craftsmen. *Bonus incentives* of several kinds had been used in the company since before the war, but there had been no unified scheme covering all workers until a company-wide bonus incentive scheme was introduced in 1952 that marked the end of a long process of evolution and refinement of techniques. It was based in the principles of work study, which aim to break work down into elements, each of which is given a time and which together comprise a complete description of the operations carried out by a particular worker. The aim was to provide workers with an incentive to attain a rate of working which (according to work study) could be maintained without undue strain. The 'standard' for the job was set at one-quarter below this rate of working and given the value of 100 units — units being the timed elements of work. The workers could therefore reach a rate of working equivalent to $133\frac{1}{3}$ units — a full day's work without undue strain — and so qualify for a bonus of one-third. This was the system applied to general workers. Craft unions still officially resisted what they saw as an attack on their skills implied in work measurement. Instead of the men with stopwatches, they accepted the assessment of 'estimators' — who were all members of craft unions and set standards by experience rather than measurement. These methods of job appraisement and work measurement, developed within ICI, provided the foundation of experience and skills on which the later agreements were based.

Basic Wage Structure	General Workers	Building Trades	Engineering Crafts
Base Rate	Negotiated centrally	Negotiated centrally	Negotiated centrally
Job Rate	Job appraisement (15 categories)	Individual job rates awarded by management (5 grades)	
Incentive Bonus	Based on time study	Based on estimation	

The resulting pay system was even more complex than this sketch suggests. In addition to the 22 categories and 4 grades on different scales, there was a multiplicity of special allowances. These ranged from the centrally-negotiated and company-wide shift allowances, disturbance allowances and weekend working arrangements to local arrangements with their roots in antiquity, differentials between local unions and special payments. In addition there was the contentious area of abnormal conditions payments. The result was a complex and fragmented pay structure with hundreds of possible combinations. Worse, it was confusing. In the welter of special payments it was often difficult for a worker to discover just what had made up his pay cheque. An incentive payment designed to relate reward directly to effort was the intention, but unrealistic in these conditions.

The system, having been set up, needed constant review. It was a significant advance on the systems that preceded it and provided a more flexible way of rewarding the complex, interdependent (particularly on process plant) jobs of the chemical industry. But the industry changes rapidly and, with it, so do the jobs. In 1958 there was a massive review by a Wages Structure Panel of which the main conclusion was that the existing payment system did not adequately reward mental effort. As a result, it was suggested that the appraisement scale should be modified to give a greater weight to the 'mental requirements' heading, and split between mental and character requirements. (This was not done.) Among the other points raised was the long-standing preoccupation with the equity of making a distinction between the conditions of employment of staff and payroll employees. Thus the two main issues that were to be considered by the 1965 Wages Structure Panel were already in the air. But if the need for radical change was perceived it was not generally accepted: there had been no energising crisis to push the system out of its existing framework. Instead, the problems were coped with by adjustment. The recommendation that the most highly skilled workers (about 10% of the total) should be paid salaries rather than be paid by the hour was rejected as being too expensive, although later a small group, the chargehands, were taken into staff.

This was the wages structure which was to be considered by the Panel in 1965: an efficient reward system, providing performance measures; managerial control and (to some degree) incentives for effort; it was objective and, as far as possible, fair in its application; it was efficiently administered by a body of management thoroughly familiar with and trained in its use. But the industry had continued to evolve, to move away from the pattern set in 1948 (and modified in 1954 and 1958). In the new conditions, the old system was becoming less and less suitable, to a degree where adjustment would no longer provide adaptation enough.

The hardware of the industry was changing. Plants increase in size and complexity; the instrumentation needed to control them becomes vastly more comprehensive. The key jobs of controlling the production units are both more responsible and more demanding — but the qualities needed

for their successful performance escape the known categories
of the payment system. A plant manager may have wanted to
reward a highly skilled process operator in ways that would
adequately reflect his value. But he was constrained by a
system of points allocation that would not allow him to
weight the mental requirements realistically. As a result he
was reduced to expedients like allotting points for sweeping
out the control room in order to boost the points under
'physical requirements' — of which there were, in such a job,
effectively none. Most limiting of all, there was no way of
measuring mental effort. The operator might be most
successful when least was happening in the plant; yet under
the old system he could only be rewarded for running about
and doing things — a state of affairs which only happened
when things went wrong. Because of the need to reward key
operators adequately, to keep them and their important
skills, there were strong inducements for managers to 'fiddle'
the system, which discredited it and reduced its effectiveness.

However, this might have been expected. All payments
systems spontaneously decay. Apart from the changing
nature of work, there is a learning effect: no sooner has a
standard been established than new ways are found of doing
the work. Short cuts are devised, tools are designed, parts of
the job are found to be unnecessary — yet the original
standard is strenuously defended against the prying attention
of the work study officers; any slack within it can be turned
to good account, either in easing the pressure of work or in
providing time to accumulate points for a still higher bonus.
The workers become more productive through their own
efforts — which is obviously no bad thing in itself, but makes
nonsense of a bonus scheme designed to yield a $33\frac{1}{3}\%$ bonus
for a day's full work. The net result is that the system
becomes slack and labour costs rise.

A third, quite different, effect, was the decline in the
incentives offered by the bonus. As part of the continuing
negotiations with the unions, ICI consolidated part of the
bonus, reducing it from $33\frac{1}{3}$ to $27\frac{1}{2}\%$. A more important
reduction of the incentive element took place as a *de facto*
consolidation: in theory, the bonus was variable in the range
from 0 to $33\frac{1}{3}$ but in practice the bonus was built into the
workers' expectations — which it was costly to disappoint —

and wages rarely fluctuated by more than 10%. Thus, subtly, the bonus scheme was transformed from a positive incentive to work harder into a penalty for not achieving standard rates. Thus the dynamics of the situation were changed.

4

Problems with People

1. The two faces of paternalism

The overt purpose of the 1964 Wage Structure Committee was to consider ways of eliminating distinctions in the treatment of certain hourly-paid (payroll) and monthly-paid (staff) employees. The subject was significant, reflecting a characteristic balance between 'pure' and 'applied' altruism: pure, as a product of a consistently ethical concern which is a theme of ICI's labour policy; applied, as a response to a problem – how to reward adequately a small group of key employees – whose solution would be to the company's commercial benefit.

The question of staff/payroll distinctions, implicitly class-based, had long worried some senior managers. The first clear statement of this unease is generally taken to be a memorandum written in 1942 by Alexander Fleck, then a division Chairman and later to be the company's Chairman (and Lord Fleck). Speculating about post-war conditions in the labour market, he wrote of the company's need for a forward-looking labour policy

'to show that this nation is not bankrupt of ideas to improve the lot of the vast bulk of its inhabitants.'

(The assumption of ICI's national role is characteristic.) Fleck then identified what he thought were the major problems and indicated some solutions:

'By a process of usage the "workers" of this country have been divided into two classes . . . normally called "staff" and "workmen". This note concerns itself with two main themes:

1. that this division is largely an arbitrary one and that there is no adequate reason for maintaining it; and
2. that its successful elimination would be a most material contribution to improve the mental attitude of the work people concerned to the whole social structure.'

It is hardly being cynical to point out that this was expected to yield benefits for the company. Fleck continued:

'A great feature would be the psychological effect produced. Most of mankind respond to the feeling that they are being trusted and react in a favourable way. If a man feels that he is being trusted by any organisation, he usually responds by thinking highly of the organisation, and in turn trusting it.'

However, nothing decisive was done although the debate continued, surfacing occasionally in reports, for two more decades. The most comprehensive report, in 1955, recommended flatly that the whole payroll should be transferred progressively to staff. Four groups were identified and a timetable proposed, starting with the chargehands, estimators and others with comparable authority and ending after five years with the transfer of the least skilled. The aim was:

'to build up further the satisfaction, confidence and a sense of security of workers; to remove the distinction between staff and better workers; to reduce labour turnover; to achieve greater flexibility in the use of manpower; to simplify the pay structure.' (*Report on Terms and Conditions of Employment*, 1955; usually called the 'Inglis Report')

The recommendation was not accepted in that form, mainly because the rate of change proposed was thought to be too rapid. The costs and difficulties would be considerable and the benefits for the company not obvious.

However, a number of more limited changes were made in the following years. Inglis's Group I was brought on to the staff in 1961; holiday scales were progressively brought closer together; similar rules for preservation and transferability of pension rights were introduced in 1964; 'clocking on' was left to divisional discretion; Labour and Staff Departments merged into a Central Personnel Department.

But the problem remained, troubling the consciences of ICI's more thoughtful managers.

In addition to this worry about fairness, there was the more practical concern — the subject of the previous section — about the best way to reward mental skills and effort. At root, the old staff/payroll distinction set mental (office) apart from manual (factory) workers. But as technology developed, plants became more automated and the skills needed to run them more mentally demanding; so that for some parts of the workforce this mental/manual distinction was losing what real meaning it ever had.

Those concerns were a manifestation of the company's tradition of paternalistic management, a dirty word in management these days, and for reasons that are not hard to find. The voluntary provision of goods and services outside the bounds of a straight commercial bargain between employer and employed has overtones of charity and defines, when it does not create, an unequal relationship: a gulf between the giver (the haves) and the receiver (have nots). The benefits are voluntarily offered but a reciprocal obligation, or the sense of obligation, is compelled to the extent that acceptance is enforced by need. A man may have no other way to some desired end — a useful skill, nourishing lunches, the opportunity to excel at a sport, or simply good health — than that offered by the company he works for in the form of education schemes, subsidised canteens, sports grounds or health services.

This is not to suggest that companies offer such things in a spirit of pure altruism. There is goodwill in such policies, but it is 'applied' altruism that persuades managers to allocate company resources for these purposes. The end result, while being good for the employee, is also in the company's interest, since it yields skilled, healthy and (hopefully) grateful and loyal employees. But the resulting relationship is unequal and socially divisive; it is also subtly coercive and inappropriate to modern conditions. People want their goods and services without strings and, if they are able to, will migrate toward situations where they can make free choices

to buy them in straightforward, equal commercial transactions.

This has not always been so. The paternalist management
policies of Brunner-Mond, the leading partner in the ICI
merger, were quite appropriate to times when market rates of
pay bought the shopfloor worker little more than basic
necessities, and when state welfare — health services, unemployment and sickness benefits, pensions and even
education — was minimal. ICI offered what was virtually a
complete way of life to the employee who wanted it. Playing
fields, social clubs, canteens, company housing, health
services and various company-financed schemes for self-
improvement were among the benefits of working for the
company — benefits which varied between divisions. They
started as a fundamentally humane means (although rigorously monitored) for providing goods and services which
would not otherwise be available to the workers. For the
purposes of this book, their importance is historical, since it
declined when they lost their motivating power: with time,
just as bonuses were assimilated, the fringe package was built
into the workers' expectations. The goods and services
offered became more generally available to the worker, who
could in the last resort expect from the State what he could
not purchase himself.

Perhaps the most important fringe benefit, if it can be
called that, was the security of employment ICI offered at
times when, and in places where, employment was highly
uncertain. ICI became the most favoured employer in areas
of high unemployment and acquired a fund of goodwill and
loyalty among long service employees that was to emerge in
quite sharp contrasts in behaviour between long-established
and new sites.

Again, the value of such security was also a function of its
availability elsewhere. In the post-war period of economic
expansion, workers learned to expect relatively secure
employment. This was not the case for managers. For them, a
'career for life' had a richer meaning — and one that brings us
to the inward aspect of paternalism. Some brief points:

First, ICI was among the earliest companies to recruit
systematically from the universities. It did so, moreover, at a
time when the dimming of Britain's imperial destiny made

industrial careers more attractive to graduates. Secondly, the men recruited found themselves in a powerfully influential cultural environment, including both class and intellectual components, of which the traditions went back to their origins in the founding companies. From Brunner-Mond sprang Alkali Division (now absorbed into Mond Division) where managers were expected to be both gentlemanly and technically rigorous. The staff club at Alkali's Winnington Hall was famous for its claret; the research department invented polythene. The chemical complex at Billingham Division had some of the same qualities, with a staff club at Norton Hall and engineering skills that attracted visitors from all over the world. Dyestuffs Division prided itself on being less fancy socially, but it saw itself (not everyone else would) as the centre of technical and managerial toughness in the company, rooted in the intensely complex chemistry of dyes manufacture and competitive international markets.

Thirdly, the company's policies of staff promotion put a premium on long service. Management was developed within the company. As a corollary, senior positions were only exceptionally filled from outside. And while this policy served the company's needs it resulted in a management structure which was shut off from the outside world.

Lastly, the jobs facing management were predominantly technical, and rewards went for technical excellence. Until the commercial environment began to change in the late fifties, the main constraints on a chemical company's success were technical. In times of high unemployment — or to be more accurate, while expectations of unemployment were still dominant in the workforce — the main problems facing managers were also technical. The solution of technical problems was a manager's job; the management of human resources could be left with safety to more junior echelons of management.

The result was a management that was highly-qualified and skilled at dealing with the extremely complex technical problems of the industry while less skilled — because less rewarded for acquiring skills — in the areas of sales, financial control and man management. Moreover, it was a management with a powerful culture founded not so much on class consciousness (although that was present) as on a sense of the

duty and responsibility owing to rank. The most accurate
model this has suggested to me is the officers' mess of a good
line regiment: a strong sense of duty, loyalty to the regiment
and obligation to the men; also the privileges that go with
rank.

It was, in many ways, an admirable and decent management culture. But it was not tuned to the management needs
of the sixties. Other skills were needed to cope with emerging
conditions. Commercial and financial skills were demanded
by changes in the environment that have been described in
detail in the previous chapter; new skills in managing people
were to be required in the programme of radical changes in
worker/management relationships contained in the Weekly
Staff Agreement. But the management — no less than other
social organisations and their associated value systems — were
to prove resistant to change.

2. *Rising expectations*

The changes in this section are closely connected with, and
have been touched upon in, the previous section. Management style is a means to an end; it is appropriate only to the
degree that it matches the needs — technical, commercial and
social — of the organisation. It follows that there is no single
optimal way of managing, although management theorists
have in the past generated heaps of paper in their efforts to
discover such an optimum. (They have learned better.)
Rather, each situation imposes special demands to which —
almost by definition — the good manager is sensitive. I have
stressed that, offensive as in some ways it is to modern eyes,
the paternalism of a few Victorian industrialists like Ludwig
Mond and, by direct descent, of ICI, should be seen in
historical context. And the assumptions of ICI's management
culture contained much that was humane and enlightened —
in the context of the pre-war conditions in which they were
formed. But the context has changed. The social environment
has changed out of all recognition: the ICI worker (an
abstraction, but no matter) is not the same man. By 1965 he
had become more affluent, more secure; he had had the
experience of some years of full employment; he was better
educated, with his horizons immeasurably broadened by

television and travel. Above all, he was not *grateful* for fringe benefits, once the largesse of a bountiful company, now accepted as his by right.

The causes of these changes are complex. The 'enabling' change, in my view, has been the steady increase in real wealth, which has loosened the grip of privation and, at one remove, the grip of other systems to which it gave power.* Full employment changes the rules of the labour market and it changes the rules of management. When a worker has the option of walking down the road to another company, the power a manager can command is sensibly diminished. He may feel that he ought to be able to command instant obedience — which would be, after all, a considerable convenience. And when he cannot, he may feel that some ancient law is being challenged — his right to manage.† But he ignores the shift in the underlying power balance at his company's cost.

More to the point of this section, full employment has changed the relationship of the worker to his job. One job, perilously held at the whim of the supervisor, is something like slavery; the availability of several jobs, even if none of them is ideal, allows a man to make a choice in his own interest where he had none. The job is there to serve his purposes, not he the purposes of the job. This is only one, arguably the most important, aspect of the way in which choice is made available more generally in the country by affluence. Surplus spending power, no less, confers power to choose.

What a man chooses has also changed, and is a function of more complex expectations. Better education — the later school-leaving age — is providing workers with mental skills they may want to use. Probably more important, mass communications (television) and cheaper travel (package

* I have developed this theme at greater length in my book *Organisation in a Changing Environment*, Addison Wesley, 1973.

† That this enforced change is often seen as a lapse on the part of the worker from an earlier state of grace is a characteristic misinterpretation. Admittedly, the near-moral ideal of hard work, obedience and loyalty to the company is consistent with the injunctions of Protestantism. But the grip of that value system was consolidated by the power employers had to impose heavy penalties — privation, no less — on anyone who did not conform.

holidays abroad) is broadening the range of 'life models' available. Without getting into the implications of the Consumer Society and the fatal seductions of over-spend, it is enough to say that the idea of what constitutes the good life is now subject to influences from far outside the immediate community — and imposes far greater demands on a worker's capacity to live it.

Curiously, the unions appear to have changed much less, in the sense that their perceptions of their roles (as far as it is possible to judge from their actions) seem to be as firmly rooted in the past as the managerial assumptions I started with. The political strength they command has become vastly greater in times of full employment and as affluence and the independent attitudes of workers have increased. But it is directed to winning battles — in defence of their members' work, particularly — which no longer have the urgency they did.

To sum up, the changed expectations of employees had effect for the company in three areas: the nature of work offered; the appropriate managerial style; and the basis of the contract with the worker. We may assume — although I think it is easy to over-emphasise it — that a better-educated worker will demand more complex satisfactions from his job. (He is just as, perhaps more, likely to demand the where-withal — more money and leisure to spend it in — to seek satisfaction away from his job.) But, at the very least, he has the freedom *not* to choose work he doesn't want to do: work that is unduly physically demanding, noisy and filthy; work that is boring, repetitive and ill-paid. One of the first effects of industrialisation is the disappearance of servants: people would rather be their own masters. Perhaps one of the first effects of sustained full employment is the disappearance of jobs so disagreeable that only a man with no realistic alternative on offer would undertake it. But it goes further than this. When the market for certain skills is tight, companies are forced to expend considerable effort to suit the jobs to the people, in ways that would have been unthinkable not long ago.

Changes in management style will be dealt with fully later. By 1965, the signs were to be found at their most explicit in the decline of the power of the supervisor — or, to put it

more tactfully, the change in his role from the height of
pre-war authority, based in power to hire and fire. By 1972,
they were to be found in the revealing complaint of a works
manager to me: that he spent more than half of his time on
people problems and had no time for the *real* business of
managing. The fact is that the salience of problems has been
shifting so that people problems are now at the top of the
pile: they are no longer looked after by the environment. But
to him they were still 'soft' and unworthy.

By the company's contract with the worker, I mean more
than the terms of the wages structure agreements. I am really
talking of assumptions about ICI's role as employer that were
implicit in labour policy. These are the two facets of
paternalism I have already referred to: treat people well as a
moral duty and as a practical necessity; reward long service
and loyalty as one would reward any virtuous act and also
because they have a real value for the company. Such policies
were appropriate to times when long service – a life spent
with one company – was the norm and steady employment
was prized above anything else. But, as I have attempted to
show, this could not survive into a time when work was
freely available and a man might seek to advance himself
more quickly – or at least to garner the interest of variety –
by moving around.

3. *The uses of behavioural science*

Strictly speaking, the behavioural sciences do not belong
among the influences important in the Rutherford Panel. The
ideas about job enrichment and participative management
commonly associated with the names of Herzberg and
MacGregor were gaining currency in the US in the early
1960s; techniques of organisation development – planned
organisation change – had not yet been developed. There
were very few people in ICI who knew of these ideas; none
with any competence to make practical use of them. None
the less, I include the behavioural sciences as a fifth strand:
the ideas were present at the beginning, although without
influence; in time they came to dominate the whole exercise.
They offered the answers to questions raised by the other
four. Improvements in productivity were the goal; massively

complex and pervasive changes in the design of jobs, wages structure and the basic contract between workers and the company were the means of attaining it. The behavioural sciences provided an understanding of what the changes involved, why they were at first rejected and, finally, the means for introducing them. The ideas are probably familiar to most readers. At the risk of anticipating the rest of the book, I shall give below a brief account of the way the theories took root in ICI, specifically in response to problems encountered in introducing the new agreements.

The start of an interest in behavioural science can be dated to a visit to the USA in 1963 by two senior managers, one of them the head of research in Central Personnel. They toured the main centres of academic research and the few companies then engaged in experiments with behavioural science techniques. The immediate product was a report on the developments they had seen, which attempted to outline 'a basic strategy for the management of ICI in the use of its people'. The ideas were before their time – more accurately, they came before the need for them was accepted – and the report was, as such reports usually are, without influence. However, it led to visits from US consultants, of whom the best known are Peter Drucker, Fred Herzberg and Douglas MacGregor. MacGregor's visit was particularly successful, but he died before he could start on the programme of work that it was to have led to. And indeed, although the seed had been sown, it was some years before the behavioural theories were generally accepted as relevant.

Managers in the company had first to learn that the traditional managerial assumptions were not altogether relevant to the new situation, and that a different approach would pay dividends. The change in attitude could not be planned. It took place as a result of trial and error, a long period of delays and disappointments during which a number of alternatives were tried and rejected – and during which the company's management slowly learned about the nature of the changes being attempted. Through this process the behavioural science theories emerged as providing a theoretical core around which to build the programme. Experiments were carried out in job enrichment which demonstrated its potential value and provided a rational counter to managers' emotional rejection; courses were provided for 'climate setters' among the managers; internal OD consultants were trained. But none of this would have been as influential if the behavioural science theories had not also performed the somewhat unexpected function of intellectual legitimation. The personnel director of a division described the process through which they became effective:

'Operationally, the behavioural science theories were enormously important since they provided a rational basis for policy decisions that seemed irrational. The whole tradition of ICI works management had come to be based in work measurement, standardisation, incentive schemes — all of them devices which provided measures and systems of control. To suggest junking incentive schemes in favour of methods based in trust and psychological motivation just about killed many managers with fear. However, along came the behavioural scientists with reasons for doing just this which were not only intellectually respectable (and they needed that) but also offered improvements all round. Once the ideas began to be grasped by managers they were eagerly seized.'

In the end the new theories came to dominate a programme which started out from quite different premises, because they worked.

5
Designing the Agreement for Trials

There were two stages in the process that led to ICI's trial agreement with the unions. The first was a management study into the company's payment structure. Their report, in January 1965, recommended that ICI enter negotiations and discussion of a joint company/union committee which led to the signature of the agreement on 'Manpower Utilisation and Payment Structure', or MUPS, in October 1965.

The Rutherford Panel

The 1964 Wages Structure Panel was only the latest, and not the most important, of a regular series of reviews. The Panel — called after its Chairman, Ian Rutherford — was set up with the quite specific intention of examining:

> 'the practicability and the implications of embarking on a "non-fluctuating" or salaried type of payment for certain payroll employees as part of the long term development of payroll and staff conditions of employment and to advise on the course of action.'

This was more than specific, it was limited to that small part of the workforce whose contribution was most appropriately .rewarded with a stable wage — put at 10% in the Inglis Report of 1955 but probably nearer 15% by 1964. Early on the Panel decided that they could not work within such a limited remit: first, because of the difficulty of identifying this favoured category of workers; secondly, having identified them, of successfully introducing new conditions of work in such a way that they could be contained and not spread downwards; thirdly, because it was not possible to make prescriptions for workers without first having some idea about the patterns of skills likely to be needed in new plants in 10 or 15 years' time. For these reasons they extended their remit to consider much more broadly the issue of productivity. It has been suggested to me more than once that the whole affair was a put-up job; that a group of managers somehow got the review brought forward — it was not due for another three years; that they manoeuvred themselves on to the Panel with the specific intention of questioning the assumptions underlying the existing agreements; and that the whole purpose was to suggest new solutions to the problems discussed in the previous chapter. I have found no documentary evidence of this sinister theory. But if it is true it merely suggests, what many people have said about organisation life, that nothing happens of its own accord.

The Panel had six members, all senior managers, who spanned between personnel and production functions with one of them, Bill Stead, the Research Manager of the Central Personnel Department. They considered a great deal of evidence, much of it in the form of research reports. Two sorts of information were especially influential: the 'ideal manning reports' and studies of other productivity agreements.

(a) Ideal manning studies

Teams of local managers were given the jobs of working out theoretical manning patterns for five works. These included a plant for making ammonia, a range of processes at Hillhouse, the oil works at Billingham, an old-fashioned dyestuffs works at Huddersfield and a paint works at Slough and Stowmarket. The works had been chosen as covering a wide range of experience and indicating some directions in which ICI was likely to develop. The teams of managers were given complete freedom in working out their optimum manning. Their basic instruction was: 'Assume there are no constraints and you are starting from a green field.' The results of this, entirely theoretical, exercise indicated a potential for dramatic savings over current levels of manning:

		Reduction in Manpower (%)	Reduction in Direct Wages & Salaries Costs (%)
Redwick Works,	Severnside	19	17.7
Hillhouse Works,	Mond Division	14	19.2
Oil Works,	Billingham	25-30	–
Huddersfield Works,	Dyestuffs	–	12.0
Slough & Stowmarket,	Paints Division	3	2.8

These studies were influential with the Panel — and later with the Main Board — and provided the solid base for their recommendations. Apart from offering a carrot of cost savings at the end of a programme of change, they demonstrated in vivid form the high cost of the current patterns of manning — much of which was determined by demarcation between unions, demarcations which manifested themselves in the form of the 'ownership' of certain jobs or kinds of work and which made a full and flexible use of the workforce impossible. That these practices imposed a high price in terms of rigidities, over-manning and duplication of work was beyond question. Yet they were also the product of a long process of evolution, the accumulation of many small victories won by the unions over employers; they were the unions' guarantee of secure employment for their members, areas of work free from competition by other unions — and they were not very likely, if at all, to be traded away. All of this was known, but it was not until the ideal manning studies were carried out that the costs to the company of such demarcations were guessed at. This information by itself provided an impetus toward a more, rather than less, radical solution, and it was to provide valuable supporting evidence for the Panel's recommendations. An early estimate of savings from the new proposals, assuming a 15% saving in manpower, put the money saving for ICI at an immediate £1.75m per year, rising to £7.28m per year in 10 years' time.

(b) Other productivity agreements
The other important consideration was the progress made by other companies in search of higher productivity. The problems the Panel were considering were common to much

of British industry; a number of other companies, all in capital-intensive (mainly oil refining) industries, were investigating ways of breaking down the union barriers to freer movement between jobs within factories. Members on the Panel visited Esso at Fawley; BOAC, to observe an advanced personnel policy in a completely different industry; and Shell, building a refinery on a greenfield site at Teesside, close to ICI's two biggest sites, Wilton and Billingham.

The most influential of these was the visit to the Fawley refinery, the site of the first productivity agreement to receive that description. It had taken the form of 'buying out' restrictive practices by a long process of negotiation in which the practices were listed and the company and unions agreed a price for their cessation. Such an agreement had the considerable advantage of improving productivity without disrupting the existing pattern of relationships. As such it was appealing to those who sought improvement but saw no reason to change the wages structure. But by the time the Panel was deliberating it seemed that the Fawley agreement had only replaced one set of restrictive practices with another, and rather expensively. Whatever the initial advantages of the Fawley agreement, it was evident that it was not the 'open-ended' kind of agreement which the Panel became convinced was needed, but a one-off agreement that offered the prospect of more of the same at some future date.

Other agreements were acquiring a greater complexity, as a more radical use of the productivity agreement framework for change was being explored. These were to emerge at about the same time as ICI's. But the main lesson from this exploration was that Fawley had been a starting-point but should not serve as a model: the company should establish new conditions that would provide a basis for continuing change; the time had gone for seeking improvements at the margin by tinkering with the old system.

A third issue was influential, possibly determining, but more as a strategic consideration than 'information': the knowledge that conditions in industries like chemicals were changing rapidly. The agreements being made in the oil refining industry would be bound to influence workers in similar industries. Specifically, at the time of the Panel's deliberations, it was known that Shell, taking the oppor-

tunity of building on a greenfield site at Teesside, was likely
to introduce conditions of work that had only appeared as
wishful thinking in the ideal manning exercises. ICI's huge
works at Wilton and Billingham, used to a position locally as
premium employer (although they had slipped back) would
suffer by comparison. Moreover, there was every indication
that the company was in for a period of wage inflation.

When the Panel reported, in January 1965, they
acknowledged that changes in the environment would enforce radical internal changes sooner or later. 'We expect that,
if ICI make no move in this direction, it will be faced with
demands from men and unions and be forced ultimately to
make such concessions. The Panel recommends that ICI
should take the initiative and try to bring about such changes
on its own conditions and at its own speed.'

At a more detailed level, a number of conclusions were
drawn from the ideal manning studies which, 'although the
teams made very different approaches to their studies and
their findings', showed 'a striking similarity in the main
features of their recommendations on organisation and
manning'. These struck at a number of time-honoured and
deeply rooted practices, and included:

1. Integration of process and maintenance plant managers
   – which had implications for the old separation
   between the chemists, who ran the plants, and the
   engineers, who maintained them.

2. The production operators should be able to do certain
   small maintenance jobs, currently done by tradesmen.

3. The supervisory structure should be simplified.

4. Some of the demarcation between different skilled
   trades should be blurred and tradesmen allowed to do
   the work of other trades.

5. Supervisors to have better training and to be of higher
   calibre in order to take greater responsibility.

The implications of these conclusions were far-reaching.
Specifically, the company would need to develop 'a better
calibre operator for the control and operation of process

plants . . . who would be largely self-supervising'. This would require a considerable degree of training — and risk. There would be considerable risks at this stage in the widespread replacement of the incentive bonus scheme by a stable wage or salary treatment, which did not provide some sanctions for managers if performance fell . . .' (This last point was to be an abiding worry of managers throughout the company.)

For the new scheme to be effective, it would have to have the wholehearted support and co-operation of the people affected — managers as well as men:

'It has to be fully realised that demarcations and restrictive practices are deeply ingrained in our essential defences of earnings, employment and craft skills. Increased money has an important part to play in their elimination, but the main means by which these inefficiencies can be tackled are greater security of earnings and employment, improvements in the status of the work and a strong and sustained effort by management at all levels and discussions with unions and men . . . to convince payroll employees that these defensive practices should be eliminated.'

The recommendations were put before the Main Board in February. Specifically, that ICI should approach the signatory unions to negotiate an agreement to be tested on limited trials. 'Trials' was something of a misnomer since, as the Personnel Director, C.M. Wright, pointed out, the changes once conceded could not be rescinded, it being 'out of the question to contemplate a return to the status quo'. It would have to be a framework agreement: because of ICI's structure it was necessary 'to devise a method, while adhering to one broad principle, that would nevertheless be capable of being applied and being accepted or rejected at different locations and in differing circumstances'. Wright warned that progress would be slow. Even so, his ideas were based on negotiations carried out in different circumstances. He guessed that formal union agreement might be obtained by early May, and local discussions started in June and July — five months. In fact, agreement was not reached until October and the first trials did not start until more than two years after that.

The Main Board accepted the proposals and an approach

was made to the unions — first to the Trade Union Advisory
Council, an *ad hoc* group of General Secretaries that met
occasionally with senior members of the Board to discuss
matters of broad policy. Sir Paul Chambers, ICI Chairman,
met the TUAC in early April and obtained their agreement to
take the next step — open discussions with national officers.
It was helpful that the proposals of the Rutherford Report
closely paralleled the principles of the Joint Statement of
Intent on Productivity, Prices and Incomes, just signed by the
unions, the CBI and George Brown, Secretary of State at the
Department of Economic Affairs. The Joint Statement had
said: 'We must take urgent and vigorous action to raise
productivity through industry' and agreed 'to encourage and
lead a sustained attack on the obstacles to efficiency . . .'
This provided a point of entry, no more, and indeed it was
probably not very influential — although a comfort to the ICI
Board, who could at least point to it in support of the
project. Not until May did the signatory unions agree to start
discussions — but the management side could hardly have
started earlier.

The first major departure in MUPS was the way in which it
was agreed — and this was the main reason for the long delay
in getting together with the unions. Not only was this to be a
new labour agreement, but the way in which it was to be
agreed was to embody the principles which it contained. That
is, it was to be a complete departure from the traditional
negotiating procedure — ·in which one side came to the other
with a demand, which was then resisted and modified in long
debate. But ICI was proposing a change in the rules — from
negotiations over a fixed set of issues to open-ended
discussions seeking the best way of dealing with a common
problem. The company was proposing that both parties
should, as it were, get the same side of the table.

The move was unprecedented. The union officers were
convinced that it was some new trick dreamed up by the
perfidious company representatives in Central Personnel.
When they did eventually agree to discuss rather than
negotiate the company representatives were no less suspicious
of the new procedures; they were no less used to the
comfortable old ways of institutionalised conflict.

The first meeting of the joint sub-committee — ten union representatives and nine from the company, including the committee chairman, John Rhodes, who was ICI's Chief Labour Officer — took place on 2 June. The ninth and last meeting was held on 24 September. The agreement, MUPS, was ratified by the signatory unions on 19 October. In between, with the general remit of finding ways 'to make the best use of our manpower' the committee had covered the ground under three main headings:

— Current problems preventing efficient use of manpower.
— The establishment of a system to provide a fair reward.
— Safeguards and procedures to secure fair treatment of employees.

The main diet for discussion was a series of papers produced by CPD, re-working much of the research material of the Rutherford Panel. The first paper was 'Efficient Use of Manpower', followed by 'Assessment of Jobs', 'Methods of Payment' and 'Extra Aspects . . .'

I shall not dwell on the workings of the committee since what is important is the agreement that emerged from it — except for one 'process' point.* So successful were both sides in using a 'problem-solving' mode of discussion that they developed a high degree of trust among themselves and became totally committed to the ideas of the resulting agreement. At the end of the process, the men involved knew and understood each other as people, accepted the logic of each other's position and yet had learned to work from the common ground that lay between them. Everyone I have spoken to who served on the committee regarded it as a high point of cooperative effort in their lives. And in some ways it was a high point, in clarity and unanimity, in the progress of MUPS. Never again were the ideas behind the agreement to burn with that fierce, bright flame. Once it was signed, the ideas that had been worked out and agreed within a small group meeting in isolation had to make their way in a world which had no part in their formulation — no *ownership*. The

---

* Organisation development consultants make a useful distinction when talking about social interaction between 'content' — the substantive issues under discussion — and 'process' — the way the group works.

people who received the new agreement had not undergone the process of change which all members of the committee, willingly or unwillingly, had undergone in the long process of discussion.

This sequence was to be repeated time and again in the next years: a small group satisfying themselves about the ideas in the agreement only to have the spark of enthusiasm and commitment all but quenched in the great lake of indifference around them. The groups progressively grew larger as the new ideas made their way, until they included the whole company; but the ideas became more diluted and, more to the point, the process was long and painful.

Some of this was foreseen at the time. At the press conference in which the agreement was launched on 19 October, Bob Tallon, the AEU representative, replied to a question asking how long the agreement would take to bring in: 'Four or five years, I should think. I cannot answer that question as it is too difficult.' Geoffrey Gilbertson took up the question: 'The important point is that it takes a lot of thinking, a lot of planning, a lot of discussion. What we are trying very much to do is to change people's attitude to work, to change the concept of what they are getting out of it. One cannot do this quickly; it takes a great deal of discussion. All our exercises and studies suggest this. So when the time comes it will have to be done slowly and steadily. There will have to be a plan for each plant, with optimum manning and discussions going on bit by bit throughout the whole company. It will not be a quick process and it would be wrong if it was.'

These were prophetic words. But not even Gilbertson, who was to play the leading role in the central management of the agreement in the coming years, could have seen what frustrations there were ahead.

An anatomy of MUPS

The agreement that emerged from these deliberations was for trials at four works — one each at the huge Wilton and Billingham sites in the Northeast; Hillhouse in the Northwest; and North Tees, a new works that was to, but never did, begin trials when it started up. It was intended to be a model for a company-wide agreement. The trials aspect of it, therefore, need not concern us when analysing what the agreement contained.

The aim was set out roundly enough in a preamble which presented as common ground the proposition: 'that an employee must be employed to the best of his ability . . .' and that '. . . he should be given the status and remuneration which will recognise the importance of his contribution to the company . . .' (The full text of MUPS is given in Appendix III.) Accepting these as the common ground between unions and ICI, the fundamental purpose of MUPS was to make it possible to measure, analyse and re-organise all the work being done by hourly-paid employees in the company. From this process (which would continue indefinitely — or until the agreement was replaced — once it had been started) would flow more efficient working and lower costs for ICI and better-designed, more highly-paid jobs for the unions' members. This would be the 'integrative bargain' aspects of MUPS: the agreement to make changes from which both sides would benefit. But no union would commit itself to anything so indefinite and there had to be a 'distributive bargain' aspect: the bargain in which benefits are traded from a limited store of goodies.

For the company, the benefits were:

(a) Flexibility. Freer movement between jobs would allow re-allocation of work across union demarcations. Permitted flexibilities were laid out in what came to be known as the 'Five Principles' of MUPS.

   i. Allowing process workers to 'use tools to carry out the less skilled craft tasks' which fell naturally into their jobs. (These were mainly minor routine maintenance jobs.)

   ii. Allowing tradesmen to operate process plant.

   iii. Providing for supervision by men from any background. (An ancient principle of craft unions is that their members should only receive supervision from men with a similar craft background.)

   iv. Allowing flexibilities between trades. (An attempt

to integrate work on jobs where more than one
skill is, often only peripherally, involved.)

v. Opening up support work (what used to be the
tradesman's 'mates') to men of any background.

But this is to reduce what was, for the company, the
most important part of the exercise to only one of its
elements. The core of MUPS was the process of analysing
work and re-designing jobs. The flexibilities were the
essential enabling conditions for this to be carried out
without restraint inherited from existing practice. (An
optimistic hope, as it turned out.) The benefit for the
company was not, therefore, flexibility for its own sake,
but the more efficient working and reduced manning that
it made possible. The estimates based in paper studies
produced a target of 15% manpower savings.

(b) A simple wage structure. The old structure had
become so complex and fragmented as to be difficult
for the company to operate and confusing for the
worker to understand. However, to move on to a
common structure of 8 grades was a major concession
by the craft unions, which previously had separate
bargaining rights and the top pay going, as of right. By
coming on to the same pay scale as general workers,
they lost the status implied by the first and, albeit not
explicitly, their 'rights' to the second.

(c) Job assessment. All jobs would be assessed and given
one of the 8 grades on the new scale. Again, this was
a major concession by the craft unions since it
replaced the old principle of paying for a skill with
one of paying for a job: the skill has been defined,
quite simply, by the fact of having served an
apprenticeship; job assessment was out of the unions'
hands. It was essential if the principle of parity across
the company was to have any meaning that assessment should be strictly impartial.

(d) There would be scope within each job grade for
varying the pay within a range of 10%. Basically, this

was intended to reward men as they learned to perform their jobs fully. But there was also a downside penalty-aspect ('.. after suitable warning, the salary will be reduced in proportion to the drop in performance . . .') which ran across the union principle of 'the rate for the job' — or, more generally, of limiting managerial freedom wherever possible. This provision was never operated because of union opposition.

By the same sort of reasoning, the agreement offered the unions a package of benefits:

(*a*) Higher pay. Pre-MUPS scales of basic rates ran from £563 to £997; MUPS scales ran from £720 to £1,100, a crude average increase of 16%. In fact, the company was very careful not to encourage any idea of 'average rise': each job was to be taken on its merits; benchmarks and norms were positively inimical to the process of assessment; and in any case, an average would swiftly become a minimum. The MUPS scales were privately estimated to involve a cost to the company of £6,250,000 if applied to the existing workforce — representing a 10% rise on the payroll of £61.1m. With labour savings of 15%, it was expected that MUPS would just about break even. However, even before MUPS was re-negotiated in 1969, there were two increases in the MUPS scales.

(*b*) Stable salary. The old, complex salary made up of several elements (of which the substantial bonuses could fluctuate for reasons outside the workers' control) was to be replaced by an annual salary, paid weekly. Overtime payments remained as a fluctuating component of the total package, although the effect of the new scale was to de-emphasise overtime and discourage its use systematically to make up take-home pay.

(*c*) Improved conditions, which meant mainly better sickness benefits. The old benefits were related to base pay and included no element of the workers'

> bonus. The new base rates, in effect, consolidated the
> bonus.

It is worth noting that the bargain was unequal in one very important sense: the two parties to it were trading different kinds of benefits. ICI was putting its money on the table in exchange for what amounted to no more than an expressed willingness to change — without any guarantees of what the changes might yield. It was here that the advantages of a more limited one-off agreement like Fawley were apparent; at least, if you were buying the rule book, you knew what you were getting. But ICI had no alternative if it wanted to break through into a new process for looking at work and one that was to be open-ended.

To view the agreement only as a productivity bargain is to forget the fundamental purpose and the deeper changes implicit in the means provided. For the analysis and re-design of work from first principles was to be the purpose; and it was to be achieved co-operatively. The 'five principles' were followed by a set of conditions, defining them more closely.

i.   The job was to be 'looked at in its totality...'
     (However, job enrichment had not yet appeared on
     the scene for the purposes of providing a set of
     principles for job design.)

ii. When manning jobs, 'the aim must be to get the right
     man in the right job... men of high skill should
     carry out as little mundane work...'

iii. 'Much re-training will be essential...'

iv. '... management will continue to use work study...
     to establish and maintain correct manning levels...'

v.   '... working practices... can continue to change
     ...'

All of these were to be 'the subject of local discussions and agreements on each work or site...' In other words, there would be no unilateral changes, dictated by management, but cooperative effort — the agreement of MUPS, in some ways, serving as a model. As a final safeguard, after local agreement was reached, 'these must be established to the satisfaction of the company and signatory unions . . .' This part of MUPS was sketchily laid out and the implications — of participation in the changes that were to take place — not spelled out. But it was the clear intent of the agreement not just to provide for the re-design of jobs but to change the assumptions underlying such processes.

The catalogue of the productivity bargain aspects of MUPS is a rather arid way of describing changes that had to be rooted, more than anything else, in changes of attitude and assumptions about roles, in particular about the nature of the worker-manager relationship. At the human level, the implications of changes proposed in MUPS were huge. It was not just that jobs were to be examined, analysed and re-designed, but also that the process of doing so was to be — which no area of managerial decision-making had been before — cooperative, as had been the process leading to MUPS itself. It was a complete departure from the ICI tradition of decision-making, of technical expertise deployed within a framework of managerial prerogative. A logical result of this process was a more participative style of management.

It could not be a one-way process. Action and reaction are equal and opposite, and the agreement contained as much potential for changing shop floor attitudes as managerial. Cooperation means 'working together'. A manager may (as Allan Flanders has pointed out) have to give up elements of his power in order to be able to manage. But it is not a one-way process: by cooperating in 'managerial decisions' the worker became involved in the structure of authority from which, by tradition, he had been excluded. He acquired, potentially anyway, some ownership of the resulting decisions and a commitment to the system that made them. It would be a step toward the staff attitudes that ICI had been nourishing since the works council scheme.

None of this was, however, apparent from a reading of the MUPS document. Such ideas, the essence of the agreement, were all but extinguished in the traditionally turgid prose of company-union agreements. The complex ideas behind MUPS were to be the subject of endless discussions: already, detailed management briefs had been prepared. But it would have been hard to discover them in the agreement itself. More, the stark phraseology and layout of the agreement presented ideas — particularly the five principles — in ways that were peculiarly threatening. To read down the list of proposed flexibilities was to read a massacre of much that local unions existed to preserve. And the benefits — of higher pay and stable salary — were put forward so woodenly as to drain them of meaning. This failure of presentation was an abiding problem through the trials, although one that was overcome when it was re-written.

The trials were set up. Everybody was primed and, as far as seemed feasible when the whole proceedings had been cloaked in such secrecy, ready to go. It very soon became apparent how optimistic these expectations were.

Basic tasks

Underlying the many activities of MUPS trials was a structure of jobs to be done in introducing the agreement which was common to all the sites. The surfaces were distractingly different — and we shall be very interested in these differences — but underneath could be glimpsed a skeleton of work to be done which, since it was common to all situations, we could usefully examine here. It has been implied, but not explicitly laid out, in the agreement itself. The sequence of steps for the introduction of WSA, which followed MUPS, is given in Appendix V.

(a) *A system of introduction.* Each works developed its own system for introduction. They started by being widely divergent but, as experience was gained, converged to a more nearly common pattern. An early lesson was the need for a 'MUPS coordinator' who collected and coordinated the management resources, decided on the broad strategy for the works and then made sure it happened. Variation in the approach taken was often quite overtly a function of the coordinator's personal style. And this meant that the system of introduction varied between the highly programmed and systematic, with all the steps defined explicitly, to the organic and unstructured, where developments were allowed to emerge naturally from the discussions.

(*b*) *A system of control.* At the same time, a system of
control had to be set up within which disagreements
could be arbitrated in a way that satisfied management
and unions that their interests were being guarded. This
had its political as well as its more practical aspects —
and, indeed, on all sites the process of introduction was
preceded by a political phase of site level discussion in
which management and unions agreed (or in a few sites
did not agree) their 'contract'. In theory, a site joint
committee was the final arbiter of conflict, deciding the
many detailed points concerning job descriptions and
flexibilities within or between unions. (The need for joint
committees gave rise to another innovation common to
all sites: official recognition of senior stewards. They had
existed *de facto* in a number of places, but the
impossibility of setting up a site-wide decision-making
body which included all shop stewards -- officially the
highest level of worker representation below the official
union structure — enforced recognition of a more concentrated system of representation.) In practice, the greatest
part of the problems that arose in the course of agreeing
job descriptions — the basic arena for dispute — were
arbitrated on the spot between the shop stewards,
workers and management involved.

(*c*) *Communication.* The first job in any introduction was an
educative one. In the early trials, particularly, ignorance
was complete among both management and workers. The
trials were therefore set off with an often elaborately-
sequenced series of meetings in which managers, supervisors, shop stewards and workers were told about the
agreement, usually by the MUPS coordinator and his
staff. These initial meetings led to discussion groups
which fanned out across the site and in which the
underlying ideas of MUPS were most exhaustively explored.

(*d*) *Analysis of work.* Once the first plants had been chosen
for introduction within a works (an important decision in
itself), the first major job was the analysis of the work
within them. The approach varied widely, from a 'top

down' initial analysis by a management team to a more 'bottom up' approach which started with the work group. The aim was the same, to make an exhaustive catalogue of all the work done in a plant, identify natural work clusters and suggest (however the suggestions arise) what might be the best way of allocating work to individuals. It was here that suggestions might emerge for re-drawing the boundaries of jobs in ways that would run across union demarcations.

(e) *Agreement of job descriptions.* In the course of the previous discussions, the main characteristics of jobs would begin to emerge. But each had to be written down in specific detail as a job description, in which all the features of a job would be listed. In this process would be involved the manager, supervisor, shop steward, appropriate experts (for example work study officers or engineers) and the worker concerned; the composition of groups varied with the system of introduction adopted. To the writing out of the job description would be brought all the experience of people most involved in the job. It was here, and in the previous section, that the ideas of people doing the jobs were elicited — an unheard-of step. The end result was an often voluminous sheaf of papers in which the job was described — sometimes to the last detail and sometimes in more sketchy outline. The last step, assessment, was in some ways the most important. Assessment of the job, as presented in the job description, was the process which turned all the previous work into hard money for the individual concerned; it will be described in the next section.

One last point needs to be made, however. I have only described the process of introducing MUPS at the level where it was overtly drafted: the design of shopfloor jobs. But, as was later said, 'People didn't realise that MUPS was a total change programme'. The ramifications of the process extended far beyond description and assessment of shopfloor jobs. The same logic was to be extended to the design of junior staff jobs (trouble at t' interface). More important, parallel to the process of introducing MUPS, there would have to be a radical re-thinking of the management systems. Specifically: the need to integrate maintenance and process management, which traditionally had separate structures; the need to plan maintenance more tightly or, as one exasperated manager said, 'just to plan it at all was a benefit'. These were themselves big jobs. The works manager of one of the trial sites commented of this: 'Probably 85% of the changes we made could have been made without MUPS.' He added: 'But MUPS was a necessary stimulus and a framework within which much else that needed to be done could be done.' The works manager of an engineering works on a large site went further: 'MUPS was irrelevant to the problems we were facing'. Too far, for his conditions were so special as to be unique within the company. But the point stands. There was much else to be done, and it was not going to be possible to confine the changes of MUPS to their immediate subject. Once the process of looking at the work being done was started, there was no way (save that of only doing a half a job) of drawing a line between MUPS and the total system.

Assessment

The whole strategy of MUPS would fall down if there were not a system of grading jobs within the company that was transparently fair, uniform and so unambiguous in application that no local 'bending' was possible. It had to be fair if it was to gain the support of the people whose pay depended on it. The agreement was national; ICI operated a centralised personnel policy: the system of assessment had therefore to be uniform to match. And it had to be unambiguous in application to the degree of rigidity if it was to be removed from the reach of local management and unions as a potential subject for bargaining. For once a system of this kind was capable of being moulded by local political factors, as the bonus incentive scheme had been, it would be fatally weakened.

The company had a great deal of experience in setting up such a system. The long development of payment systems described in Chapter 3 provided a fund of experience and expertise which was almost unique in the country. The management were thoroughly familiar with the techniques of

work study and job appraisal — on which the job assessment
scheme was to be built. And although the bonus incentive
scheme had been in places weakened and bent, it had been
for the most part efficiently controlled. The National Board
for Prices and Incomes looked at the scheme in 1969,
specifically 'the company's contention that by its close
central control of its wages structure it has been able to
control and contain wage drift.' They concluded:

> 'On the whole our examination of individual sites within
> the ICI complex corroborates this finding although as
> would be expected the situation varies somewhat from site
> to site. There is no doubt that in certain areas there is
> substantial competition for tradesmen from the engineer-
> ing industry and this may, as already notes, have had some
> effect on the pay of ICI's tradesmen. In general, we are
> satisfied that whereas the company has not wholly
> contained wage drift, the control which is exercised is
> more effective than is common elsewhere . . .'

This report was, of course, written when the MUPS trials
were substantially advanced. But it refers to control systems
in operation for some years. And it was on this experience
that the job assessment system for MUPS was based.

It was still to be a factor comparison method but there
were some further refinements — not in the basic method,
but in the make-up of the final assessment (engrossing further
shifts in the skills composition of jobs) and the way in which
the assessments were carried out (to accommodate some of
the fundamental, 'cooperative' features of MUPS). As Table 1
shows, weightings were adjusted to give greater weight to
mental requirements, skills and knowledge factors, all at the
expense of physical characteristics.

What concerns us here is the shift between the last two
columns. Weightings for 'Mental' and 'Personality' were
increased from 22½% of the total to 32%; 'Skills' increased
much less, from 55% to 59%; and 'Physical' more than
halved, from 22½% to 9%. It would be hard to find a more
eloquent statistic to describe the way in which the nature of
work in the chemical industry has changed. In addition,
'conditions payments' were to be removed from the rating

**Table 1. Weightings in Bedeaux, Job Appraisal and
Job Assessment**

	Bedeaux (1935)	*Job Appraisement (1948)*		*Job Assessment (1965)*
Mental	24	16	22½	15
Personality	—	—	—	17
Skills & knowledge	49	40	55	59
Physical	15	16	22½	9
Conditions	12	28	—	—
	100	100	100	100

scheme altogether. The reason for this was, basically, that
conditions are part of the context of the job and to be
distinguished from those factors that are a function of
the job's content. More practically, people are highly
sensitive to small differences in their working conditions; to
build this sensitivity into a pay scale that went up in eight
large steps was impossible — or, if it was tried, would very
likely distort the assessment process. There was a strong case
for having the conditions part of payment (Abnormal
Conditions Bonus or ACB) separate from job assessment,
where the salary scales took into account conditions normally encountered in the chemical industry, and this was done.
There were two practical problems to be overcome in
introducing this new scheme. First, the new weightings and
main-heads meant that the pay scale required calibration. In
effect the assessment of MUPS grades was simply grafted on
to the structure of marking that had been developed in job
appraisement. But bench-marks had to be established and 23
jobs were written up and presented to the company
assessment team by the management of the three trial sites
between November 1965 and February 1966. They had been
chosen to cover the range of likely jobs and skills and were
assessed with three guiding assumptions:

(i) That where the jobs had not changed, the old appraisal

marks were taken as correct, with appropriate modifications.

(ii) That the jobs were to fall within the eight grades.

(iii) That a commonsense relationship between new rates of pay and existing values had to be established. For example, it was pointless to offer the same money for a job that had been substantially enriched.

These preliminary assessments were refined as experience was accumulated and a firm structure of jobs built up. By July 1968, more than 200 jobs on ten different sites had been examined. On four occasions during this period the company assessors met to compare notes, discuss results and bring their ideas in line so that a standard view of job values was maintained.

The second big problem was that of training assessors. It was a huge problem. By the time the process was finished all the company's payroll were to be assessed; an army of assessors would be needed. The nucleus was a company assessment team composed of people with considerable experience in job appraisement who did the initial assessments. Onto this team were grafted new people who, at first, simply observed and then (after some 20 assessments) began to participate and produce their own marks. These were thoroughly discussed in the closed sessions of the assessment procedure and tested against the arguments of the other assessors. The trainee assessor built up his own standards and when he had marked 40 or so jobs — and with the approval of his team chairmen — he became an established assessor. In this way, company-wide standards were successfully maintained.

Assessment itself started with the presentation of the job, which was done with whatever aids were needed to put across particular features: slides, film clips, videotapes and — almost always — a visit to the work site to see what was involved. The presentations were lengthy, since it was in the interest of the worker (or presenting team: in some works it became an almost professional routine) to give as full an account of his job as he could manage. As a result, some presentations took a whole day. The job was then exhaustively analysed and discussed with the presenters until the assessors felt they fully understood it. The assessors then assigned marks under the four main heads. These marks were discussed in closed session so that differences of opinion could be identified. In fact, with experience, the differences rarely amounted to more than 3 or 4 points. If they remained, there would be further discussion with the presenting team, followed by another marking session and yet further discussion until the points were agreed. It was, and had to be, a painstaking process and, as I said at the beginning of this section, transparently fair. Inevitably, doubts were raised in the minds of people who felt they'd been put at too low a grade. It was always open to demand a re-assessment – which happened quite often – or, when agreement still could not be reached, to take the issue into the disputes procedure. More fundamental worries were expressed by shop stewards about the use the management assessment team might make of their opportunities to mark jobs down as a way of keeping wages low. But these never survived a closer understanding of the process or, which happened in a few cases, an invitation to sit in on the team's closed session.

This had to be the case. The assessment procedure had to be demonstrably impartial, neutral and objective. Unless it could stand up to the most hostile and searching scrutiny the whole basis of MUPS would be threatened.

PART III

Introducing MUPS: From Naive Learning to the Beginnings of Professionalism

The MUPS trials and the introduction of WSA that followed
have to be seen at two levels: from the centre and at the
periphery. They were company agreements, centrally designed to provide a framework within which a number of
diverse locations could separately seek common ends. But the
action, the work of changing and the change in working that
it was all about, took place at the 80-odd locations where the
detailed introductions took place. This was where the
problems that were to hold up introduction for six years
were encountered and dealt with in the small group of union
leaders and managers which had put MUPS together; problems to which MUPS provided answers in which the people
most directly affected had no ownership.

The account of what happened is divided into two parts:
this part, which describes the introduction of MUPS; and Part
IV, which describes the re-negotiation and introduction of
the Weekly Staff Agreement that followed. Both deal with
process of introduction. The *achievement* of MUPS and WSA
for the company and its employees is the subject of Part V.

The periods covered by the chapters of these two parts
overlap since, although strung along a chronological line, they
describe issues or groups of events to which there was no very
clear boundary. Chapter 6 runs from the signature of MUPS
to the end of 1966. It describes the shock and withdrawal
that greeted the new agreement at the three trial sites – a
period I have called one of 'naive learning', since it
represented the confrontation between the old assumptions,
which provided the framework for MUP's launch, and the
quite unfamiliar problems of organisational change that
MUPS brought in its train. Chapter 7 covers the first
successful introduction of MUPS and runs from end-1966 to
1968. Covering the same period, Chapter 8 continues the
story of the opposition to MUPS in the big sites of the
Northeast and near-crisis they caused the company, and more
particularly for the MUPS experiment. Part III ends with an
account of the lessons drawn from the MUPS experience and
the use made of them to professionalise, or routinise, the
introduction of WSA. At the end of Part III the company and
signatory unions have decided to bring an end to the MUPS
experiment, although allowing existing trials to continue, and
to re-negotiate the agreement.

6

Naïve Learning

MUPS was launched after the signature of the agreement, on 19 October 1965. It was circulated to the 4,000 workers at the three trial sites — Hillhouse in Lancashire, a works each at Wilton and Billingham, both in the Northeast — where it was received with, at the best, reserve. It had been expected that introducing the agreement would not be easy: a major reason for choosing the works in the Northeast was to take on the challenge of introducing MUPS under difficult conditions. But no one had expected a response that shaded down from cautious interest (at Hillhouse) to outright rejection (at Wilton).

Was it the money? It is easy, when constructing a Better Life, to lose sight of the fact that people work for money. Fred Creek, senior ETU shop steward at Billingham, afterwards said: 'The fellows leafed through the agreement until they reached the part which told them how much they were going to get. Then they chucked it aside: it wasn't enough.' Jack Lofthouse, for a large part of the trial period Chairman of Heavy Organic Chemicals Division (which had responsibility for the contentious Wilton site), said: 'I could have told them that the rates were not attractive. With the levels of bonus and overtime craftsmen were getting, the MUPS rates were simply not attractive enough to interest them in the changes that were being proposed.' But, true as it may be, this is hindsight: at the time the agreement was made, there were good reasons for fixing the rates at the MUPS levels. Moreover, once it became obvious that the pay scale was set too low, it was raised.

Resistance was much more than a matter of money. Time and time again, talking to people about the first response to MUPS, I have been told that the simple fact of the agreement having been made centrally, and in secret, was a cause of intense resentment. 'How could they know about the problems of the Wilton site?' said Paddy Tombe, senior AEU shop steward at Wilton and the centre of much of the opposition to the agreement in the Northeast. The people most involved had no ownership of the complex new agreement, which arrived without warning or preparation. It has been suggested to me that this interpretation of the early opposition has some of the attributes of a myth, a *post-hoc* rationalisation of a much more deep-seated rejection. The agreement was both vague and threatening. It was vague because it could offer no clear 'deal': until the new jobs had been thought through and assessed, no one knew for certain — although they had to make guesses — where he would land in the grading scale. MUPS was threatening because the list of 'five principles', set out in stark clarity at the very beginning of the agreement, struck at the main defences of the craft unions' position, apparently at the *raison d'être* of craft status. The reaction was not uniform between unions. The agreement was widely talked of in the Northeast as a 'General Workers' Charter', an apprehension that was to stiffen the opposition of skilled unions and build up the expectations of General Workers to a point where reality was bound to disappoint.

At Hillhouse, the initial discussions with shop stewards revealed misunderstandings; and after three talks with management, the AEU shop stewards stayed away altogether. They later received instructions from their district committee not to take part in talks, and this was not resolved for another six months, and then only partially. At Wilton the AEU shop stewards walked out of the first meeting and effectively boycotted all discussions on MUPS, although productivity discussions were started, under a different heading, in 1967. At Billingham the initial response was less extreme than at Wilton, but there too the AEU shop stewards were instructed by their district committee (the same) not to take part in discussions.

The depth of this opposition quickly became apparent. A fortnight after the agreement had been signed, the AEU's 'ICI Advisory and Consultative Committee' met to interrogate Bob Tallon about the agreement. The committee is a group of 15

senior shop stewards from ICI works, without formal power
but carrying influence as representing the views of AEU
members. The questioning at the meeting on 3 November was
keen and even hostile. At the end a resolution, proposed by a
group of shop stewards from ICI's Northeast sites was passed:

'that this Advisory Committee requests the Executive
Council to inform the ICI that this document in its present
form is unacceptable to the AEU and must be amended to
include the recognition of skilled craftsmen, and that in
consequence the AEU are prepared to enter into negotiations with other craft unions for the total abolition of
the demarcation problems and the interchangeability of
craft supervision provided that the company give guarantees of protection of employment and salary grade
considerably in excess of that set out in the Agreement for
fully skilled craftsmen.'

In this way the local union structure set themselves in total
opposition to the agreement which had been approved by
national union officers.

The Engineers were to be the most obdurate opponents of
the agreement. In 1967, the NBPI Report on Productivity
Agreements (Command 3311) commented in a note on
MUPS:

'The hostility to the agreement which has held up the trials
has come almost entirely from certain sections of maintenance craftsmen and among them especially from some
members of the AEU. Since greater flexibility is the heart
of the agreement maximum strain has been placed on the
traditional craft outlook. The proposed site joint committees with their tasks of examining the components of jobs
and the redefining of jobs have been seen by some as
endangering the craftsman's status and creating a threat of
craftsmen being swamped by process workers. Moreover,
there is a potential loss of craft independence since the
trials involve a single salary structure for craft and
non-craft and joint discussion between shop stewards of all
unions on the implementation of flexibility.'

It had been one thing for the national organisation to accept the benefits of the changes in MUPS. But it was quite another thing to gain acceptance of these changes at the local level where they had vivid reality in terms of jobs available, status and ancient privilege. There were complicating factors at the local level — differences between the sites in union/management relationships and the local 'political' environment.

The resolution of the AEU's advisory committee was followed at the end of November by an abrupt change in direction by the boilermakers' union (Amalgamated Society of Boilermakers, Shipwrights, Blacksmiths and Structural Workers). In a letter from Dan McGarvey, the union General Secretary, the company was told that 'the General Executive Council have had under the most serious consideration the above scheme (MUPS) and I would respectfully advise you on behalf of our Boilermakers, Blacksmiths and Shipwrights sections that we have decided to reject same . . .' A circular letter went to local union branches which concluded with the instruction that 'you must not enter into any discussion with the company on their proposals'.

In a discussion with a company representative shortly after, the boilermakers' objections were made more explicit. Most fundamentally, the rules of the union specifically forbade the union members to allow other people to handle their tools so that the craft/non-craft flexibility provisions of MUPS could not be allowed. The union objected to the secrecy in which the agreement had been put together and, lastly, considered that the MUPS salary scales comprised an inadequate money offer for what was being asked. The union announced its intention at that point of calling a meeting of ICI's signatory craft union representatives in order to press the company to suspend the agreement.

A background note prepared in CPD at this time discussed the opposition that was building up to MUPS at the local level. It concluded — three months after the MUPS launch — that the company had lost initiative pressing the agreement forward and that the current policy was not bringing success. Clearly there was a need to make the company's position more explicit to the craft unions, and in particular to give reassurances about the effects on their members. A meeting was held with AEU officers in which a number of assurances were given by the company: no trials would be started for at least three months; any redundancy would be handled by re-training and re-allocation; the limits within which craft workers might be subject to supervision by general workers were spelled out. Moreover, the company revealed that preliminary paper assessments of engineering jobs had yielded no assessments below grade 6. The AEU officers said that the executive council was not planning to vote on the resolution passed by the advisory committee before 1 March. Meanwhile, they would encourage their members to take part in discussions about the agreement with management on the trial sites. In effect, a moratorium was called on the trials, during which discussion, aimed at bringing about changes in attitude but not on substantive issues concerning the work, would be allowed to take place freely.

Local resistances were not, however, to be overcome from the centre so easily. AEU shop stewards at the two sites in the Northeast, Wilton and Billingham, continued in their refusal to take part in talks. This meant that site joint union/management committees, the pivotal group without which the detailed discussions on job description could not start, were not set up. At Hillhouse, the AEU district committee imposed a similar ban, linking it more overtly to the resolution of the advisory committee. Discussions were taking place at a number of levels in the works; but without the participation of the AEU they could not lead to anything. 1966 ended with no prospect of a breakthrough into more substantive negotiations on the agreement.

This situation continued for another year, although the precise form of the deadlock shifted from week to week as discussions started here, only to be abandoned, or signs of promise were reported there, only to be extinguished — all on a number of different fronts: site, plant and union.

Site differences

This suggests a good deal more uniformity than was the case. The experiences introducing MUPS on the three trial sites were widely different in ways that vividly reflected local differences between them. The outcome was a spread of

three years between the beginning of MUPS working at
Hillhouse, in January 1968, and the start-up at Wilton and
Billingham. This spread of experience was a feature of the
attempts to introduce MUPS and its successor across the wide
range of conditions encountered in ICI's many sites. But that
is still to come and in any case, when it did, only repeated in
different forms what had been encountered with the first
trials.

Of the three initial trial sites, Billingham and Wilton were
very similar in basic characteristics. Both are large sites (Wilton
covers 1,100 acres), each comprising several works —
of which each is a self-contained factory, employing from
1,000 to 4,000 people. At each site some 10,000 payroll and
4,000 monthly staff were employed. (At the time: Billingham subsequently shut down a number of its works.) They
are built around different kinds of products — Billingham
around fertilisers and Wilton around petrochemicals — but
are members of the same technological family, in terms of
basic design principle and the sorts of jobs and working
conditions they offer the people who run and maintain them.

If this last point seems tautological within the 'chemical
industry', one has only to remember the range of processes
and products covered by that term — and briefly discussed in
Chapter 1. Both sites are extended complexes of inter-related
chemical plants set in a hissing, steaming mesh of product
and service pipelines. Around the core reaction of
cracking naphtha to make ethylene a series of satellite
processes has grown up to make use of the many by-product
streams. Similarly, at Billingham, although the primary
objective of the site was the manufacture of fertilisers, the
by-product streams are worked up to yield a range of
products spanning from building products by the thousand
tons (cement, plasterboard) to fine chemicals. It is the
ultimate expression in hardware of chemical logic; in
chemical engineering terms the sites are highly efficient:
Billingham was a Mecca for chemical engineers in the
inter-war years; the Wilton flowsheet has been used as a
model for a number of later petrochemical complexes. But
the cost of such complexity is extreme rigidity since no part
of the system can be changed — for example, in response to a
sudden change in the market — without affecting the rest of

it. However, this feature was not of such significance to the
MUPS experience as the physical nature of the resulting
factories: the jobs of operating and maintaining the plants;
their huge size and relative emptiness. Although inter-
connected through the system of pipelines, the works, and
even plants, operated more or less in isolation from each
other. Within them, the process workers — members of the
general worker unions (mainly T&GWU in the Northeast)
— worked in small groups, shift teams; the craftsmen worked
by themselves, dealing with running maintenance problems,
or in the sizeable engineering works — employing more than
2,000 at each site — that had responsibility for the large jobs
of periodic maintenance and construction. Thus there was,
inherent in the nature of the plants, a significant difference in
the relationship that the members of the two groups of
unions had with their work.

Probably the most important similarity lay in employing
people from the same part of the country. Both are in the
Northeast, 13 miles apart on opposite banks of the Tees
estuary. And both draw their workforce from an area which
is one of the oldest industrial communities in Britain, with
attitudes and politics that are crucially related to this fact.
Coal mining, iron-ore mining, iron and steel manufacture,
shipbuilding, heavy engineering and the railway workshops at
Darlington have been dominant employers for more than a
century. Perhaps they were no less humane during their
profitable years than other Victorian employers, which is
saying very little. But the companies and their workers in the
whole region suffered acutely during the twenties and
thirties; three of the six dominant industries listed earlier
have closed down in the past twenty years. And local
tradition contains a still-lively memory of the suffering and
privation of those years. How lively the memory can be
emerges in discussion even now; it was illustrated in the case
of an outstandingly able worker who refused promotion
because he did not 'want to be part of the management of a
company that put my Dad out of work during the Depression', by then thirty years in the past.

With such a history of unstable employment and long
periods of privation, it is not surprising that the main role of
the unions should be defensive. Nor is it surprising that the

initial reaction of craft unions — the best organised and most
powerful and most militant — should be rejection of a
change, MUPS, that threatened the defences of demarcation
and union ownership of jobs that had so painfully been
accumulated in the previous years. That in the times of full
employment following the war, when Wilton was being built,
this power had been used to build in a high level of
overmanning at both sites was not an argument that could be
expected to carry much weight with unions. Their job was to
defend their members against the possibility of a return to
the old days of unfettered managerial prerogative, lay-offs
and high unemployment. Given the suspicion and lack of
trust existing between company and employees, to argue that
the overmanning was threatening ICI's existence was simply
to invite an unprintable answer. We shall return to ICI's
experience at these two sites in Chapter 8, for they stood at
the political (small 'p') extreme of ICI's attempts to
introduce MUPS. For the moment let it suffice that no
amount of argument could affect the hardening determination of the local unions that MUPS would not be
allowed to pass: particularly within the powerful shop
stewards' committee at Wilton, and still more particularly in
the AUEW, whose district committee had jurisdiction over
both sites.

On the face of it, there was not much more progress at
Hillhouse; MUPS was still a year off agreement there by the
end of 1966. But the situation was very different. For in the
Northeast there was a complete ban on talks of any kind and
the management got no further than site-level discussions
about whether, and with what safeguards, they could *start*
talking about MUPS trials at the Olefines and Product Works.
But at Hillhouse talks continued in some form, however
tenuous and unofficial, throughout the year following MUPS
signature. At first the AEU district committee had banned its
stewards from talks — although the district secretary had
informally suggested that the management should continue
with their manning studies in the plants selected for the first
trials. The ban had followed the AEU's ICI advisory
committee resolution of November. It was not until the AEU
representative, Bob Tallon, had visited Hillhouse in March
1966 that the committee allowed AEU shop stewards into

separate discussions. And in September, they allowed them
to take part in joint discussions. (This would have happened
sooner, but it was World Cup Year and no evening meetings
took place that Summer.) That is, they could take part in
meetings where whole areas of work were analysed, not just
with management but also with members of other unions
affected. It was essential to MUPS that the work should be
analysed, in chunks that formed natural wholes, in order that
the best patterns of allocating work within those chunks
should be agreed. To carry out this fundamental job,
union-by-union, would merely perpetuate the division the
process was intended to examine. By the end of 1966, the
process of working up manning proposals for the trial plants,
writing up and agreeing the job descriptions was well under
way.

But then Hillhouse is quite a different place from the two
other trial sites: relatively small and in a different part of the
country. Readers unfamiliar with Britain's industrial history
may shrug this fact off as at best peripheral. However, small
as the country is, it is as diverse socially as it is geographic-
ally. And although Hillhouse has not the strong local features
of the Northeast, this very lack played a part. The works is in
a suburb of Blackpool, the traditional holiday centre of the
Northwest. The main local industry is entertainment; other
industry is of recent origin. The unions are neither so
defensive nor so militant as those in the Northeast – or in
other areas with a long industrial history. A local manager
described the resulting management/union relations as 'tough
but reasonable': no sentimentality in the struggle for advantage, but conflict is not allowed to reach the point where
talking stops. It is a basic reasonableness, the manager
maintained, that is characteristic of the area. He cited the
trouble AUEW members took to make it possible for the
works to keep going during the one-day national strike
against the Industrial Relations Act called in 1971 – the kind
of 'reasonableness' that is the despair of revolutionaries. One
is reminded of Arthur Koestler's story of Lenin's cutting off
the subsidy to the British Communist Party on hearing of a
football match between striking workers and the local police.

The other important intrinsic difference was the physical
one of size. Two divisions had works on the site: Plastics,

employing 1,208, and Mond, employing 1,675. This had two
effects that I was able to observe. First, the 'management
presence' was more real at the smaller site, more palpable
than at Wilton particularly, where the huge and alienating
size of the site, the diffusion of control to a number of
management centres, made management in some ways less
visible. This was partly a consequence of the managers'
greater freedom of manoeuvre on the smaller size. (We shall
come to Wilton's management problems later.) Secondly, the
'political' structure at Hillhouse was smaller than at Wilton.
The 25 or so senior shop stewards at Wilton formed a site
committee which was large enough to be politically self-
sustaining. At Hillhouse, the five senior shop stewards were
not enough to form a political 'critical mass' within which
the urge to resist could be sustained and nourished. It is
perhaps a surface effect: as the rate at which crystals of sugar
dissolve accelerates as they dwindle, so might attitudes of
resistance be more easily dissolved away by the management
environment in a smaller than a larger group. Whatever the
explanation, the 'big site problem' was the biggest and most
obstinately persistent headache ICI had in its attempts to
change the organisation.

Hillhouse had a number of special factors in its favour. It
had a tradition of good management, part of which was a
well-controlled bonus scheme and overtime that was at the
relatively modest level of 6%. It had a high proportion of
long-service employees with some sort of commitment to ICI:
turnover ran at a steady 10%. The works manager had been
involved in the MUPS negotiations, so the scheme for
introduction was well-prepared; and managers fully understood what was intended. The result was a carefully managed
and meticulously planned approach to the exercise. But this
much is hindsight. At the beginning anyway, Hillhouse
seemed to offer more hope of success in introducing MUPS
than the other two sites.

Managing at the centre

Seen from Millbank, it was an intensely frustrating experience. Both management and the unions' national officers had
underestimated the amount of change involved and the

strength of feeling ranged against the agreement. In particular, they had not expected the circumstances in which MUPS was agreed to provide the strongest initial grounds for rejecting it. Getting round these objections was going to provide the committed men at the centre with a succession of hopes and disappointments that was to continue for some years yet.

The central clearing-house was the Joint Union/Management Committee — effectively the committee that had negotiated MUPS in 1965 and which had been kept in existence to provide the central forum to which problems in applying MUPS would ultimately be referred. It was the most visible expression of the 'joint problem-solving' approach which MUPS was intended to introduce through the company. And it depended crucially on the union members. This is not being unfair to the management members, for their compliance — if not their enthusiasm — could be taken for granted. The important forum, within which the company's authority was deployed, was the management steering committee.

But the union members, even if they could not deliver their members' cooperation, could have stopped the agreement. Instead they worked hard to help it through, particularly those who had been through the experience of putting it together in the first place. Probably, the most consistently influential member was Jack Williams, the T&GWU representative and secretary of the joint committee. 'A highly improbable person to find in that place', he was later described to me by an outsider. 'Union business tends to be very serious, even rather solemn, but Jack took nothing seriously — not the T&G nor ICI.' And he worked to get the agreement accepted by the union members. (Another member called him 'a right-winger', perhaps because of this.) An important figure was Dave Basnett, later General Secretary of the G&MWU. Both of these were representatives of general workers' unions, which expected to benefit. On the craft side, Gus Cole was a valuable bridge to the ETU, which he represented. And Eddie France 'exerted an influence out of all proportion to the weight of his union', the building trades operatives. A much later arrival was Len Edmonson, representative of the AUEW. Not having shared in the process of putting the agreement together (the original AUEW member, Bill Bradley, had died just before it was signed) he was not convinced of its value to his members until he had been able to exert influence to introduce what he felt to be necessary safeguards. Thereafter he played a central role in the introduction. It would be invidious to single out names from the long list of managers who played a leading part at the centre. It is more to the point to underline the power situation within the company which enabled MUPS to proceed. This was, first, the support of Sir Peter Allen, ICI's Chairman during the most crucial years of introduction; secondly, the commitment to the MUPS ideas of Rowland Wright, who was personnel director at the beginning. It is often said that no programme of organisation change can succeed without protection from the top and these two Main Board directors provided it. One might add that not even the most necessary changes take place without some individual to push them through. MUPS had this in Geoffrey Gilbertson, a man crippled by polio nine years before the MUPS negotiations but possessed of energy, willpower and ruthless persistence, all put at the service of a total conviction that MUPS was right for the company. He had been involved in the stages leading to MUPS and was brought to the centre from Billingham, where he was a division personnel director, by Wright in 1967 to take charge of the programme. But at this stage (1965-6), very little was understood of the nature of the change being attempted. The package had been put together and it had been left to the, often bemused, management of the trial sites to make it happen. And this meant that, at the beginning, very little did happen.

Not unexpectedly, the reports to the joint committee at its first meeting after the MUPS launch had been of widespread acceptance by general worker unions. The reaction of the local craft unions was not uniform. For the most part, the ETU representatives were prepared to take an active part in discussions while the opposition was led, as first signs had indicated, by the AEU. These union differences are best understood in terms of the power balances between the unions, the traditional status of craft unions and the threat imposed not just by the agreement but by the continual shifts brought about by technological change.

One of the main reasons for negotiating the agreement at all was that larger and more complex plant required greater skills on the part of operatives which could not be properly rewarded under the existing scheme. At the same time, much of the skilled work in maintenance was only defined as such, legalistically, because it involved the use of tools. It is generally accepted, even privately by union representatives, that the genuinely skilled content of 'skilled' work on the sites in the Northeast was between 40% and 20% of the total. The great bulk of the work — as with unbolting the autoclave lids at Hillhouse, making low-pressure pipe joints, removing safety guards over electrical apparatus, tightening joints or unblocking pipes — involved skills no more complex than could be imparted in half a day's training. These facts may have been privately acknowledged but could never be officially accepted: demarcations, however 'illogically' defined, represented jobs for the union members. The agreement seemed to offer the prospect of handling these jobs, in whole or in part, to unskilled workers and this was not something the skilled unions were prepared to allow, least of all in areas where security of employment was prized above money, as in the Northeast. Of the main craft unions, AEU members were most threatened by this while the ETU members felt far more confident. Technological development, with highly instrumented plants and increasing use of many types of electrical equipment, offered to electricians guarantees of increasing work. (Even if it hadn't, electricians were to some extent protected by laws which required certain jobs to be carried out by technically skilled men.) Lastly, there was an ideological element among a small but important part of the opposition. Against dogma there is no argument.

The unions' opposition to MUPS should not be seen as a wholly negative episode, however. On both sides of the negotiating table there were antique attitudes to be unlearned and discoveries to be made about each other. Craft unions may have had to adjust to the emerging conditions of the industry, but managers had as much to learn. 'At the start, the whole basis of negotiation between the unions and managers in the divisions was unrealistic', said a manager who had worked in the Central Personnel Department during most of the MUPS exercise. Negotiations between unions and management — over which changes in working practice were to be traded in exchange for better conditions, more responsibility and more pay — often foundered on the assumption of management that the workers had 'no right' to restrictive practices in the first place. That is, managers 'instinctively maintained a fiction that the restrictive working practices which had for a long time provided the base from which unions operated had been voluntarily conceded by the company. The corollary of the fiction was that they could be withdrawn at management's discretion so that the question of negotiating their withdrawal for better conditions did not arise.' (We could call this a quasi-moral view and wrap it up in the phrase 'the right to manage'.) There was much more and, indeed, it can be argued that the attitudes of management have since proved far more enduring and resistant to change than those of the unions. The long periods of frustrating discussions-about-discussions or total non-communication provided the setting in which the need for change was demonstrated. It can even be argued (an argument that belongs in the Department of Silver Linings) that, if the agreement had been more easily introduced, it would have been less valuable.

There was a great deal to be learned in this first period, but it had to be by trial-and-error: there was no way of defining the problems except by encountering them, and then adapting to them. It is for this reason that I have called the period to the beginning of 1968 one of 'naive learning'. The process of joint discussion which led to MUPS was unconventional. But the framework of assumptions within which the resulting agreement was launched was traditional: the answer had been agreed at the centre and it was up to the periphery to put it into practice. It had been done hundreds of times before. But solutions to problems which involve fundamental changes to people's lives raise resistances that are not generated by capital investment (or, for different reasons, by managers). The company and unions blundered into this minefield in almost complete ignorance of the difficulties in store. The shock and pain as the mines went off was considerable. The inability of management at the trial works to deliver offended deep-rooted assumptions about the role of management and threw into embarrassing relief the powerlessness of the unions' central organisation. It was not until these were acknowledged and confronted that the process could move into a more consciously and *expertly* problem-solving mode.

Ten meetings of the joint committee were held during 1966 in which the problems encountered at the trial sites were discussed. By the end of the year, in spite of a number of false starts, realistic discussions were under way only at Hillhouse; there was sporadic activity at the Sulphate/Nitrate plants at Billingham and virtually nothing at Wilton. The original plan, of choosing sites which were known to be difficult in order better to display their success as an example to the rest of the company, was proving to have been too ambitious. It was becoming very important to have some success to demonstrate or the agreement might be in danger of foundering altogether. This analysis was generally accepted in the joint committee and it was decided to seek nominations from the divisions for new trial sites.

7

First Successes

The possibility of extending the trials were first raised in the joint committee in May 1966 when union officials reported that, visiting non-trial sites in the company, they found 'an interest in MUPS and a genuine desire among employees to learn more about the concept and progress of the trials'. The growing difficulties at Wilton were noted, and it was suggested that the site could be left 'in cold storage' and attention be given to bringing other sites into the trials.

From the beginning, it had not been intended to confine MUPS trials to the original three works. A note to the management steering committee in July 1966 raised this issue and listed the arguments for extending the trials as: any success would be a stimulant to the agreement; it would start the process of obtaining cost savings; by demonstrating the benefits of the agreement a success would serve to mobilise union support. Against this initiative, it pointed out that: the original sites had been chosen to cover a range of fairly typical conditions which could not usefully be extended with new sites; it would not be in the interests of a controlled introduction of MUPS to encourage the rapid spread of the agreement; a rejection could be doubly damaging.

By September of this first, frustrating year, the idea of adding to the trial sites was accepted to be the most hopeful way of keeping up the MUPS impetus. But — an early lesson from the first trials — the decision to come into the trials should be, as far as possible, voluntary. This is, groups of employees should be given the opportunity to put themselves forward as trial sites. Individual unions would then take soundings and if these were favourable the joint committee would decide whether or not trials could take place.

The divisions were approached and asked to put forward

nominations for trials. In December, the list below was put forward to the unions. The works all conformed to the main basic requirements that:

(*a*) They would provide a suitable spread of technology, skills and other features that would make them valuable examples for the rest of the company.

(*b*) Management was willing and resources were available for preparation and discussion for the trials.

(*c*) The local management considered that there was a favourable union climate for introduction at the sites.

The sites listed were:

1. British Visqueen, Stevenage
   (Plastics Division)   550 payroll
2. Dumfries
   (Plastics and Nobel Divisions)   1,000 payroll
3. Stowmarket
   (Paints Division)   700 payroll
4. Severnside & Immingham
   (Agricultural Division)   650 & 60 payroll (resp.)
5. Gloucester
   (Fibres Division)   2,200 payroll

It is notable that these sites were predominantly small and isolated, offering a better chance of success than the large complex sites which had proved such a difficulty. Gloucester was the largest, but the average size was under 1,000 – which was in sharp contrast to the more than 10,000 people involved on the Wilton and Billingham sites. It had become apparent that some of the main problems encountered on these sites were a function of their sheer size and the 'goldfish bowl' effect of introducing radical change at one works, watched with friendly or jealous interest by the rest of the works.

The Main Board agreed to extension of the trials, and when the joint committee met again at the end of February, the unions agreed to take soundings among their members. The first reactions that came back were favourable. By May

Jack Williams, secretary of the signatory unions, was able to inform the company formally that the unions were prepared to go ahead with trials discussions at Stowmarket and the joint committee formally accepted it as a trial site. Similar formal acceptance of the other sites was obtained in due course. By now, however, informal discussions were proceeding at the nominated new trial sites. (For reasons gone into more fully later in the chapter, informal talks had already been started at Gloucester and Stowmarket.)

The introduction of new sites marked a complete change in the strategy for MUPS. Of the original three trial sites, only Hillhouse was still in the running and even there, there was grave disappointment. The works manager, Albert Hollis, had reported with confidence that Hillhouse would start trials in May. Almost at the last minute, these were held up by a dispute with the AEU over the assessment of fitters. In contrast, rapid progress was made at Stowmarket and Gloucester. These were now seen as offering the best prospect of starting trials. Following the logic of this development, the joint committee decided to press ahead with extending the trials still further, to show, by example, the benefits of the new agreement. With the example of these successful trials before them, it was thought more likely that the obdurate large sites — which were now seen as posing quite special problems — might be persuaded to join in.

Towards the end of 1967, this policy looked as though it was bearing fruit. An internal progress report to the personnel director summed up the situation as at November 1967. Talks at Wilton and Billingham were still at a standstill but the trials at Hillhouse were firmly expected to start on 1 January. Two of the new sites, Gloucester and Stowmarket, were working hard to start trials at the same time. The Hillhouse trials were expected to serve as a useful example in the Northwest, while Gloucester and Stowmarket, although valuable examples within their own divisions (Fibres and Paints), were thought not to have much influence outside. Estimates of savings at Hillhouse and Billingham were still expected to amount to some 10%. For the first time, the report indicates serious worries about the possibility of ever introducing the new agreement on Teesside. 'The prospects of a continuing deadlock on MUPS on Teesside must concern both the company and the union national officers. It is a situation which leads inevitably to thoughts of alternative routes to MUPS, or even alternatives to MUPS itself.' But the steering committee saw no alternative to continuing with MUPS, other routes offering many difficulties. 'In immediate terms, a change from MUPS on Teesside would involve a major problem of communication to management, payroll and unions throughout the company. This would come when managements at many factories in the company are working successfully along MUPS lines and it could appear to them only as a distinct and discouraging change of direction. The company would be publicly retreating from its commitment to an agreement offering a national lead in industrial relations and the involvement of workers in productivity.' And, '. . . any change of direction at this stage, even if it were limited to one area such as the Northeast, would, by merely indicating the possibility of an easier alternative, damage the possibilities of success that still exist at the other trial sites.' The committee concluded that the trials at Hillhouse, Gloucester and Stowmarket should be allowed to demonstrate the benefits of the agreement. This was, indeed, the route the company chose, although the difficulties encountered in the Northeast were serious enough to cause concern — and occasionally despair.

With considerable rejoicing, the first plants came on to the trial agreement on 1 January 1968. These were Stowmarket, with 750 payroll, Gloucester, with 1,850, and Hillhouse, where the approach was not to bring the whole works on but to bring it on plant-by-plant so that initially 300 people were concerned. Heartened by this success, Jack Williams suggested that it would be useful to keep the pressure up by allowing still more new sites to volunteer. The decision to make application voluntary, the expression of a spontaneous wish, was shrewdly judged. First, and most important, it removed the element of compulsion from the transaction — or more accurately, of management pressure which, by identifying an item of policy as 'belonging' to the management, automatically turned it into a bargaining issue. Secondly, the voluntary approach filtered out those works where there was no wish to proceed, increased the chances of success and so kept up the momentum of change.

The four trial sites that had been nominated with Gloucester and Stowmarket were reporting progress, but there was a good argument for adding still more to their number; there was a momentum in introducing a trial which needed maintaining. The point was taken and agreed by the joint committee. An announcement offering the prospect of broadening the trials still further was made throughout the company suggesting 'that management and union represent-atives at each works in the company should now discuss the MUPS proposals with a view to assessing whether there is support from the management and employees for the works to be nominated as a trial site. Requests for nominations should then be submitted through company and union channels for consideration by the joint committee.' As a result of this the works at Pontypool and Darwen were nominated as trial sites in March; in May, two further works, Kilroot and Clitheroe, were approved, and unions had made requests in respect of a further seven works.

These new trials provided positive and hopeful results from the MUPS experiment. As we shall see in the next chapter, the hope they offered was nearly overwhelmed by the problems in the Northeast. But they offered more than merely the hope that, having succeeded once, it might be possible to succeed again: they provided experience of success, where there had only been experience of failure — which offered no clues for the way forward. Yet, each of the successes was quite different, not just because of the environmental differences discussed in Chapter 6 but because the managers adopted quite different approaches.

Hillhouse

The new sites had been chosen with conscious cunning, as offering the best chances of success. Two of them, the Nylon Works at Gloucester and the Paint Works at Stowmarket, were first past the line with Hillhouse. They could hardly have been more different than the big works in old industrial areas which had become the centre of opposition.

The contrast between Hillhouse and Gloucester is, how-ever, more instructive, since each represents typical aspects of the ICI scene, and the management approaches to the problem posed by introduction of the agreement were quite opposite.

Of the two, Hillhouse lay closer to the middle of the ICI range of location, size and technology. Among its advantages was the fact that, it having been decided early to include it among the trial sites, a degree of preparation was possible. Part of this was unintended: Hillhouse was one of the five sites that prepared 'ideal manning studies' for the Rutherford Panel in 1964. As a result, there was at the works a group of managers, a dozen or so, who had been through the exercise of critically analysing the existing patterns of work. The manager in charge of the exercise, Ken Sharpington was made the MUPS Coordinator for the site; he later said of the group that 'their appetites had been whetted by the opportunity to think in a de-constrained manner about work which had hitherto been set in a fairly rigid framework of traditional constraints'.

The immediate rejection of talks on MUPS had been a setback. However, a manager who was closely involved later said: 'The delays turned out to be very beneficial for us. They gave management the opportunity to re-think many of their assumptions about MUPS. If it had been a more rapid implementation, I am convinced that it would have been far less effective.' Sharpington agreed: 'The initial setback was a godsend, since it allowed us to develop a system of change . . .' And he did, indeed, work out a detailed sequence of steps which were to be followed in the plants.

First, however, the agreement was to be circulated throughout the works and its implications fully discussed. (The process was called 'training' for management and 'preparation of attitudes' for shopfloor workers.) In a detailed schedule of meetings fanning out through the works, the word was to be passed from top to bottom. Concurrently, management and shop stewards agreed on the first plants for application. These had to be typical enough to provide a precedent for the rest of works and to have management/union relations good enough (which meant basically, cooperative shop stewards) to offer a high chance of success. Two plants were chosen: the carbide furnace, in the Mond Works, and Corvic 1 and 4 in Plastics. The first was something of an anomaly in a chemical works, being more like a blast furnace. It had been chosen, partly at union insistence, to avoid the temptation of choosing too easy an option, but it was soon dropped (the furnace was shut down) and replaced by Chlorobenzenes. The Corvic plant employed 270 men in a batch process, polymerising vinyl chloride to the plastic PVC in autoclaves. It offered scope for rationalisation of the basic operation: opening up the autoclaves (secured by bolts, therefore defined as a 'skilled' job) and cleaning them out (an unskilled job). Chlorobenzenes was more of a typical chemical plant, run by teams of process workers and maintained by itinerant craftsmen. Here the scope lay in re-thinking the management systems and re-designing the work for more flexible operation — for example, allocating work within the process teams and making it possible for some small jobs of running maintenance to be carried out by unskilled men. It was probably as well that the carbide furnace dropped out of the picture since the work was not obviously susceptible to this sort of re-organisation: it was manual, repetitive, heavy and dirty; it employed men, attracted by high bonuses possible under the old incentive scheme, who were earning far more than the MUPS rates.

A management team then examined every aspect of the work in the chosen plants as a basis for developing detailed proposals for new manning requirements. This was by way of being a feasibility study. More substantive discussions took place in the next stage when the process of analysis and generation of manning proposals was repeated in job-by-job discussions involving managers, supervisors, shop stewards and the individual workers. Problems with implications for the site or involving union principle (e.g. crossing demarcation boundaries) were discussed and agreed in a working party of managers and senior shop stewards. The manning proposals were then submitted to works management and, in the case of AEU jobs, the district committee.

This process was the heart of the MUPS introduction. It was where the ideas and experience of the men involved in the work could be elicited and brought to bear on the, inevitably more theoretical, ideas of managers. In many cases, the old job standards contained much jealously-guarded 'slack' which would only be offered up in discussion — and then only when an atmosphere of trust was created. It was a question of making the switch from the traditional negotiating mode of discussion ('I've got something you want: how much will you pay for it?') to a problem-oriented mode ('What is the problem? How can we devise a solution to it that will satisfy us both?'). Once the message got across, that the slack was no longer something to bargain with, this information was willingly put into the discussion. For example, one job contained the requirement, carrying its points towards the job standard, that the operative should climb a ladder at intervals to take a temperature reading. It emerged that the measuring instrument was visible from the ground and that nobody had climbed that ladder for years.

Another issue these re-definitions of job boundaries raised was the one of supervision, although this was a question of union principle that concerned stewards more than shop-floor workers. (Most unions have traditionally refused to allow members to take instructions from members of other unions.) But it was an important part of MUPS that supervisory staff should be reduced – to provide scope for job enrichment as much as to cut numbers. In the original Corvic manning report, 10% of the savings were expected from cuts in supervision. The draft manning proposals for Chlorobenzenes estimated that one-third of the total savings would come from supervision. Chlorobenzenes was a special case, however, since the greatest savings were expected to come not from the usual categories of MUPS savings but from re-organisation: integrating process and maintenance functions, which had more implications for management than shopfloor.

The emphasis in this process was very much a matter for individual works – particularly in the trials, where there was no experience. The systematic methods of the previous two sections were very much Hillhouse's own. Other works devised other ways: a great deal of the analysis and job design at Gloucester, for example, was carried out in work discussion groups.

The last stages of the introduction fell firmly into the general framework prepared by the company. Job descriptions gathered in the preceding stages; the descriptions were agreed; and the resulting jobs were 'presented' and assessed. The process of assessment, which was (and is) the keystone of the new pay structure, is described at the end of Chapter 5.

Sharpington's meticulously detailed schedule was pushed back and delayed until the time taken was four times what he had originally estimated. But this was, we can now see in retrospect, something to be expected. Everything about MUPS was new, but it arrived in the guise of a traditionally-negotiated agreement. There had to be a process of learning, during which both unions and management assimilated the implications of the new way of bringing about change. To intensify the newness of the experience, Hillhouse was for nearly a year, 1966/7, the only works in the company at which MUPS talks were going on. To the immediate problems of guarding the pass at Hillhouse, therefore, was added the far larger problem of guarding the interests of management and unions throughout ICI. Both sides were acutely conscious of their responsibilities as setters of precedents which could, if too easily conceded, be used to the disadvantage of their fellows elsewhere. The result was a heavy-lidded caution, an unwillingness to take risks. That the works-by-works introduction of MUPS meant there could be no question of precedents, good or bad, was something that had to be learned.

There was a third factor which held back progress: even with the painstaking preparation and discussion, the workers were reluctant to commit themselves to something whose effects they could not judge. The company had ruled that there could be no commitment to rates of pay until the jobs had been presented and assessed; the people involved were unwilling to agree to the new jobs until they knew what they would mean in cash. This was met by circulating job-by-job estimates of the pay implications of tentative grades.

It was also a calculated risk for, nebulous as it was, the letters made explicit much that had carefully been kept ambiguous. And there was no way of knowing whether the mood of the men would be disappointment (expectations were running high) or enthusiasm. In the event, the letters provided just the sort of statement of the meaning of MUPS that was wanted. The inducements were substantial and the attitude change marked: a mass meeting in November 1967, of AUEW members held shortly after they had all been

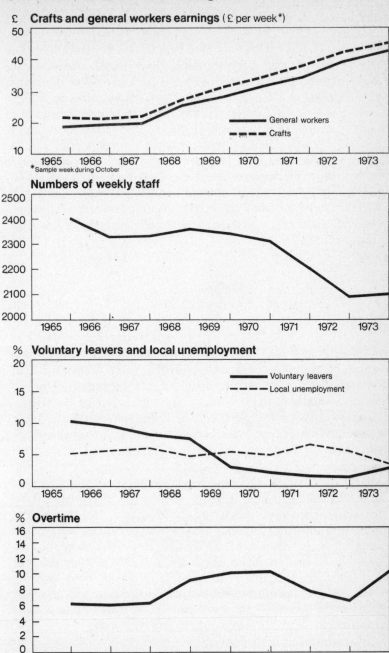

Fig.4 Hillhouse: indicators of change

Crafts and general workers earnings (£ per week*)
£

— General workers
- - - Crafts

*Sample week during October

Numbers of weekly staff

% **Voluntary leavers and local unemployment**

—— Voluntary leavers
- - - Local unemployment

% **Overtime**

circulated with these letters, voted overwhelmingly to accept the agreement. The effort of making the calculations had been backbreaking. 'Those damned letters nearly killed us', the personnel manager said later. But it had provided the necessary impetus. The Chlorobenzenes and Corvic plants led the way for the Hillhouse site and were working on MUPS conditions on 1 January 1968; the rest followed over the next five months. It was a hard-worked and gritty success and for this reason an important example within ICI. For it demonstrated that system, patiently applied, could be used to introduce a complex programme of human change. The more detailed aspects of change will be discussed with other works later; an indication of the changes in Hillhouse results — in as much as they are reflected in statistics — will be found in fig. 4.

Gloucester

A more spectacular success was achieved at Gloucester, much the most studied, visited and discussed of the ICI's works. (A detailed sociological study of the introduction of MUPS at Gloucester will be found in Cotgrove et al.) Within ICI it was certainly the most influential of the early trials, for two reasons. First, the results achieved far exceeded even the most optimistic expectations: the attitudes of shopfloor workers and union/management relations exemplified the cooperative spirit which was one of the main objectives of the new agreement; all the targets set for manpower reduction were easily passed. In 1973 Harry Penny — the MUPS coordinator and now works manager — estimated that it would require twice as many shopfloor workers pre-MUPS to achieve current levels of production. The workforce benefited correspondingly, and average salaries of weekly staff increased from £21.80 to £38.70 per week in the five years to December 1972. Secondly, it had been assumed that the regimented, rigidly controlled processes of fibre-spinning were not an appropriate subject for MUPS-type changes. But Gloucester showed that even such jobs, resembling a mass production assembly line, could be transformed.

A counter-myth is subscribed to by some managers, that the successes of Gloucester were entirely due to a chance combination of favourable factors. Certainly, Gloucester had some advantages. The area was not one of those relics of the industrial past whose legacy was so bitter elsewhere. It had been the home of the aircraft industry – which boomed during the war and then subsided; it was near the Forest of Dean, whose coal mines were closing. Unemployment had risen and a new employer was welcome when British Nylon Spinners built the works in 1960. Unemployment had not been high for long, and it was relatively separated from other industrial communities. The other special factor was, ironically enough, the work – which had been thought to be an insuperable obstacle. For, unlike most chemical plants with their complex patterns of different jobs, Gloucester had relatively few jobs. A works employing 2,000 men might have several hundred jobs to agree and assess, but when it came to it at Gloucester – with its banks of identical machines – 65% of the workers were covered by two job descriptions, enormously simplifying the work of analysis.

A more substantial advantage was the tradition of open communication that had been established with the works' founding, for two reasons: the ex-aircraft workers were notoriously strike-prone and a major communication effort had been necessary; and the management had identified a need to keep the workforce informed about changes in fibre technology. The production of fibres is fairly remote from the end products. But small infractions of the rigid rules of production could have disastrous (and expensive) effects which were not visible until the end of the chain of subsequent processes. The importance of maintaining standards had to be brought home, and was, in lectures and discussions known as 'Palm Court sessions'. These were started as a one-off educational programme but developed into annual meetings where all workers had the chance to hear about the workers' results and prospects.

To these special features of Gloucester should be added a last one: that the most important work of introducing MUPS had been carried out before the works had been accepted as an official trial site. This was indirectly a result of ICI's acquiring the Courtaulds half-share in BNS in 1964. The questions raised in people's minds about their future with the gigantic and impersonal ICI were only to be allayed with information. And when the Palm Court sessions came round again in 1966, the MUPS agreement was taken as a text from which to preach the lesson that ICI was basically benevolent.

It was a highly significant move. MUPS was presented to a workforce for which it could have no immediate meaning: it was a topic for unstressed, free-wheeling discussions; not 'What are they going to do to us?', but 'What interesting things *they* are doing over there . . .' With nothing at stake, management and union representatives could discuss the merits of the new ideas and feel no need to take up defensive positions. Moreover, this fortuitously low profile enabled MUPS ideas to slip into the Gloucester consciousness under the early warning system of local resentment which had triggered off resistance at other sites.

Thus, the initial work on the agreement was entirely informal. The agreement was issued to the workforce on 20 October 1965, but Gloucester was not a trial site until 16 months later. But in that time, 30 'events' are entered in the MUPS diary, having to do with setting up working parties, meetings, training sessions, reports and manning studies. It allowed the management to make a small unstressed start.

As at Hillhouse, a great deal of the special features of the MUPS introduction at Gloucester can be traced back to the MUPS coordinator, Harry Penny. But where Ken Sharpington had been meticulously systematic in his approach (the Hillhouse system was described as 'mechanical' by some other managers), Penny was inspirational, almost evangelical. For him, attendance at the first Warren House training session had been a revelation. The theories discussed – and the ideas behind MUPS – were seeds that crystallised his own perceptions, and he returned convinced that this offered the way to the sort of working life people should have: cooperative, rich and full. He initiated the works discussions on MUPS and was largely responsible for the spontaneous mood of MUPS-preparedness that developed. The first action was to set up a management working party to have a look at five projects. One of their conclusions was that MUPS might not be inconsistent with nylon spinning after all. Specifically, the studies indicated that large savings in supervision were theoretically possible. It was an important conclusion, since it contained the seeds of major changes. A high ratio of supervisory staff was assumed to be essential to maintain standards; the corollary was the relatively mechanical, content-less work left for the operatives; any work that was at all complex was done by the large numbers of assistant foremen who were less supervisors than senior hands. If it was accepted that some of the quality control could be given to the operatives, much else could be changed as well.

The reports were not formal and certainly not binding. But they received important support from the conclusions of syndicates of supervisors set up in March. (This turned out to be another of the initiatives peculiar to Gloucester.) As in other parts of ICI, the compliance of supervisors in the introduction of MUPS could be, and was, assumed even though the enrichment of jobs at the upper end of the grades scale could only be achieved at their expense. The Gloucester management was more alive to this problem than in some other works and turned to it in early March with a series of talks on MUPS ('Theory and Implications') after which syndicates of supervisors were set up to examine their own work areas along the same lines. These reported in May, with some surprising results – of which the most surprising was the almost unanimous rejection of the two-tier supervisory structure. Much of the work of the assistant foremen was not supervisory at all but more in the nature of checking controls and speeds, setting instruments – all in the interests of maintaining standards. There was a case, which the supervisors accepted, for handing over some of the work and retaining more strictly supervisory functions for fewer men.

The supervisory ratios varied, but they included anomalously high levels. They ranged from 1:20 in a non-machine area to 1:8 in spinning – where there were 3 foremen and 10 assistant foremen for 100 men. This point was taken by the supervisors' syndicates and they also made some requests. They wanted to work within a 'span of control' of 5 supervisors to each manager; they also wanted help with functions that fell outside their strictly supervisory role – in training, special investigations and communications between groups. The first was not conceded, but the second was and 'Project Officers' were created to perform these interstitial functions.

The syndicates had been given the job of working out their

own supervisory structures. The result was that, for example, in Drawtwist the 13 foremen and assistant foremen were replaced by 8 foremen, who worked to a shift manager. In the works as a whole, an establishment of 32 foremen and 164 assistant foremen was replaced by one of 76 foremen and 20 project officers. The reduction in numbers was not lightly undertaken nor was it easily achieved. The works had some flexibility in the presence among the assistant foremen of a number of trainees (foremen went through a 12-month training course) who could be returned, grumbling, to the condition of process workers; appointments as project officers absorbed some more, which may have been why the suggestion was taken up; probably more important, there was to be a continuing need for training up to MUPS job descriptions, for which the displaced assistant foremen were well-suited; and lastly there was natural wastage.

Penny held regular meetings with the supervisors to keep communications open and they were not invariably happy occasions. (He found himself introduced at the beginning of one session by a placard which read: 'The Last Appearance of the Mushroom Boys: Kept in the Dark and Fed on Bullshit.') But talks to supervisors today elicit no signs of bitterness — quite the opposite. The fact that they had been fully involved from the start gave some control over their destinies; the ones who departed have been described to me by the supervisors as those who 'couldn't stay . . . unable to cope with the new situation'. And the resulting jobs are evidently more satisfactory than the old, which 'were supervisory only in name and involved a lot of doing. Now the operatives do the doing, watching their own standards, and we supervise, co-ordinating our work groups for maximum efficiency.' 'We are able to manage supplies more efficiently and to anticipate shortages.' 'We take action to maintain the flow of work and only intervene when the group hits an obstacle.'

The importance of this episode was that senior managers had their own ideas about inefficiencies and the savings which could be achieved in supervision. They had the choice of, in the old style, simply turning these conclusions into fact by making managerial decisions and accepting the cost of low morale. Instead, they turned the whole problem over to the supervisors themselves, giving them the job of designing their own supervisory structure. The result was cooperative and participative in a real sense.

Shop stewards were centrally involved in the discussions and syndicate work. In June 1966, the annual Palm Court sessions were focussed on MUPS, so that the agreement and its underlying purpose were familiar to everyone in the factory. By now there was keen interest in the agreement and an impatience to try it out. But, not being a trial site, the management was unable to move. However, the factory had been able to take a step in the direction of MUPS when, in May, clocking was abolished for shiftworkers – an action which always has managers and supervisors shaking their heads and predicting ruin. Perhaps as a demonstration of the spirit at that time, time-keeping actually improved. 'It led to a big improvement in the atmosphere', a process worker said later.

The enthusiasm did not last. The government introduced a wage freeze; Fibres Division announced 1,200 redundancies (200 at Gloucester), marking the first of what was to become a continuing series of crises in the synthetic fibres industry worldwide. National unions declared that they would consider no productivity changes of any kind without financial reward. In the factory MUPS discussions ceased altogether and union attitudes hardened. Changes suggested by management were rejected, even when they only involved supervisors. However, some sort of dialogue was maintained since, with the government's wage freeze, MUPS offered the only way of improving earnings.

The breakthrough came, in Penny's view, at the end of the year – or at any rate an event occurred which marked a re-awakening of shopfloor interest in MUPS. The T&GWU was arranging a one-week course for shop stewards and asked the works manager for the release of Gloucester's T&G stewards, for facilities – the Palm Court – and some contribution from management. The course was held at the end of 1966 and Penny took the opportunity to give lectures and start discussions on productivity. 'It was essential that we should not come after the unions but that interest and requests for discussions should arise spontaneously from their side. The shop stewards' course provided just the opportunity I had been waiting for.' One sign of the re-awakened interest was the unions' agreement to changes designed to produce saving in supervision, recommended earlier in the year by the supervisors' working parties.

By now the works management was aware, through the grapevine, that the joint steering committee in Millbank was considering adding new trial sites to the list as a way of keeping the MUPS exercise going. Both unions and management applied to have Gloucester included, through their own official channels. Partly to keep up momentum — and partly to pre-empt the claims of other works by demonstrating local enthusiasm — a working party was set up to examine the spinning area in depth. Harry Penny became chairman of the committee, which had four full-time and two part-time members. These were managers whose skills and experience covered work study, engineering and development. With supervisors seconded in two-week stints, but without shop-floor participation — since the T&GWU was maintaining an official 'no talk' policy — the work of analysing jobs in the spinning area was completed in three months. It pointed to the possibility of making substantial savings through changes in manning and the partial elimination of supervision.

Although lack of official T&GW union participation forced it to work in something of a vacuum, the committee at least had the support of local shop stewards and the shopfloor. In some ways the lack of official support was a blessing since it further reduced the pressure to take action on MUPS and allowed time for other training and preparation. In fact, shop-floor discussions in the spinning area did not start until May when official T&G approval had been obtained. By then there had been considerable activity. A series of talks and discussions had been held with junior managers and supervisors on the technical aspects of MUPS such as job appraisement and work elimination; a good deal of effort had gone into training foremen in group discussion leading; and some discussion groups had been formed in engineering, since the craft unions allowed it. Some minor changes recommended in the working party report were introduced in spinning.

Gloucester had been nominated for a MUPS trial on 1 March, with the immediate support of craft unions. But the T&GWU district office was unable to take part in discussions without clearance from their national office. After a number of informal contacts, a meeting was arranged with all process (T&G) shop stewards at the end of April and their agreement obtained.

The next step was to prepare for and start discussion groups. This was done with some care. The working party prepared a brief for each supervisor, covering the jobs in his area that would be discussed by his group. He had already received training in group leading, of which the main purpose was to prepare him to lead *from behind*. The natural reaction of workers whose experience of management did not include much interest in ideas from the shopfloor was 'It's all decided. Tell us what's planned and we'll tell you what we think of it.' It was common through the company that it always took some time before shop stewards and operatives could be persuaded that there was not some master plan locked away which would be produced with a flourish when everyone was worn down with useless talking. A paper, 'The Gloucester Concept of a MUPS Investigation', comments: 'The importance of not presenting a blue-print is two-fold: firstly, to gain acceptance of the idea that operatives should have a real chance of discussing their work and . . . proposing improvements; secondly, to provide an atmosphere free from the restricted horizon of the blue-print . . .'

Once the message got through, the discussion groups went 'like a bomb'. Meeting for about half-an-hour at a time in work groups of about ten, the men discussed work in their area, possible ways of rearranging it and the implications for individual jobs. Members of the working party were available to talk about specific aspects — which were taken as valuable opportunities to explain the relevance of behavioural science theories, particularly the Herzbergian 'not by bread alone' thesis. Proposals came from the working party in the guide-lines, but (quoting from the same paper) 'It must be clear . . . that the proposals are open to modification. Indeed it will probably be found that there are a number of respects in which the future pattern cannot emerge until operatives' views have been obtained.'

Ideas were fed back to the working party and responded to with bulletins in which the working party indicated points of agreement or difference. When this stage was completed, and the general pattern of work in the area fully discussed, the discussion groups sent representatives, usually shop stewards, to 'gel' sessions. In these, the four shifts got together to pool ideas from discussion groups about a given area of work. The sessions often took more than a day since knotty problems about the transfer of work between unions were discussed between union representatives – for which reason management was not represented. In the next stage, the working party put together a draft job description, working from the conclusions of the 'gel' session, which was then circulated to the shift workers for further discussion. When the job description was finally agreed, it was ready to be assessed. Finally, training programmes were worked out to supply the skills called for in the descriptions. The process was elaborately repetitive and time-consuming, consciously so. Only by moving slowly, acting with complete transparency, involving people and gaining their agreement at every stage could there be any guarantee of commitment to the changes.

But this is somewhat to anticipate the course of MUPS at Gloucester. The first job description – for polymer handling – was not drafted until mid-June, 1967, six weeks after discussions had started in Spinning; it was formally approved three weeks later; and it was not assessed for a month more, on the first visit of the assessment team in mid-August. Meanwhile, working parties had been set up to cover other parts of the works and discussion groups were proceeding down the path blazed by the Spinning Area discussions. 'Blazed' is not an exaggeration, for the discussions in Spinning aroused a good deal of sometimes jealous attention in the rest of the works. One progress report of the period comments: 'The enthusiasm in Spinning has been highly infectious. We are inundated by demands for detailed discussion . . .'

The process was being controlled by a joint steering committee, chaired by Harry Penny, in which management and senior shop stewards made the policy decisions about the MUPS introduction and dealt with problems arising in the work areas. Jack Sweet, a Drawtwist shop steward, said later that the steering committee was largely responsible for maintaining good relations in the works during the exercise. It was a place where knotty problems could be talked out and 'pressure got released'. And it was the central decision point where permission had to be obtained for any major initiative. Without the control the steering committee provided, the enthusiasm of the early stages could easily have led to hasty decisions.

The cooperation of shop stewards was essential and perhaps should be added to the special factors of Gloucester listed at the beginning of this section. Unlike the other ICI works in the trials, Gloucester did not have troubles with the issue of flexibility. Whether because of management skill, or local character, or because the lack of a long and bad industrial history provided unfavourable conditions for the process by which, elsewhere, defensive attitudes were institutionalised in local union traditions, there was already a significant degree of flexible working in the factory. As we have seen, the sticky periods in negotiations arose mainly from the local T&GWU members' need to be convinced and not, as elsewhere, from the anxiety of craft unions about the loss of the protection from demarcations. The most important result of this more open attitude was the vital willingness always to talk. However, it went further. The shop stewards' syndicates, of which the setting-up marked the beginning of shop steward involvement, made a valuable contribution to the subsequent discussions about jobs; they played a central role in the area discussion groups and in the drafting of job descriptions.

Also, 'we were fortunate in not discussing MUPS in the new ways of working in a negotiating situation', Penny says. Only in the last months of that year, when the works was working toward a deadline of 'going on' by 1 January 1968, was there any pressure. But by then the process was in full swing: four working parties were in operation by the end of May; a further three set up in August brought all jobs in the factory under discussion; and later teams were able to draw on the experience of the first.

It was an outstandingly successful introduction and, with the impressive successes at Hillhouse and Stowmarket, went a long way to stiffen the resolve of senior management during the mounting troubles of 1968. We shall be examining the results achieved in a number of works when we consider the effects of MUPS (and its successor, WSA) on the company. It is enough at this stage to say that it amply fulfilled the expectations of its designers. The visible part of the productivity bargain yielded manpower savings of more than the target 15% for the company and substantial pay increases for the workers. At a less visible level, the jobs had themselves been enriched and the organisation of work improved. The first feature was more apparent at Gloucester, where workers in jobs that had been tightly controlled found themselves with considerable new responsibility extending even to the basic decisions about scheduling their work. The second feature dominated at Hillhouse, where scope for job enrichment was more constrained by technology (and in any case less necessary) than at Gloucester, but the opportunity for improving the planning and organisation of work yielded considerable benefits.

To complete the set, we should have a look at Stowmarket; but only a brief one, for the Paint Works there is *sui generis*. The conditions are quite untypical of ICI and the experience of introducing MUPS, while interesting in its own right, contains few clues to an understanding of problems elsewhere. The works is small — the size of about a quarter of the Hillhouse workforce — but it is, even so, one of only two major industrial employers in Stowmarket, which is twenty miles from the nearest industrial centre, Ipswich. The works was therefore strongly placed as a premium employer in a place where there was little alternative employment of a similar kind. The isolation and lack of an industrial tradition in the area further strengthened the management in relations with the unions; there was no long folk memory of privation to contend with and no habit of resistance. Lastly, the manufacturing process is relatively simple, mainly a matter of mixing and packing. The level of skills among process workers is not high and the demands of maintaining the relatively simple plant do not require a large force of craftsmen. In spite of these advantages, there were serious resistances to the agreement that were overcome through discussion and analysis — 'joint problem-solving', in fact. But a closer look at the process will tell us nothing that we cannot learn from the other two trials.

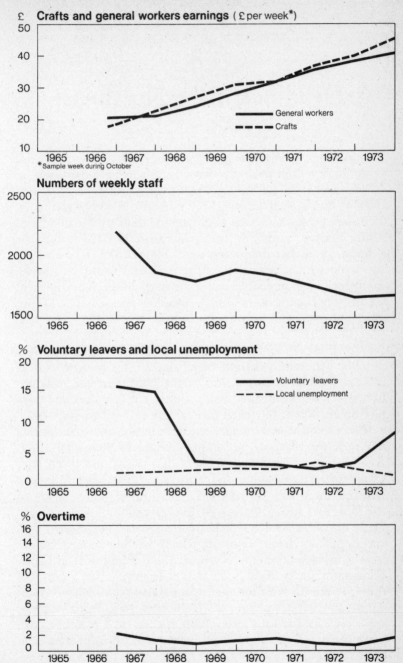

Fig.5 Gloucester: indicators of change

Crafts and general workers earnings (£ per week*)

* Sample week during October

— General workers
--- Crafts

Numbers of weekly staff

Voluntary leavers and local unemployment

— Voluntary leavers
--- Local unemployment

Overtime

8

Deadlock in the Northeast

The system of volunteering for trials set up by the joint committee would probably have been adequate, by itself, to allow works on to the agreement in a controlled manner, until it had seeped into and permeated the whole company. A dozen works had been accepted for trials by the middle of 1968, and were making their way towards MUPS. But the process of further increasing their number had to be brought to a stop for the situation in the trial sites in the Northeast, far from being amenable to the strategy adopted by the joint committee the previous year, was rapidly worsening to a point where it was endangering the whole agreement. New trial sites did what had been intended and introduced movement into a situation that had become perilously static. But they did not generate a current of change strong enough to flow around the big, resistant sites of the Northeast and – as was hoped – wash away the obstructions. The big sites had been put on the shelf, but they obstinately refused to stay there.

The situation was already foreseen in a steering committee report to the company personnel director in November 1967. At that time, it had become likely that two, if not three, sites would soon be working under the agreement. The influence of Gloucester and Stowmarket – because of the isolation of the sites and special nature of the operations – was thought likely to be limited to their own divisions; but a great deal was hoped for from Hillhouse which 'would almost certainly have a big effect in the Northwest and might also influence Billingham or even Wilton, although only after a lapse of time'. A month later the three sites started on the agreement. Although the example of Hillhouse was influential, as expected, it was the quite sharp success of the other two, particularly Gloucester, that became most influential and even decisive.

For the rest of 1968 — or until time came for re-negotiating the agreement — the emphasis was on pressing forward with new trial sites. But the frequent disappointments were beginning to tell; other possibilities were considered. In January 1968, Rowland Wright, the personnel director, was reporting to the Board:

'Management in some parts of the company had become disillusioned . . . and suggestions have been made that we should consider alternatives such as individual plant-by-plant bargaining or separate negotiations with the craft and general worker unions . . . we have no evidence that any form of half-way house is likely to prove a practicable proposition.

'The suggestion that we should make progress by plant bargaining has many dangers: unless conducted against a background of agreed principles the result will inevitably be the highest common pay factor for the lowest common productivity across any one site. Loosening intercraft demarcation would be useful but not worth the MUPS pay scale and, if the general workers were left out of any deal, we would face massive unrest.'

The strongest movement for making a separate deal — and the best reasons for doing so — developed at Wilton through 1968.

The importance of the Wilton site in ICI's MUPS experience cannot be exaggerated: from being an expected sticking-point — and for that reason all the more worth including as a trial site — it became an obsession and a positive source of danger to the company, draining management energy, greedy for all attention and the centre of a shop steward movement opposing the agreement.

Wilton was important for other reasons. The site represents the largest concentration of investment in the company. It has crucial strategic value in terms both of capital — and hence in effects on the company's results and stock market standing — and, physically, as a control point in many of the chemical processes. It also has a more psychological importance. In Wilton were concentrated ICI's most modern plants, making petrochemicals. Wilton was a large part of ICI's claim to a place in the modern chemical world. Through the 1950s, all the major chemical companies – and quite a few cash-swollen oil companies – invested heavily to keep up with growing demand and with their competitors. The result was worldwide over-capacity and, with the 1958 US recession, dumping in Europe followed by the price wars of the 1958-62 period. ICI's investment in Wilton virtually stopped in those years. But the chemical cycle picked up again and, by the time MUPS was launched in 1965, ICI had invested more than £300m on the site and was still investing at a rate of £50m a year (all in 1972 pounds). There is now more than £500m invested at Wilton, representing a quarter of the company's assets.

The economics of such heavy investment were compelling. The logic of complexity in chemical plants has been described: the more completely the company could make use of its proliferating streams of products and by-products, the more efficient and profitable would the operation become. Allied to it is the logic of scale: in continuous process industries there are almost unlimited benefits to be gained from building bigger plants. But the social logic of an organisation is not coincident with its economic logic, dominant logic or business endeavour, and it was the social logic of Wilton that was to dominate the introduction of MUPS – and after – to such a degree that the economic benefits of the new ways of working have yet to appear.

This was more than just a question of size, although the difficulties for an individual of feeling cosily identified with something as overwhelming as the steaming towers of the 1,000 acre Wilton site, still less the company owning it, do not need much emphasis. It was also a product of the *rapidity* with which Wilton had grown, the *diversity* of its workforce and the almost constant *change* which characterises the site. (The effects of technology on attitudes have been discussed in Wedderburn and Crompton.) It was a function, too, of the locality, its history and the unions – 'militant' or merely 'well-organised', depending on your point of view. Always a potent presence, union activity took on a more political tinge when the senior stewards organised themselves into a site committee which, by the time MUPS was launched, had an office off the site and circulated its own news-sheet.

There was plenty of unrest to work on. The site employed people from closed-down coal mines, ship yards, the defunct Cleveland Steel Works and the run-down railway workshops. Not only did they have no particular allegiance to ICI, they imported an unsettling history of employment in industries with more past than future. Moreover, in boom times, Wilton was competing for labour with local industries — in particular the neighbouring Dorman Long Steel Works — which had long habits of taking men on at high rates and laying them off during the frequent downturns in business, so that the labour market was also fluctuating. Local unemployment went from less than 2% in 1952-7 to a peak of 9% in 1962. More of a problem still was the presence on the site of armies of contractors' workers: highly-paid casual workers who were seen to be at once a threat, doing work that might be done by the company's own maintenance and engineering workers, and a promise, of higher pay which 'fairness' demanded should also be paid to the ICI men working beside them.

These factors are reflected in labour statistics for the site, although much muted and filtered by aggregation. In the year of MUPS' launch, turnover on the site was 17%. Always sensitive more than anything else to prevailing unemployment, turnover had recovered from a 4% low, reached during the 1962 recession, having been as high as 20% in the palmy fifties (see Fig 6). Time lost through absenteeism and sickness averaged 7% for 1965.

The site average for overtime during 1965 was 12%, a more difficult figure to interpret, but important, since it reflects not just the pressure of work but also the pressure from workers for more money — pressure which had the more force since they were able to point down the road to Dorman Long or Smith's Docks, which offered high levels of overtime.

12% is a higher level than it seems, since by far the greatest part of overtime was accounted for by the 4,000 workers — craftsmen and support, mostly on day work and mostly on maintenance. These were quite regularly notching up 18-20% overtime in 'systematic' weekend work. The result was that, in combination with bonus payments that had crept up to as much as 40% (when the levels had been officially set at 27½%), the Wilton workers, craftsmen in particular, were taking home pay packets that bore little relation to their base rates. More to the point, their earnings were far higher than the MUPS pay offer.

All of this would have mattered less if the Wilton management had not been so deeply divided, and in some cases competitive, that they left a power vacuum for the union organisation to fill. Given the policy of uniformity in pay and conditions, what was needed, and what was lacking, was the will to devise, coordinate and carry through policies for labour on a site basis.

The roots of the problem are to be found in a decision — 'disastrous' according to some, 'inescapable' according to others — made at the beginning of Wilton's development to allow the several divisions present each to be responsible for its own works. If it was disastrous, it was so because the decision immediately introduced tensions between the loyalties of managers toward the site and toward their parent divisions that could only be decided in favour of the divisions — which controlled the managerial reward systems. The site had originally been run by its own 'Wilton Council'. But by 1965 Heavy Organic Chemicals Division had been given responsibility. Inescapable this decision was not; disastrous it was, for the dynamics of the site management were now completely wrong: there was no individual with an interest in running the site as a unit, nor with the power and authority. On the contrary, there was a confusing and conflicting web of responsibility and power in which none of the interrelated systems matched. The workers were recruited by the site personnel office but worked within a works — which were sizeable enterprises in their own right: Terylene Works alone employed more than 4,000 people in its heyday. The only body with a structure appropriate for operation on a site-wide basis, the power and the will to do so was the unofficial committee of senior shop stewards.

Trials were meant to take place at Wilton's Olefine Works, but attention was held at site level for two years, and it was another two years before significant progress was made toward the detailed plant discussions that were the cutting edge of MUPS introduction. Wilton, in other words, never emerged from the political phase — of management and unions testing each other's positions — that marked, to greater or lesser degree, the beginning of all introductions. The Wilton experience was political from beginning to end; the shop stewards were able to block any moves toward substantive discussion until, when they came, they were nugatory.

When the agreement was launched, it was immediately rejected by the AEU shop stewards. As in the other trial sites there was an elaborate sequence of meetings to make sure that people were briefed about the agreement. When the turn came for the senior shop stewards to have their first discussions on the agreement, the AEU representatives walked out, refusing to take part. This refusal was shortly afterward made official. The AEU was shortly afterward joined by the Plumbers union and the Boilermakers. Without the participation of leading unions, joint discussions on the agreement could not take place and the whole project was effectively brought to a halt.

However, as planned, the Olefines Works started its long build up to the MUPS trials with a series of manning studies carried out by management on a plant-by-plant basis. These were intended to serve the same purpose as the studies at Hillhouse and Gloucester, where management teams produced ideas for change as a basis for discussion at work group level. But without the participation of the craft unions, they could not move into the discussion of jobs on a plant-by-plant basis within the works. They petered out within a few months. Meanwhile the discussions at site level — about whether there should be discussions — fizzled and sputtered inconclusively.

The reasons for the opposition were familiar: the 'not invented here' resistance to changes being imposed from the centre; and, more fundamentally, the deep worries among craft unions, particularly engineers, about the threat to their protected position. At the same time, the agreement did not offer enough in the special conditions of the Northeast to make a more direct appeal to the workers through their pay packets. This was a sharp contrast with the story at the first trial sites, where MUPS rates were attractive from the start.

By the time MUPS was launched, the bonus rates at Wilton had drifted to an average 33% on base rates — considerably more in individual cases — although the bonus rate was meant to be no more than 27½%. Overtime was high for day workers. For shift workers, pay was made up with a shift disturbance allowance. As a result of these additions to the base rate, the earnings of an engineering tradesman on day work was as follows during the first part of the MUPS exercise:

October 1965   £24. 14s.
April 1966   £26. 4s.
October 1966   £23. 4s.
April 1967   £24. 6s.

Against this background, the basic MUPS offer of £20 per week for Grade 7 (at which tradesmen were to be assessed) offered no inducement to change. Not all the unions objected equally. Process workers were almost jubilant at what was seen as a 'general workers' charter'; the tensions were not eased when they, for long the underprivileged members of the working class, took the opportunity to taunt tradesmen about the loss of their ancient privileges. 'We'll be taking over the site soon . . .' is said to have been the general tenor of these exchanges. Electricians were relatively indifferent to this, since theirs was a skill defined not by tools but by an area of work and this was partly defended for them by statute. It was the engineers who were, or seemed to be, most under threat. A large part of their work was defined as 'skilled' by virtue of the use of tools, often very simple ones. In real terms only a small part — variously estimated at between 20 and 40% — required engineering skills of a sort which the average handyman might not command. The fact was known, although never officially admitted, and it was defended in straight power-political terms: ownership of work meant jobs; sharing of the work with unskilled workers, however rational, meant handing over jobs to other unions and changing the balance of site power that membership defines. Aligned with the AEU were most of the other craft unions, the less numerous 'black trades' (Sheet Metal Workers, Boilermakers and Plumbers).

The differences between unions became almost immediately apparent. In January 1966, the ETU and ICI jointly arranged a course for ETU site shop stewards at the Union's College at Esher. The initiative had come from the shop stewards. The result was one of those extraordinary occasions with which the progress of MUPS in ICI is irregularly studded, when the meeting reached a high pitch of open

Table 2. Wilton Shop Stewards 1971

Union	Shop Stewards	Members	Members/Shop Stewards
TGWU	197	7,071	35.8
AEF	62	1,627	25.6
ETU	29	509	17.5
PTU	13	215	16.5
SMW	3	53	17.7
Boilermakers	11	220	20.0
Woodworkers	4	41	10.2
Painters	1	14	14.0
Building Workers	1	18	18.0
	321	9,668	

discussion and involvement in issues that would normally have aroused stock defensive responses 'back home'. Problems were not talked away but defined, discussed and listed for future action. The result was a far deeper understanding of the meaning and aims of MUPS — which the ETU shop stewards, led by the senior shop steward, began to spread in a series of plant meetings on their return.

But this was one of those false starts which, seen in retrospect, could have been built on, but for reasons which seemed good at the time diverted into the sands. Hearing of the success of the Esher course, other unions began to ask for similar facilities and opportunities for their shop stewards to discuss the agreement. The site management was enthusiastic, but the request faced the company with a dilemma: could they allow the interest to develop spontaneously, organically, when the AEU was maintaining such a rigid 'no talk' posture? The Teesside management coordinating committee, presiding over the two big and a number of smaller sites, said they would approve of training conferences for individual unions or for all the unions, but no halfway houses. The risk of splitting off the AEU from the other unions, isolating and confirming them in a policy of obstruction, was seen to be too great. The company decided that at all costs the AEU had to be kept in the union community and the AEU shop stewards kept open to influence from their peers. It was a monumental mistake of judgment. The missed opportunity was never to come again.

In this highly political situation, the nature of the leadership became more important than the underlying issues. And the unions had extremely powerful leaders, intelligent and dedicated men whose main interest was not the objective economic rationality of ICI's long-term interests, even though this was presented as being coincident with their own members' need for jobs. Their interest was their members' immediate interests — which meant more than anything else the preservation of jobs, and of status, procedural distinctions, demarcations and any other structural defence against a fluid labour situation on the site. The leading figures on the union side were Paddy Tombe (who had been largely responsible for the November decision of the AEU advisory committee), a senior shop steward from Terylene Works and John Grace, a T&G senior shop steward. There were also others, some 25 senior shop stewards in all, hardly less able and together comprising the only unified political unit on the Wilton site. It was at site level that the Wilton debate was to be conducted for the next three years.

The two sides settled down to an extended period of trench warfare, which was to stretch through the signature of WSA in 1969 until the first workers on the site went on to the agreement at the end of 1971 — six years after MUPS was launched. Trench warfare favours defensive strategies: nothing could tempt the unions from their prepared positions; the shop stewards' perception was that almost any change — except a straight increase in pay, which they were always willing to accept — would be to their disadvantage. Therefore it was left to the management to take the initiative while the shop stewards could more safely remain with the status quo. It was hardly an engagement at all, since the unions — with the AEU very much in the lead — simply refused to talk. Even the visit by the joint committee from London in May 1966 had no more effect than had the attempts of site managers to find their way around the seemingly enigmatic obstacles.

By the middle of 1967, the deadlock at Wilton had been accepted as a fact of life at the centre and joint committee policy was beginning to re-form itself around the idea that only new trial sites would provide the impetus to keep MUPS on its feet. But the frustration of local management and those unions, mainly general workers, interested in MUPS was still mounting.

Then, in October that year, Jack Lofthouse made a speech which unleashed a furious protest from the unions and generated enough energy to break the deadlock. The speech was made to the Wilton site council, part of the works councils structure, and spoke warningly of the effects on future investment plans of continuing high costs at Wilton. It was reported in the factory newspaper, the *Wilton News*, and picked up by a local newspaper where, greatly compressed, it appeared under the headline 'ICI THREAT TO TURN ITS BACK ON TEESSIDE'. More inflammatory still, the report said, 'He accused the AEU of holding up progress by refusing to open talks. Other unions at Wilton were willing to negotiate.'

The story brought an immediate reaction. It was a 'premeditated, treacherous, unprovoked and unjustified attack' on the AEU. Paddy Tombe said in an interview that it was completely unfair to blame the AEU: '. . . we would be dishonest as a trade union if we went into talks which we knew would not work . . .' The row mounted and reached a climax in a furious meeting between Lofthouse and fifteen AEU shop stewards. Out of this 'savage' meeting came the first breakthrough at Wilton.

The confrontation led to an agreement with the shop stewards to look at productivity on a plant-by-plant basis — but not within MUPS. This was not the first time that the AEU had tried to put forward the idea of a separate agreement. However, the opportunity offered by the October meeting was taken, even though it was to lead to unbinding, uncommitted, non-MUPS talks on productivity. Nothing else offered a way forward. The main priority for the Wilton management was to start talking, discover areas of agreement and build on them. From head office it seemed a risky business, possibly jeopardising the whole project by a sort of productivity Balkanisation. The site management was aware of these fears and, in November, David Jones — HOC deputy chairman with special responsibility for Wilton — sent a message to London which ended: 'The Wilton management appreciate the risk and intend to establish a system of control so that these dangers will be minimised . . .'

With some reluctance, the joint committee agreed that the productivity talks should take place. Four works were nominated for the talks — Olefines, Terylene, Nylon and Plastics — which were to be *only* on the subject of productivity. In effect, the talks were to comprise the manning studies and job descriptions stages of MUPS introductions elsewhere.

Without minimising the difficulties that were encountered, the talks that ensued were successful and engaged the interest of the people involved — an interest that seemed, from its liveliness, to have been latent all the time and held down by the deadlock on the site. (There may have been an element of competitiveness in this: Gloucester, Hillhouse and Stowmarket had now all accepted the agreement which was seen to be successfully in operation.) The discussions were not equally successful. There were still strong resistances, even to non-MUPS discussions. But it was talk; it was movement.

At a meeting of the joint committee in London, John Harvey-Jones expressed the hope that 'in the end, the process of free discussion and explanation would lead everyone at Wilton to see MUPS proposals not . . . as arbitrary rules predetermining their fate, but as a commonsense framework . . .' It was not to be. Any hopes management might have had that the talks would by themselves lead to changes in attitude on fundamental issues were disappointed. If the talks were to lead constructively forward, there would have to be a change: either in the shop stewards' opposition to MUPS; or in the company's refusal to allow a separate agreement to be worked out on the Wilton site. The talks came to an end in May 1968. The gap between the two sides could not be bridged.

Some months after the productivity talks broke down, Geoffrey Gilbertson wrote of the company's opposition that any agreement made at Wilton would have to be better than MUPS, and would therefore instantly give rise to a demand for better conditions throughout the company. 'Either this would happen, in which case an agreement would in effect be negotiated at Wilton for the great majority of ICI employees, or the position would be reached when the only logical thing was for each factory to negotiate its own agreement . . .'

This was a bitter disappointment for management, nearly

punch-drunk with the seemingly endless frustrations of introducing MUPS. And the frustration on all sides was reflected in tensions not just between company and unions but within the company — between Wilton (or rather HOC) management, the personnel department at Millbank and the other divisions. Each represented a separate logic, each could claim a large measure of truth — but Wilton was the odd one out.

By early 1968 MUPS was growing daily more dangerous for the company. The agreement had become a political issue around which a strong movement was forming. The shop stewards at Wilton had a strong organisation which printed a newsletter off the site, attacking both the company and national union policies. They went further. From late 1967 onwards, even while the productivity talks were in full spate, Wilton stewards — or, more particularly, Paddy Tombe and John Grace — were visiting other ICI sites to mobilise and coordinate opposition to MUPS. In September of that year, news came of the formation of an ICI craft shop stewards' committee, with Paddy Tombe as secretary. The attempt to gain support for an all-union stewards' committee for the whole company received little support, but strong links were made through 1968 between works in the Northeast: the three Teesside sites, Nylon Works at Doncaster and Dyestuffs at Huddersfield and Grangemouth. It is difficult to assess the strength of this movement and the reality of the threat it posed to the company. But there is no denying the fright it gave to management.

It was becoming apparent that, far from being able to leave Wilton to ripen on the shelf while concentrating on more tractable works, the site would obstinately refuse to be left to come to its collective senses. None the less, the company, site management and joint committee — and also, though very differently, the unions on the site — still sought ways around the deadlock. These were effectively brought to an end by the visit to Wilton in July of the company's Chairman, Sir Peter Allen. A strong supporter of MUPS, he was worried by the way the trials were developing. As Chairman it was his job to question the benefits of even his own convictions. He talked to management, to the works council and he met a group of Wilton shop stewards. It was a tough meeting and convinced him, first, that there would be no progress at Wilton with the current agreement and, secondly, that the time had come to assess its benefits and decide what the next moves should be. He called a meeting on his return and set in motion the chain of events that was to lead to the setting up of the Callard Committee.

At about the same time, the Wilton stewards produced their own productivity proposals, what they called a 'mini-MUPS', which put forward conditions for a Wilton agreement. It had been assembled, with the help of Wilton management and Tony Topham of Hull University, out of the experience of the productivity proposals. Even if it could have served as a basis for a separate agreement (a route that had already been rejected) it was pre-empted by the consequences of the Chairman's visit. But as a footnote on the Wilton episode, it should be remembered.

For the last half of the year, there was little activity – none centred on MUPS – while the main scene of action shifted to London, the deliberations of the Callard Committee and an intense period of political activity around the issue of Wilton's management. As a result, a number of changes were made in October 1968: John Harvey-Jones took over the management of the site as a deputy chairman of HOC with Brian Jenkins as personnel director; and a Wilton site coordinating committee was formed in an attempt to deal with the inter-divisional tensions on the site, and represented a return to the earlier days of the Wilton council.

The first priority of John Harvey-Jones was to 'win credibility for Wilton management with the company' and first actions were designed to cut across inter-divisional competitiveness and to forge a strong site management team.

The institutions either already existed or had just been created for achieving this, but it needed some decisive action in order to make them work. Thus, a works managers' committee had been in existence for some time but was largely ineffective in agreeing, still less in carrying out, site policy given the strong loyalties that the managers felt to their divisions. Probably more important, since it enabled the works managers' committee to work meaningfully, was the formation of the Wilton site coordinating committee. This was a response at the centre to the failure of the policy of giving site-management entirely to HOC. Deputy chairmen of divisions represented at Wilton were ex-officio members of the coordinating committee which provided a forum for aligning divisional policies toward the site at the highest level.

One of the first actions of the Wilton site coordinating committee was to approve a proposal from Harvey-Jones that the management be sent on Coverdale training courses — a one week course in group dynamics, leadership and decision-making. The benefits for Wilton of the course were that it provided all managers — some 1100 were sent — with a common set of skills for dealing with problems of handling discussions in groups. Of more immediate benefit, it provided Harvey-Jones and Brian Jenkins with the opportunity to talk to the managers of the site away from the site. 'As far as I am concerned, this was by far the most important part of the training scheme', said Harvey-Jones. 'Brian and I got them at a place where we could really get at them and tell them about the need for management on a site basis and the way in which inter-works rivalries handed the initiative over to the shop stewards.' It was an expensive but highly successful effort. At a trivial level, it meant no more than that the managers of the site had shared this one experience — of going through the course and being talked at by Harvey-Jones and Jenkins. But it was more important that, for the first time, a thread had been woven through the management of the site which provided some sort of unity, however tenuous.

Two other events marked the swinging back of the balance of power, both of them took the form of confrontation with the unions in which management successfully held their own. The first was the dismissal in September 1969 of Paddy Tombe, the AEU senior steward and, up to the time of his departure, by common consent 'the most powerful man on the site'. A story of his going would be a book in itself, replete with accusation and counter-accusation. The dismissal went to arbitration and the company's action was upheld. The second event was a strike of T&G workers in February 1970. This too the site management successfully stood against and the strike fizzled out after four days.

Harvey-Jones is convinced that these two events marked a turning point since they demonstrated that it was, after all, possible for management to take some initiative. If such a

statement seems a grotesque reversal of normal roles, it is a
reflection of the Wilton situation. Through 1968 and for the
first part of 1969, the shop stewards, in Harvey-Jones' words,
'ruled the site'. No individual manager was prepared to take on
the stewards, who were able to act with increasing impunity.
It was because he grossly overstepped rules which were being
constantly, but less obviously, flouted that Paddy Tombe was
eventually dismissed: this demonstrated more clearly than
anything else could have that there was a limit to the
freedom which the stewards could take. To take on a strike
was a similar demonstration that the company did, after all,
have power in its dealings with the unions. The power had
always been there; what was needed was a determined
individual who was prepared to use it. But Harvey-Jones
would have achieved little if he had not been at the same
time developing a sense of site identity and site loyalties to
replace the exposed, fragmented management that had
developed on the site.

There was a long way still to go before the unions finally
agreed to cooperate in the introduction of the new agreement, and still longer until the last substantial group of
workers was covered, by the end of 1971. But to retail the
events that led to the final denouement is only to repeat
much that had happened before. However, two events are
probably worth noting.

In July 1970, the WSA coordinating group decided to try
and break the deadlock by taking a leaf out of the Hillhouse
book and circulating some provisional guesses about manning
and assessments. Discussions had been proceeding since the
WSA had been signed but they always suffered from the
disadvantage that they were abstract and gave the workers
very little to compare their present situation with. The
personnel department decided to issue 'WSA Organisation
and Manning Plans' for all the work areas on the site. The
plans were put together by the managers involved and, in
effect, distilled the manning conclusions from the WSA
discussions of the previous year. As at Hillhouse, it was a
device to present the agreement to the workers in a concrete
form where they could begin to grasp the benefits for them
on an individual basis. To provide such demonstrations of
what was going to happen under the agreement was bound to

increase the pressure to go on the agreement for those unions who had already given their approval, particularly the T&G (from which a strike had already been threatened for this reason a month or two earlier).

Secondly, capitalising on the dynamic for change generated by the O&M plans and, somewhat reluctantly, bowing to the practical need to allow the 'willing' unions to proceed, the company decided in September 1970 to make a radical change in policy and allow the unions to make individual agreements to go on. This was far from being an easy decision. To have unions going on to the agreement piecemeal was going to create an untidy situation, more tensions and strain within the workforce and would result in a work situation that would be extremely difficult to control. Probably more to the point, if WSA meant anything, it meant a complete re-think of the work in particular areas. This was not possible on a partial basis; all the work in an area had to be considered in terms of the best way of carrying it out; to allow one union to go on to the agreement while another union, whose work was logically also affected, remained outside, could result in an inefficient introduction. However, there was no real alternative. The situation was once more becoming dangerous. The discussions and the O&M plans had unleashed considerable spontaneous demand for the new agreement — or rather, for the pay the new agreement would carry. The demand has to be satisfied, if a fresh crop of troubles was not to replace the old. Billingham had already experienced a protest strike of T&GWU members against AUEW obstruction; there was no reason why the same might not happen at Wilton. In any case, the situation of workers on WSA rates side-by-side with workers on the old scales was too unstable to last. ETU members voted to start discussions in October; other craft unions accepted over the next months; the AUEW voted to start talks in a mass meeting in April 1971, leaving only the Plumbers holding out — which they did for another year.

It was a Pyrrhic victory for both sides. The management got their agreement, or the form of it; the craft unions got their pay increases. Neither side got much else. There was little change in the direction of more flexible working; Wilton remains, by international standards, overmanned and ineffici-

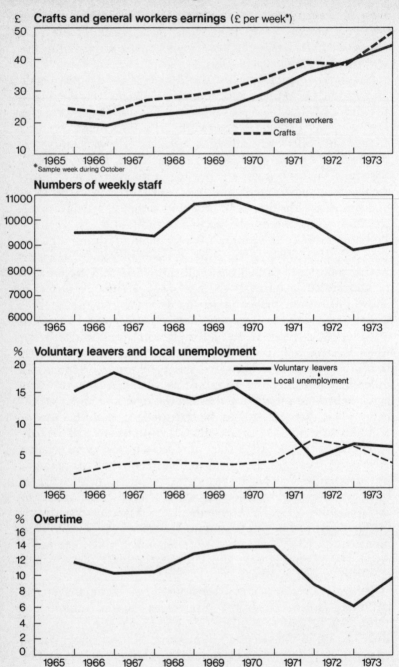

Fig.6 Wilton: indicators of change

£ **Crafts and general workers earnings** (£ per week*)

*Sample week during October

— General workers
--- Crafts

Numbers of weekly staff

% **Voluntary leavers and local unemployment**

— Voluntary leavers
--- Local unemployment

% **Overtime**

ently-run; many jobs remain untouched, un-enriched. The managers, stewards and supervisors were all exhausted by the experience, so that when it neared its end the form of the agreement became more important than its intention. It is not easy to see who gained from the long and bitter fight. Quite possibly, everybody lost.

Billingham

To tell the story of Billingham is to repeat much of what happened at Wilton. There was the same long deadlock and the same failure to gain site agreement to proceed with talks for trials in the Sulphate-Nitrate Group of the large Products Works. (These titles are pretty opaque and only to be penetrated with explanations whose length would not be justified: as at Wilton, the trials never started.) However, although in Chapter 6 we concentrated on the substantial similarities between the two sites, it was the differences that told, for the outcomes were very different. Both are large sites, complex and drawing their labour from the same region. But in their histories, the places they occupied in the local communities and their commercial futures the two sites were sharply constrasted. Some key differences:

(*a*) Billingham was set up half a century ago by managers from the elite Alkali Division and soon developed its own intellectual — i.e. engineering — mystique based in a justified pride in technical achievement. Social life centred on Norton Hall, an old house overlooking the green, in the pretty town of Norton, where many of the senior managers live, which was bought by ICI and used as a social club and guest house. Dinners were formal and the clarets excellent; accents were predominantly Public School. A rather artificial society formed around this isolated chemical factory in Durham, stable, self-perpetuating and based in a consciousness of superiority that, by the time of MUPS, had become a myth.

The hierarchy inside and outside the factory was based in work relationships. Managers were primarily technical experts, rewarded for solving technical problems. Human problems were, to put it crudely, solved by a combination of paternalism and the prevailing high unemployment.

(*b*) One important product of Billingham's technical and commercial strength was that it could offer steady employment in periods of high unemployment. Moreover, it offered better working conditions, fringe benefits and prospects than local competitive employers. Jobs with ICI were prized; long service became a commonplace; Billingham became — and still is — a 'company town', dominated by the company that provided most of the local employment. By 1965, the company had been at Billingham for nearly 40 years; many of the employees were second-generation ICI men. There were inevitably frictions, but there was a deep-rooted relationship and, fundamentally, trust.

(*c*) Everything depended on Billingham's continued success as an employer. During the period of the introduction this was at first called into question and then thrown out of the window as the site had to make drastic adjustment to changing markets and technologies, and the workforce was drastically cut. The most characteristic Billingham process — the one for which it was built and which made ICI's technical reputation — was the high pressure synthesis of ammonia, the basis of all fertilisers. The market was chronically oversupplied, prices always under pressure and the need to reduce costs paramount. By 1965 Billingham's coal-based process had given way all over the world to oil-based processes and, in addition, a low pressure technology was being developed that would replace many and expensive high pressure units with a few, gigantic units — with consequent changes to the maintenance needs. Billingham developed an oil gasification technology and made the change, first in raw materials and then in synthesis technology. Both brought huge problems: 400 men were employed in the coke ovens alone; teething troubles with the new units lasted for years.

(*d*) Billingham never suffered from the management vacuum that opened the way for the naked assertion of union power at Wilton. It had started as a single division site. Other divisions were latecomers on a scene that was well-established by the time they appeared. Dyestuffs, Plastics and HOC had works on the site but the Agricultural Division management was well in control and there was no question of the conflicts and competition that characterised the Wilton scene getting in the way of a unified policy — or not to the same extent.

Initially anyway, these insulating differences did not weigh heavily against the physical similarities touched on in Chapter 6, still less (for human factors often rose above such mundane constraints) against the political matrix in which Billingham was set. It was in the Northeast and drew its labour from a population with the same experience as Wilton. More specifically, the AEU members on the site were bound by the same district committee rulings. This meant that the AEU shop stewards and members were not allowed to take part in discussions.

None the less there were discussions. The process started in the Sulphate-Nitrate group with seminars and discussion groups that eventually gave everybody, from senior managers to the shopfloor, the opportunity to discuss and learn about the agreement. Further discussions took place with shop stewards at their request; with the AEU stewards informally. Meanwhile, the management job of making a preliminary analysis of the work was being carried out, mainly by people from the work study department, 'but all the important critical examination is a joint effort involving both management and work study. The procedure . . . is a small group which has the appropriate section manager as its chairman. The other members are the plant manager concerned, another plant manager and the work study officer. The second plant manager . . . is free from the sometimes crippling knowledge that "it has always been done like that . . .".' However, the AEU stewards did not take part in these discussions.

The joint committee visited the Northeast from London in early April 1966 and pressed the balking AEU to agree to taking part in the joint consultative mechanism: a trials working party that would oversee the process of suggesting changes to working practices at a detailed level; a joint trials committee, that would meet less frequently to oversee the working party; and a site committee to spread the information about what was taking place at the trials among unions and management. The joint meetings started in May but stopped again in July after a mass meeting of the AEU, called by the district committee at Middlesbrough. Len Edmonson later reported to the joint committee that his members in the Northeast wanted reassurances about the future status of time-served craftsmen; about separate negotiation for craft rates; and about safeguards for 'the present holder of a piece of work'.

The job of work analysis and drafting the new jobs continued but joint negotiations, without which they had no force, did not start up again until December 1966. Even though only a few senior stewards took part, progress was rapid. Manning proposals and job specifications were drawn up; preliminary assessments of some jobs were carried out by the company assessment team. There was another break in February and March when the AEU and T&GWU fell out over the union membership of craft assistants (what had been the fitters' mates): both laid claim to them. But by October 1967 this part of the process had reached a point where more substantial union approval was required. There was 'a large measure of agreement . . . on new manning and the re-organisation of jobs . . .' But the AEU shop stewards wanted the approval of all members on the site. They were submitted to mass meetings of ETU and AEU members on the site — and they were rejected, totally by the AEU and (as the senior ETU steward put it) 'negotiably' by the ETU.

This was a tremendous disappointment. The reason advanced at the time was the 'fishbowl effect'. However, this was not how the setback was formulated by the unions at the time — and indeed, it may be a rather glib, *post hoc* explanation for a much more deep-rooted source of opposition: the basic fears of the AEU about the effects on their position of accepting the *principle* of flexibility at all. Managers may have been reluctant to accept this explanation because there was little they could do about it. The AEU mass meeting passed resolutions calling for all craftsmen to be assessed at the top grade. More to the point, a shop steward later said, they needed safeguards to prevent management from taking liberties; and they wanted some work back in exchange for the work they were letting out. It was the old question of defensiveness and lack of trust: the unions had to learn that short-term defence of their work may not bring long-term benefits; the managers had yet to earn trust.

The outcome of this period may have been the same as that at Wilton, but the processes were quite different. At Wilton, the debate never got beyond the preliminary political stage. At Billingham, there was always talk; that is, rarely did disagreement reach a point where discussions ceased altogether. And the talk was substantive, about issues and problems which were mutually agreed to be of importance. Why this should be so when at Wilton, so close, it was impossible to start real discussions cannot be simple. However, an important factor must be the existence of large numbers of long-service employees, among the shop stewards as well, who felt able to trust the company that far. The senior ETU steward, Fred Creek, said: 'We may disagree but we've got to keep talking. There's no point in cutting off altogether.' This attitude was closer to that at Hillhouse than at Wilton. But the blockage remained. The MUPS trial was shelved and the WSA introduction that followed was a similarly three-legged affair, with discussions and analysis proceeding without AEU approval. One self-contained unit — the anhydrite mine (of which more in Chapter 11) — got to the line by itself only to be reminded by the district committee of the blanket ban on negotiations. There was a protest strike by the T&GWU in September 1969 against the AEU ban. As pressure mounted from other unions, the management first offered a 'deadline' formula — under which employees covered by the agreement by October 1970 would be paid as though from August — and then (more strikes were threatened) allowed unions on piecemeal. Although far from ideal, it was the only way to release the pressure of employees' expectations.

The interpretation of the Billingham experience has been challenged by managers with experience of the Northeast. 'The troubles at Wilton drew attention away from Billingham', said Jack Lofthouse. Jim Bell, personnel director at Billingham, agreed: 'It had always been expected that Billingham would be a trouble spot.' But in contrast with Wilton it appeared quite cooperative. Bell added: 'If the difficulties hadn't originated at Wilton, they would have started up at Billingham.' None the less, there were important differences for it is not disputed that Billingham ended up with more from the agreements than Wilton. We shall be

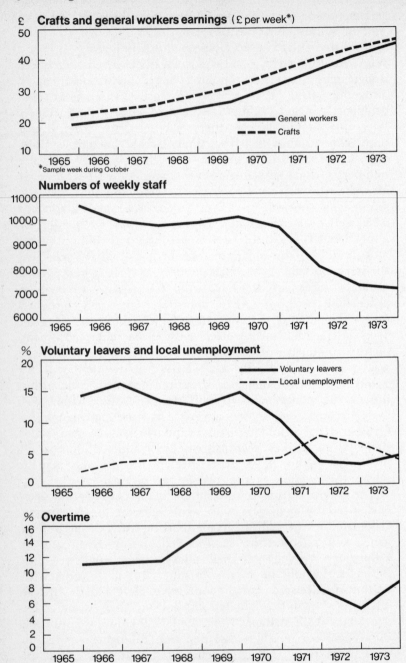

Fig.7 Billingham: indicators of change

Crafts and general workers earnings (£ per week*)

*Sample week during October

General workers
Crafts

Numbers of weekly staff

Voluntary leavers and local unemployment

Voluntary leavers
Local unemployment

Overtime

looking at the results achieved at different works. The main difference was that they ended up with a spirit of cooperation and group working which became important when Agricultural Division had to face up to its commercial crisis, in 1971-3.

By taking the stories of Wilton and Billingham to their end, I have run the narrative past its due place in the book. We must now retrace our path to mid-1968, when it had become obvious that the MUPS trials had served their purpose. The successes had shown what could be achieved; but the deadlock at Wilton and Billingham, and the political situation developing around it, made it imperative to seek another way forward.

9

The Lessons from MUPS

This brings us to an important point in the progress of the agreements, from trials to full introduction: the point when the threads of experience from MUPS were being gathered together and, for the first time, some systematic — or rather *usable* — sense was being made of it. For this reason, I shall pause in the narrative to consider what these lessons were, since the conclusions they led to set the scene for the full-scale introduction that followed.

Re-defining the problem

It is now a truism of management theory that there is a connection between a manager's assumptions about people and his style, the way he deals with them. An analogous connection is that between definitions of a problem and the solutions offered for it — which are largely determined by the way in which the problem is defined. Among the 'solutions', or help, provided by the Central Personnel Department was a series of training conferences for managers involved in the trials. And it was very much a reflection of the assumptions about the problems of introducing MUPS that these took the form of providing answers to such questions as: 'What are the objectives of MUPS?' and 'What is the thinking behind it?' Not that these are trivial questions or their answers unhelpful. The Warren House conferences for senior managers involved in the trials ran from the launching of MUPS to mid-1966 and supplied important information about an area in which most ICI managers were wholly ignorant. They covered some of the basic behavioural science theories and emphasised their relevance to MUPS; they tied MUPS into the company's commercial situation in ways that the

managers would understand. These were answers that fitted
into the framework of traditional managerial (and union)
assumptions within which MUPS was launched. They
assumed that, if a reasonable and logical answer was provided
to a problem, reasonable men would perforce accept it.
However, there could be no answers to questions that had
not been asked, nor solutions to problems that had not yet
arisen. These had to wait for the intense self-questioning that
followed the shock of the first two years' near-complete
failure.

The change in viewpoint was epitomised in two meetings
held in the first half of 1968 — which crystallised an
important set of changes in the way problems were being
defined and MUPS introduced: from an emphasis on cog-
nitive (thinking) to affective (feeling) data; from the *ad hoc*,
trial-and-error early phase of naive learning to a more
conscious and expert method. Trial-and-error was to remain
important: conditions at the sites were too different to allow
any rigid single approach, however expertly designed, to
succeed. But as experience accumulated it was inevitable that
some lessons more general than the importance merely of
being flexible would emerge. Also, the need for a firmer line
and more expert help from the centre was apparent if the
'framework' logic of MUPS was to have any meaning.

The first meeting involved 18 managers from the trial sites
directly involved in MUPS; it was an informal initiative,
expressly conceived as a forum in which the experience of
the sites was to be pooled. The managers met with members
of the CPD staff in April at the Ariel Hotel. They had all
shared the common experience of managing MUPS introductions, and this experience was the agenda of the meeting.

The conclusion provided no startling insights into the
process, nor any key to future action. A report on the
meeting commented:

'The differences and the similarities are of equal interest,
but the significance of neither can be properly understood
without relating them to the local management and
factory situation. It is this last factor which makes difficult
any attempt to analyse or assess MUPS experience. More
words and time need to be spent describing the manage-

ment's starting point in each case ... Nevertheless the common themes in the experience ... point steadily towards the same problem areas ... Experience elsewhere can indicate some possible choices and some possible hazards ... For managers beginning on MUPS therefore a presentation of trial site experience should enable some problems to be seen ahead in clearer terms, and some advance actions to be taken.'

The conclusions were, at this distance, obvious enough and even banal. No programme of action emerged. Rather, signposts were set up identifying areas of difficulty:

* The need to prepare management and include supervisors in the process. (The managers agreed that their most conspicuous failure had been in the treatment of supervisors.)
* The importance of rigorously and systematically analysing the site situation.
* The need to have, and to deserve, trust.
* The importance of growing MUPS locally. (That is, the danger of bringing in outside resources to introduce the agreement.)
* The fundamental role played by discussion groups and the value of careful preparation in setting them up.

What was important at the Ariel meeting was not, however, these conclusions but the beginning of an attempt to draw lessons from MUPS that could be generally valid for the company. The meeting was a failure in not achieving its purpose. There was no programme, no method of MUPS introduction. But an unexpected conclusion of the greatest importance did emerge from the discussion: the implicit acceptance by the managers that the *process* of introducing MUPS was at least as important as the *content* of the agreement. At one point, the report says, apropos management education: 'Every manager will learn more and change his style in some degree as he tries to apply MUPS ...' It was too soon to realise that the process of introducing the agreement might in some ways be a more powerful instrument of change than the agreement itself.

The second conference took place two months later and

was almost a mirror-image of Ariel. It was an official, corporate event and it was a 'working conference' (or, as similar events were later called, a 'workshop') of 20 managers involved, or likely to be involved, in trials. The aim of the conference was to help each of the managers to find ways of dealing with the problems he foresaw in introducing the agreement. It was run by two consultants from the USA, Ed Schein and Hollis Peters, and took the form of presentations and discussion in full session alternating with work sessions in pairs and small groups. It was to be a model (and had been consciously contrived as such) for a series of working conferences and in which several hundred key managers took part at Warren House in the next two years.

In contrast to Ariel – the first coordinated attempt by managers to *look back* into their experience and *generalise* – this was the first conference where there was a more objective attempt, *looking ahead*, to *diagnose* the problems of introduction and to seek solutions to them. No general solutions emerged (another of the lessons from Ariel) since each manager had a highly personal list of key problems and each had to seek his own solution to them. But the conference showed that there might be ways of helping a variety of people to cope with the central problems of MUPS introduction that fell short of handing out a rigid set of prescriptions.

The discussions centred on the issue: 'MUPS isn't working; what do we need to change?' Much more important, there was an awareness of the importance of 'irrational' factors in the rejection of MUPS – by management as much, although less obviously, as by the payroll. These were explored in the more introspective discussions of the workshop, and can be grouped under three headings:

(*a*) Insecurity, which in management took the form: 'What will happen to me?' (Mainly for supervisors) 'Will my job vanish if the jobs below me are enriched?' 'To manage I must have rules, but MUPS seems to promise an endless series of re-negotiations of rules; nothing is fixed any more.' 'What do my superiors really want? What will they reward?' 'Who carries the can if it (my piece of it) goes wrong?' The insecurity of the workforce was always more apparent, particularly in return for benefits that seemed, at best, unclear. Also, the 'fishbowl' effect of trials at isolated sites created uncertainty in the union members about their roles as precedent-setters.

(*b*) Power, authority and responsibility were major factors since the managers' role required them to use these. This covered basic worries about controlling and/or motivating payroll without the bonus incentive scheme. Also, 'If I give responsibility away, will it be misused? And, if it is, can I take it back again?'

The unions' worries were equivalent. Demarcations were a powerful form of control over work and employment; flexibility threatened to take this away. They knew how to make the existing system work but, 'If it changes, where will we be?' Moreover the unions had been restricting management power as a goal for more than a century. Would the new agreement put the clock back?

(*c*) Assumptions about people, which revolved around issues of trust. The management assumptions could be crudely caricatured in terms of MacGregor's Theory 'X': people do not want responsibility; they will always avoid work; and must be either bribed or driven to it; they lack self-control; work has to be simplified to fall within their limited abilities.

The unions had been formed, almost in opposition to these ancient managerial preoccupations, to meet the power of management; the history of the battle had been long and bitter and nothing that had happened encouraged a belief in what managers were suddenly saying about participation. Moreover, if they allowed the agreement through, what was to prevent management using it as a basis for forcing continuous change?

Before any progress was going to be made with the agreement, the blocks had to be identified by each individual, to be confronted (even if they could not be argued out of existence) and ways of dealing with them outlined.

If this analysis comes perilously close to being psychological in orientation, it should not come as a surprise, since the workshops were devised and run by behavioural scientists and Organisational Development (OD) consultants. However, it is more difficult to assess what part this more theoretical view of organisational change played in subsequent events. A sharply different view is provided by Bruce Neal, who played a leading part in the Warren House workshops:

'It is easy to over-emphasise the role of behavioural science. The problems were defined in those terms, but this was not by itself enough to provide a dynamic for change. For that, you needed power; it was power that Geoffrey [Gilbertson] used to push the divisions along from the centre . . . As for the Warren House workshops, my own view is that the behavioural science inputs were only minimally influential. The key decision was identifying the people we should go after [what became known as the "key climate-setters"] and then to expose them, within the framework of an agenda drawn from the problems identified in the trials, to Geoffrey and other experts. It was in those dialogues that you could see people's ideas changing . . .'

This last point is an echo of the use made by John Harvey-Jones of the Coverdale training sessions through which all the Wilton managers were put.

Job enrichment

Ideas are like politicians: often interesting for their own sakes, but important only when in power. What brings them to power? No invisible hand sorts them out, selecting the best for office. The market is inefficient and the best may be left languishing while meretricious substitutes and elderly incumbents cavort and posture in the limelight. However, at times of crisis, nations find the leaders they need. And people find the ideas they need when uncertainty becomes too threatening. The senators of ancient Rome may have picked their way across the field to where Cincinnatus (modestly, but with watchful eye) was ploughing with some of the same relief and hope that sustained ICI's managers on their way to an understanding of job enrichment – hope that the ideas were good enough for the job; relief at having found reason for hope. The role of the leader is twofold: he must lead, of course, but it is no less important that he gives his people the secure sense of being led. Ideas have a dual function as well: more or less accurate predictors of puzzling events, they also serve to colonise the unknown, domesticating it and setting it into a comforting framework of familiar rationality.

Ideas derived from the behavioural sciences — about job satisfaction, participation, motivation and management style — assumed increasing importance during the introduction of ICI's agreements. It is not belittling the intrinsic strength of these ideas to suggest that growth reflected, as much as anything else, their legitimating role. For they provided intellectually respectable reasons for a move from well-tried and familiar methods of control into less familiar territory. And when so much was changing, a firm framework of ideas was badly needed.

A concern with job satisfaction was one of the strands leading into the MUPS negotiations, but weak. The main sources of energy for the change, the issues around which a coalition of unlikely allies could form, were solidly set within the familiar framework of existing ideas: the need to reform the pay structure; the commercial crisis that could threaten the company in the future. These were issues which were generally understood, and prepared the ground for change. But the sorts of change proposed raised problems which were not easily fitted into the familiar framework and were indeed radical and threatening innovations. It was as though the package of MUPS was a Trojan horse, an object familiar enough in itself but filled with unfamiliar ideas. Once through the breach in the walls made by the trials, the ideas came swarming down.

The most radical innovation was the replacement of the old payment structure with stable salaries. An important tool available to managers for maintaining and increasing production had been removed; they would have to learn how to manage in a non-incentive situation. Flexibilities — the main overt focus of MUPS, were no threat to managers since the move represented a new freedom for managers to improve methods of work — which, presumably, they had wanted to do all along. (This is a gross simplification for it is by no means obvious that there was, what is implied, an unremitting pressure to improve the allocation of work.) However, the cooperative method by which flexibilities were to be agreed — epitomised in the MUPS negotiations themselves — cut through the tangle of assumptions surrounding the accepted role and prerogatives of managers. The agreement itself was a semi-managerial 'solution' to a problem, cooperatively arrived at perhaps but launched within the old framework of unilateral command. Lastly, the whole exercise represented a shift in the role of managers, from technical problem-solving to dealing with people.

The ideas of behavioural science knitted many of these threats and opportunities together. For they teach that people want responsibility and, given work that is more complete, will seek satisfaction in it; that the job of managers is not to drive, but to lead; that the old picture of the reluctant worker, heavily supervised in his minimally-demanding job and putting out more effort only in return for crude money incentives, is inadequate. The changes offered by MUPS fitted neatly into the prescriptions of the behavioural scientists, which in turn enriched and deepened the bald and necessarily simple prescriptions of MUPS. Above all, the manager, worrying about the loss of the incentive 'carrot', was able to set it in the context of a different style of management, where sticks and carrots were no longer necessary.

Readers not already familiar with the relevant theories are advised to refer to some of the books listed in the Bibliography. This is not the place for an exposition more detailed than an ungarnished list of the most influential groups of ideas: developed in the USA by Abe Maslow, Douglas MacGregor and Frederick Herzberg.

Maslow developed a theory of motivation, known as the 'hierarchy of needs', in which he suggested that everybody has similar needs (the brackets enclose some of the more familiar manifestations):

> Self-Actualisation (creative)
> Ego (status)
> Social (love)
> Safety (stability)
> Survival (food, shelter)

The categories are not exclusive and indeed overlap. They describe clusters of goals towards which, or to the satisfaction of which, people direct their energy. The important part of the theory — for it is obvious that different people have different goals — is the way in which the needs are felt: the individual is driven to satisfy the lowest unsatisfied need; only when it is satisfied does the next highest need in the hierarchy become operative. The implications for a manager are important: that the workers' needs are potentially more complex than the simplifications of industrial life allow (not that this — the earliest complaint against the dehumanising effects of industry — is new); more important, that the needs will change with changing economic circumstances. Turning this argument around, there are available to managers a far wider range of rewards — means for satisfying the workers' needs — than the strictly economic view allows.

Closely related to Maslow in his conclusions, Frederick Herzberg derived his 'dual factor' theory of motivation from empirical observation. He asked people what it was in their work that satisfied them and what dissatisfied them. He found that the answers formed not a continuum but two separate groups. Moreover, satisfaction was not provided by lack of the 'dissatisfiers' — which led to an absence of dissatisfaction — nor dissatisfaction by absence of 'satisfiers' — which only led to a lack of satisfaction. Herzberg called the first group 'hygiene factors' by analogy with those health factors, e.g. the excellence of the water supply, whose absence causes ill-health but which will not, in themselves, bring good health. These were such factors as money, working conditions, company administration and technical supervision — all concerned with the *context* of the work. The second group he called 'motivating factors', because they act more positively, and included such factors as achievement, recognition, responsibility and the work itself — all concerned with the *content* of the work. From this work he drew conclusions about the way in which jobs should be organised if workers were to gain satisfaction at work and not to be bored and alienated. And from it emerged the concepts of job enrichment — extending the job vertically, so that it is more complete, the worker has more responsibility and more control over the decisions affecting his work. Also related are the concepts of job enlargement — extending the job horizontally so that the worker has a wider range of tasks, avoiding some of the monotony of over-specialisation. Herzberg's theories provided a framework within which the process of analysing work and agreeing job descriptions could be carried out.

The third main group of ideas complement Herzberg's, in that workers and their jobs (enriched or otherwise) do not exist in isolation but in the context of possibilities allowed by management. Douglas MacGregor considered the ways in which managers approach their work and concluded that a manager's style is a function of the assumptions he has about other people. He developed what is probably the best-known of behavioural science theories in management, two extreme types of managers working from opposed sets of assumptions about people which he called 'Theory X' and 'Theory Y'. The 'Theory X' manager looks upon his subordinates as dim, lazy, passive, selfish and resistant to change; they don't like work and can only be induced to do a job by a combination of bribes and threats. To match these assumptions, work should be highly organised and planned, split into small, undemanding, easily-supervised fragments. The 'Theory Y' manager assumes that, given the chance, workers will enjoy their jobs; that, far from avoiding responsibility, they positively welcome it; that they are capable of bringing to their work qualities of enthusiasm, imagination and intelligence traditionally reserved for hobbies, for 'work is as natural as play'. Following these assumptions, a manager sees his job as providing maximum opportunity for the worker to make a contribution and gain satisfactions from his work; he encourages continuous growth in the workers' knowledge of the job; he provides a challenge by getting the worker to set his target and leaving him a large degree of self-supervision in attaining it. In short, the worker whose job has been enriched must have a 'Theory Y' manager if he (and his employer) is to gain full benefit.

It is easy to see how seductively relevant these theories were to the situation that ICI's managers were facing in introducing the new agreement. The whole basis of management, the focus of attention, had been one of bargaining over hygiene factors. The time had come to raise their sights to a

more complex view of people in a working situation. MUPS
provided such an opportunity, since it allowed the re-design
of jobs in forms that would correspond to the more complex
needs of workers no longer held in the vice of unsatisfied
survival needs. Moreover, the work demanded it: an organisation and supervision appropriate to the industry of half a
century before was not appropriate to the technologically
advanced, highly instrumented chemical industry of the
present day. There was a strong normative element in the
behavioural prescriptions: not only were the managers not
failing in their duty by relinquishing the old controls, they
would be positively virtuous — humane, far-sighted and
courageous.*

Two points need to be made about the normative aspects
of job enrichment: historical and social. It is tempting to
draw the conclusion from the work of the behavioural
theorists that the old ways were ineluctably bad, but this is a
misleading simplification. They were as appropriate to their
times — and, seen in the context of their times in a company
like ICI, as humane — as the work councils. But like the
works councils, they had survived beyond their time; there
was no mechanism for continuously updating them. Organisations, particularly large and successful organisations like ICI,
are protected islands (or rather continents) of stability in a
social and political environment that is constantly changing.
The changes are small, but over time they amount to the
sorts of shifts in power that only revolutionaries dare to
dream of. The change between the conditions in which the
mold of ICI management was first set — before the war — and
the mid-sixties amounted to just such a revolutionary shift,
and only a revolution was adequate to accommodate it
internally. It is quite a general point: the world changes
constantly, but our perceptions, the ways we model reality,
change discontinuously — and disruptively, often painfully.
(Read the correspondence columns of the serious news-
papers.) The second point concerns the class bias of the
theories, which embody a middle-class work ethic that is not
necessarily generalisable. It is a criticism that has been

*Cf. the success of Dr Spock's manual of permissive upbringing: mothers do not
want to deny their children; to be told that spoiling is virtuous was impossible to
resist.

levelled at the work of Herzberg in particular. Work may be as natural as play to people whose lives — their sense of achievement — are bound up with their work; it is not obviously true of people for whom work is traditionally instrumental. This is only to say that the job enrichment thesis can become reductive: there are more routes to self-actualisation than through job satisfaction; it is also possible to pursue a quite rational course of minimising work and seeking self-actualisation away from the job.

The ideas, appropriate as they were, were not easily or quickly accepted, for the reasons described at the beginning of this chapter: they threatened too much. But they were tirelessly preached throughout the company by members of CPD, who travelled to groups of managers, supervisors and shop stewards; outside consultants were brought in to provide special skills and more neutral authority; the workshops at Warren House provided more concentrated learning experience for a relatively few managers. One of the most influential arguments used was a programme of experiments on job enrichment carried out in ICI by W.J. Paul and K.B. Robertson. Prevented from looking at shopfloor jobs by union worries about 'MUPS by the backdoor', they looked at job enrichment among groups of junior staff and concluded that the theories had relevance in Britain and offered practical benefits. The study had been published (a reference is given in the Bibliography) and I shall not discuss the conclusions. What was important was its value as a statement of the new ideas in a form which ICI's rational, technical problem-solving management could not reject. It presented them in a guise which they were required, by training, to take seriously — another Trojan horse.

Balance of power

It had become apparent during the trials that there had to be, located somewhere in the company, single responsibility for driving the agreement on, coordinating and controlling its progress. And this could only be at the centre, where there were already reserve powers over personnel matters. Nominally, this had always been the case. But during the period of 'naive learning', there was little the centre could do to take a lead except adopt exhortatory postures. At that time, managers of CPD knew rather less about the problems of introducing MUPS than the works who were doing it; such ideas as they had were being proved wrong at every turn. The locus of action had therefore moved out to the works. But the situation could not be allowed to drift along without losing the main advantage of having a strong central capability – to generalise from particular experiences and coordinate – and, in spite of the official status of MUPS, it was running out of steam.

The change was marked by the arrival at the centre of Geoffrey Gilbertson. Gilbertson had been closely involved in all of the events leading to MUPS and was chosen to succeed John Rhodes in CPD. He moved down from Billingham in October 1967 and took over as 'Personnel Manager – Labour Relations' in the New Year. It was an important time for, as he says, 'By now MUPS was faltering. There was no planning, no organisation, no ability to look forward. More damaging, there was no conviction at the centre and, as a result, no drive from the centre, pushing the divisions.' He had been brought down for the job – over a number of protesting, if not altogether dead, bodies – at the insistence of Rowland Wright and at once proceeded to assert the role of the centre in managing the trials.

'There are three elements in a change programme of this sort,' he later said. 'And they must be got right. You have to be able to mobilise the *power* of the organisation. If you haven't got the active support of those in authority, you can't carry the organisation with you. Part of the power picture, you must have the *resources* to do what is necessary and they must be allocated down the line. There'd be no point in the centre issuing orders, for example, if the divisions were not prepared to put the people and training resources behind them. And lastly, there has got to be *zeal*.' Zeal was Gilbertson's particular contribution, and he was no amateur at using power.

It had become necessary to 'get the power situation right' by the assertion of central authority. And in March 1968 Rowland Wright sent letters to division chairmen spelling out the future organisation of MUPS in some detail. In it he made a number of points, all of which indicated the need for the centre to assume a more positive role:

(*a*) The need for speed and massive mobilisation of resources.
(*b*) The importance of MUPS 'as the keystone of future labour policy'. Hence 'personnel policy as a whole must be developed in harmony and therefore requires coordinated direction'.
(*c*) The need for watchfulness, given the strain MUPS would impose on the system.
(*d*) MUPS had to be a joint effort and both Millbank and the Divisions had their own roles to play. But '... the right type of guidance from the centre is both welcome and essential ... as also is the provision of a central clearing house for detailed points of policy and practice ... while allowing full rein for local initiative and opinion, in the end the Company must decide the most favourable course of action ...'

He then went on to spell out the organisation structure and responsibilities for MUPS introduction, of which the most important part was: 'The Personnel Manager (Labour) is to be recognised as the focal point of the project, with responsibility for coordinating and progressing all MUPS activities ... He is Chairman of the Company's Trade Union Joint Committee and will have resources allocated to him to provide the support necessary for Divisions to succeed in implementing the policy.'

It was a fairly bald statement of the role of CPD. But it was not — what it might have seemed — inconsistent with the divisions' own wishes. How much power should remain at the centre was always a lively subject of discussion — too lively for it to have been the subject of a massive, final policy decision. And when the matter was officially examined, as periodically it was — by the committees which are always roaming around ICI looking into different aspects of the organisation like little bands of surveyors anxiously checking the fabric of some grand, crumbling pile — the message comes back that the divisions are pretty happy with the present balance. It is not hard to see why. Irksome as it must be to have important decisions taken in remote Millbank, it is not impossible to influence CPD so that the divisions' needs are felt. And CPD serves the very comforting purpose of standing between divisional management and a direct confrontation with the unions.

An important initiative of CPD's about this time demonstrated this balance. In September 1968, three liaison officers were appointed, each with a full-time responsibility for making contact with three divisions. They were a communication link, part of the central control system but, as one of them said later, 'The divisions saw us more as protection than as intervention. We were the unofficial but authoritative guarantors that their actions fell within the lines of CPD policy. It was a job we could do without raising the official bogies that would have been risked with an approach through official communication channels.' A classic example of a 'lateral' link in an otherwise unwieldy 'vertical' organisation.

More of an innovation was the liaison officer's role as 'outside helper'. This is the familiar 'third party consultant' role of the OD consultant, the expert who is involved with none of the parts of a team and merely sits in to help group processes. He is not concerned with the content of the decisions taken, only with the need to make the process of arriving at them as efficient as possible.* It was an unfamiliar approach in a traditionally-run company, where decisions are arrived at and carried out within a hierarchy of power to which the notion of a 'helping role' is alien. But it was not a pure example of third party consultancy since the liaison officers were a part of, and much helped by, the power system of the company.

At the risk of anticipating the rest of the story, this is probably the right place in the book to see where this line of reasoning took the 'behavioural' aspects of the change programme. Gilbertson arrived at the centre and soon acquired, what he did not have in remote Billingham, the conviction that the CPD ought to adopt a much more positive role — not just in the MUPS introduction, but in the agreement that was to follow. Pressures had to be applied to keep the system moving; an environment sympathetic to change created; and the willingness to change fostered in individuals.

* Readers interested in this approach will find a lucid account of it in Ed Schein's *Process Consultancy*, in the Addison-Wesley Series on Organisation Development.

The primary requirement, of 'getting the power and authority part of the equation right', was, as we shall see, achieved during the re-negotiation of MUPS. The new agreement had the full authority and approval of the Main Board behind it; a significant number of Board members had acquired direct experience of and commitment to it; and the danger posed by the Wilton situation was confronted and a solution proposed in a new management organisation. There was now no disputing the authority with which CPD could press the divisions to introduce the agreement. However, it had early on been shown that power and authority was not enough in a change of this sort. If managers were not fundamentally committed to the changes, no matter how they were situated in the management structure there were a thousand ways they could resist. 'Early on,' said Arthur Johnston, an internal OD consultant, 'well before WSA was signed, we decided on our change strategy. We identified three areas of action for Bruce Neal and myself: bringing about attitude change in what we called "key climate-setters"; providing expert resources for works which needed them; and getting the commitment of the division boards. We succeeded in the first two but failed in the third.'

The key climate-setters were the senior managers — five or six at each works — whose attitudes and understanding of WSA would be crucial to successfully introducing it. It was for them that a series of Warren House workshops was devised. In all, more than 400 of the managers who answered to the description went through the workshops. It was, as Johnston says, 'a big intervention in the management system', training a significant part of the company's management in diagnostic skills and providing them with a different way of looking at organisation problems, and at their own relationship with them.

But it could not be left at that. With that programme had to go another of resource development, 'so that when the managers returned to their works, with their attitudes unfrozen* they would be able to call on expert resources to help them.' This meant that internal OD consultants had to

---

* A bit of OD jargon which refers to a model for change widely accepted among behavioural scientists: Unfreeze-Change-Refreeze.

be trained within the company. ICI therefore set up and ran two six-week courses of its own in 1969 and 1970. A number of other companies (Shell and Unilever among them) took part, making it a cooperative effort, and some 50 consultants were trained, to staff OD departments in the divisions. However: 'The idea was good,' said Bruce Neal, 'but we were probably too late. I doubt that the consultants were ever an effective force.' In the introduction of WSA, maybe. It would probably be fairer to say that the effectiveness of the OD capability varied widely between divisions, virtually disappearing in some but remaining strong in others.

The third strand of this change strategy was the least successful. It was an attempt to proselytise among division boards so that, when the climate-setters returned from Warren House in a fluid condition, there would be a more sympathetic 'back-home' environment for the processes of organisational change. (A recurring problem with such programmes: there is usually little difficulty in bringing about change at the individual level.) Some two-day conferences were arranged, modified versions of the workshops. But they never caught on among division directors in the way they did among the more junior 'key climate-setters'. Perhaps the directors were too involved in the company's power system to allow themselves the risk of engaging in what has been called 'interpersonal authenticity'; perhaps they were just less susceptible.

The most effective short-term intervention at the centre remained the Warren House workshops. The provision of the internal OD consultants was a longer-term investment. In effect, it moved some of the OD push out to the divisions — where there is still a carry-on in the form, for example, of team-building activity as a preliminary to commissioning a new plant or of bringing in outside consultants as a fairly routine check on the functioning of management groups, and some division boards. The total amount of 'behavioural' intervention has been considerable and the way has been prepared for the continuing use of these techniques. As Dick Beckhard, an American OD consultant, said: 'It is probably the only company of its size on this side of the Atlantic where only a handful of the main board directors *haven't* been on T-Groups.' One may argue about the precise significance of that statement; there is no arguing with the conclusion that, at the least, these once-exotic techniques have been absorbed into the familiar armoury of management tools.

Divisional divergency

The need to develop and spread expertise was one argument for pulling more power over MUPS back to CPD at Millbank. A more concrete reason for setting up a single command headquarters was the practical difficulty of designing a single policy for a group of divisions with widely divergent, and sometimes only tenuously related, interests. In its most general form, it is the basic problem of organising and managing modern industry, the split between economic and human reality; between the advantages of scale and managers' needs for autonomy and accountability; between the systems that must be set up to control large organisations and the way these systems limit the capacities of the people who must operate them.* A discussion of the reasons why companies grow big is beyond the scope of this book, but it hardly needs to be demonstrated that great size confers very mixed benefits. In a company like ICI, a conglomerate in which individual divisions are as big as some other 'giant' British companies, the mixture is more evenly balanced than many. The only unarguable advantages of size are power-political, a source of market strength *vis à vis* competitors and of bargaining strength *vis à vis* suppliers of finance, raw materials and labour. Rationalisation economies, from the sharing of such common services as research and marketing, are open to question. And production economies are real but cut off at a size well below that of the whole company; for convenience we might accept that they cut off at divisional level. (This list leaves out the personal motivation of senior managers who, according to such commentators as Robin

---

* In my book *Organisation in a Changing Environment*, I have argued that the processes which have resulted in ever-larger organisations are an inescapable part of our economic system but that the wealth their success has generated has played a leading part in changing the expectations and demands of the people that work within them. MUPS was the first step in ICI toward meeting these newly-visible needs.

Marris, pursue size as the easiest route to power and security.) Any large company is, as a result, held together by the advantages of size but is in danger of flying to pieces, driven apart by the disadvantages. We may assume for the sake of this argument that the fact of a company's holding together is proof that the advantages at that moment of time outweigh disadvantages. In such a diverse assembly, the only unifying view is that from the centre, but any decision taken for the benefit of the company as a whole will evoke a mixed response.

To be more specific, the political centres below the Main Board are divisional boards, each responsible for the affairs of a very different business, each given the job of increasing its profitability. The decision to introduce MUPS was a company decision, taken along both a time dimension (it was necessary to adjust to changing social conditions) and a technological dimension (the process technology of the chemical industry both required it and offered the right circumstances for making such a change). This is where the fact of ICI's being a conglomerate is important. Although it all fitted into the definition 'chemical industry', the circumstances of the divisions were far from homogeneous. To the extent that this effect was expected, it was anticipated by casting MUPS in the form of a framework agreement, with detailed local negotiation. But the framework could not allow flexibility enough to prevent the division boards from accepting MUPS with something less than enthusiasm. They could see a uniform increase in labour costs to be set against a flow of benefits that was anything but uniform.

The two main constraints influencing the divisions' reactions were commercial and technological: the 'right' sort of process technology provided conditions in which MUPS offered obvious advantages; profitable businesses provided room in which extra costs could be absorbed – and vice versa. Two divisions – Dyes (later Organics) and Nobel – had neither of these. Although completely different, both were fighting for profits on sales of their main products in markets which were declining or highly competitive or both. And in neither did the technology conform to the company norm.

Traditional dyes manufacture is a somewhat paradoxical combination of the most advanced organic chemistry, involving the elaborate design and tailoring of molecules for particular purposes, and a process technology that is rudimentary and of which parts are disagreeable and need minimal skills from the process workers. A well-controlled incentive bonus scheme was seen, probably accurately, as the best way of attracting the combination of low-grade skills and a willingness to work hard in poor conditions. MUPS threatened to turn all of this on its head, at one stroke increasing wages and removing the incentive element which, given the margins the division was working on, would turn a small profit on dyes sales into a thumping loss. For this reason the division chairman, Bill Mavin, resisted the new agreement to the limit of his powers, and was supported in this by his managers — nearly all of whom had come through the Dyestuffs mill and were steeped in the divisional mystery.

Nobel Division (now Nobel Explosives Ltd) operated processes in Ardeer, Scotland that had not changed in their basic features since Alfred Nobel founded it a century before. The division 'mystery' centred on issues of safety — in production and in the product (as reliability). At the same time, the danger from rare terrifying explosions led in obscure ways to a system of massive bonuses; the isolation of the site combined with lack of change in the technology to freeze many labour practices in a mould set before the First World War. An agreement like MUPS was even more threatening in this environment. At the time of writing, the successor to MUPS is only just being introduced.

The two divisions stood at one end of a distribution. Between them and the modern process divisions were strung the rest, enthusiastic or unenthusiastic to a degree that was determined by management perceptions of the relevance to their special conditions of the new ways of working, and the costs. The simple point having been made, it is a far from simple picture. Two divisions in strong commercial circumstances (Paints and Fibres) were able to introduce the agreement successfully after initial misgivings about their 'inappropriate' technologies. Petrochemicals had a good technological base and was relatively unconstrained by market conditions but was in the vice of the Wilton labour problem. Plastics had the right technology for the agreement but, selling in a very competitive market, was hard up against costs. Agricultural Division, also technologically well-placed, was in the middle of massive changes at Billingham. And all of them had special problems affecting small groups of workers, such as the large groups of girls in the packing lines of Pharmaceuticals, who did not obviously fit into the MUPS framework. This diversity within the company and the initial reactions to which it gave rise added considerably to the difficulties of introducing the agreement.

The internal strains arising from the Wilton situation were of a different sort. It was not the diversity of the divisions' needs but their dependence on Wilton: chairmen of divisions whose key raw materials came from Wilton looked at the continuing troubles there with alarm; they applied pressure through Millbank, and on their own works managers at Wilton, to get things under control — first things first. It was at this time that Wilton managers became used to being looked on as the 'bad boys' of the company, letting the side down. There had always been tension between divisions and Wilton; the site had too strong an identity and the divisions could never be quite sure that 'their' managers remained loyal to the divergent divisional interests. So the way had been prepared for an anti-Wilton movement to grow among senior management within the company. And the problems of MUPS provided the issue which it could form around.

Lastly, at a more procedural level, the position of the divisions was anomalous. They stood between Millbank's Central Personnel Department — where the agreement originated as a matter of management policy — and the works, where it was to be worked out in its details. They had formal and real power over the personnel policies of their own works, yet they had not been involved in the origins of MUPS nor, at the beginning, were they a necessary part of its consummation. It was not surprising that, as a result, strong direct links soon developed between the centre and the works which, to some extent, by-passed the divisions. Partly this was a logically inevitable reflection of the realities of the situation; partly it was the result of an attempt in Central Personnel to inject more push into the flagging project. How this was done, and how at the same time the contract between divisions and the centre was re-negotiated, is the subject of the next two chapters.

Conclusion to Part III

The period covered in this part is central in the MUPS/WSA experience. Only 8% of the workforce was covered by the agreement by September 1968; the next two years were to see far more activity — by the end of 1970 more than 90% would be covered. But the learning that had made subsequent progress possible had all taken place in those first, painfully slow-moving, three years. The company and unions — leaders of change — had entered the period within the framework of old assumptions about their respective roles; they had attempted to introduce radical changes into the very texture of employers' working lives, as though what was proposed was very little different from any other major change — in wages structure or even a large capital expenditure programme. They emerged from the period having learned about the real nature of the changes that were proposed, and having acquired a whole new range of skills for bringing them about.

It is not possible to make clear separations between the many different changes taking place either in time or within the organisation: all overlap, sprawl into each other and all are interdependent. None the less, I think we can identify three major periods:

1. The first was a period of 'naive learning'. Company and unions had hatched the agreement in secret and sprung it on the trial sites: the usual way for 'management initiatives' requiring union concurrence to emerge. Both sides, company/management and unions/members, worked within the framework of traditional assumptions about their roles. Above all, the great majority of the management — involved and observing — received the agreement and the job of introducing it as an economically rational change in labour policy.

The opposition encountered from the local unions had been expected — particularly in the militant Northeast — but not their apparently unbudgeable opposition to any form of managerial reason, based in managerial calculations about the workers' self-interest. At a similarly rational level, the union representatives argued that the company was not offering enough for the changes it asked. But beneath these rational surfaces were strong emotional reasons for rejecting the new ways of working that were not to be made explicit for some time.

Fortuitously, this delay was beneficial and served two main purposes. First, it provided an arena within which the ritual conflict between management and unions could be played out and ancient stresses relieved; it aroused interest in MUPS, generating energy for discussion — both of these providing the means for changing attitudes of both management and unions, providing a deeper understanding of the agreement and of the logic of each other's positions. Secondly, it provided an opportunity for management to prepare itself more thoroughly: by learning about the agreement; by studying the work at an appropriately detailed level; more broadly, by providing indicators of the true magnitude of the change involved.

2. The second was a period of transition. The rational-economic assumptions of the first phase were still prevalent but the management at the centre (the management steering committee) was beginning to test alternative strategies in order to find ways around the local union opposition. The effort of attitude change through discussion — about the agreement and about the nature of the work — continued; the attempt to take the Northeast by frontal assault was abandoned in favour of a policy of encirclement. But the expectation that successes in the new sites might influence the large, obdurate sites of the Northeast was based in a misunderstanding of the political nature of the opposition and of the special dynamics of large sites.

3. The third was a period of awareness and the beginnings of professionalism. It was a change that was articulated in reports and explicitly accepted. 'For the first time,' says

Arthur Johnston, 'managers saw themselves as part of the problems.' As much as anything else, this was a change in the framework of assumptions underlying the introduction, from the manager-dominated first phase to a more open and flexible — almost participative — phase.

From all of these considerations, a strategy began to emerge which had three aspects:

1. *political*: to regain and maintain the power balance with the unions at difficult sites;
2. *rational-economic*: to maintain control over the form and direction of the agreement;
3. *emotional*: to deal with the blocks to ownership of the agreement in management and payroll.

These correspond, not quite matching, with Gilbertson's three principles: Power, Resources and Zeal.

A pattern of change was beginning to emerge which repeated itself through the company over and over again, a pattern which is characteristic of the development and growth of any system of ideas. It can be seen in the chart of numbers covered by the new agreements on p. 189, which has the characteristic shape of the 'S'-curve. (The same shape describes the early part of a product cycle, or the growth of any population in a finite environment.) The first part shows no growth: the product is being developed — as it was in the first joint committee of 1965 and then in the early stages of each individual trial site.

When it comes, growth begins slowly — the period of the 'first takers', pioneers testing the unknown. In the trial sites these were the first plants which, very tentatively, demonstrated the benefits of the new ways of working; at a company level, it was the trial sites themselves that did the job.

Once it has started, the numbers covered by the agreements rise as quickly as the machinery of control and approval set up by the company and unions can allow. In the cases of Gloucester and Stowmarket, the works went on as a whole; at the company level, once the first trial sites were demonstrating how the agreement worked, a scramble developed to get on.

But the growth cannot continue at this high level. As it approaches saturation, it begins to level off, leaving only the hard cases to make their slow way through. The last part of the product cycle — or of the growth of biological systems — would show a decline as new ideas emerged to compete with the old, and usurp them. But it is too soon for this to happen yet.

The curve I have referred to describes the growth of numbers covered by the agreement, people who had gone through the system of work analysis, the agreement of job descriptions and assessment. But these followed the agreement of the people to take part in them, and that followed acceptance of the ideas. The key to the growth of MUPS working lay in the spread of the ideas behind it and this followed quite naturally the cycle I have described: of a start with a small group which convinces a larger group; the bigger the group convinced, the more powerful for action became the ideas. It follows that the crucial part of the process — in the company; at each of the trial sites; and at each of the plants within the works — was the early part of gaining a foothold and convincing the first takers. It is for this reason that so much attention has been devoted to this part of the process: in some ways, what was to follow was far less important.

The process was now well under way. Wilton or not, the benefits of the agreement had been demonstrated to the rest of the company. What was needed was final approval of the form suitable for a company-wide agreement, and then to make it part of the ideas of all employees. This is the problem the company and unions handled in the period covered by the next part.

PART IV

MUPS is Dead: Long Live WSA

In this part we continue with the account of the process of introducing organisational change. The trials had demonstrated the merits of the ideas in MUPS, but the company had run into a political opposition on the big sites that was evidently not going to be amenable to persecution. A new agreement was negotiated – the subject of Chapter 10, which runs from July 1968 to June 1970 – and introduced throughout the company in the next two years, described in Chapter 11. It may seem perverse to devote only one chapter to the introduction of WSA, a process which by any measure of physical progress – numbers of people, jobs or sites covered – covered vastly more ground than the process to which I have devoted three chapters of Part III. But the balance is realistic, for two reasons. First, in terms of learning and of change, the greatest part of the crucial work within the company was carried out during the trials (corresponding to the 'development' and 'first taker' phases of a product cycle). Secondly, as expertise in dealing with the problems of bringing about organisational change was acquired, the process became more routine, more professional. The transition from works trials to a company-wide agreement was marked also by the devolution of power over the processes of introduction from the centre to divisions; the process became more diffuse and individual events merely repeated, with local variations (some of which are briefly described), what had gone before. Part IV ends with Chapter 12 in which I discuss the problems of keeping WSA an alive and vital part of the company's affairs.

10
Re-negotiating MUPS

This chapter covers the period from July 1968 to June 1970. It starts with decisions by the company to set up a Board committee to review MUPS and make recommendations for the next stage — whether to proceed along the same path or develop a different strategy — and by the unions to request officially that MUPS be re-negotiated, and ends with the signature of the Weekly Staff Agreement. The MUPS trials were continuing in parallel with this new process and only ended with the signing of the new agreement in May 1969.

The key events are those setting the scene for the final effort of introduction. First, a commitment had to be made at Board level that the company would continue down the road on which it had set off with the MUPS trials. Secondly, the signatory unions had to be convinced that this was right for their members and the agreement re-negotiated. Both of these re-negotiations would have to provide opportunities for the views of the constituency — union members and shop stewards, works and divisional managers — to be known and play a part, generating the ownership of which the lack had been the greatest initial weakness of the MUPS trials. Lastly (and the second major lesson from the trials) managers had to be prepared for the change and trained to bring it about.

These three 'events' cover the three main strategic issues with which we concluded the previous chapter. They provided the framework within which the introduction of WSA took place.

Callard Committee

The starting point of the transition between MUPS and its

successor was Sir Peter Allen's setting-up a Board committee on 15 July with the terms of reference: 'To review the progress of the company's manpower utilisation and payment structure agreement with the unions, to examine proposals for accelerating its objectives and to make recommendations to the Board taking into account both immediate and longer term considerations.'

The committee was chaired by Jack Callard, a deputy chairman. It had five other members from the Board: Rowland Wright in his personnel role, three representatives of divisions (Mond, Fibres and HOC) with close experience of MUPS, and Stan Lyon, representing the management services function. It acquired a seventh member in Geoffrey Gilbertson, who was appointed as the secretary but swiftly got a member of his staff to perform the secretarial duties.

The results were not the foregone conclusion that the terms of reference might suggest. Although convinced of the rightness of the thinking behind MUPS, Sir Peter Allen had to consider whether the costs did not outweigh the benefits for the company. There had been outstanding successes at Gloucester and Stowmarket to demonstrate that such agreements could work. But MUPS had also brought into being the running sore of the Northeast, the potential dangers from the ICI national shop stewards committee and the costs and disruptions of having so manifestly failed to carry through company policy — an unambiguous demonstration of the power that local unions could exert in the face of a disunited management. Moreover, Sir Peter was under strong pressure from divisions like Dyestuffs which saw heavy costs and few benefits to flow from the agreement. And no one was happy about the threat posed by continuing conflict at Wilton.

In practice the committee had little option but to allow MUPS, or something like it, to continue. It would have been impossible to dismantle the trials except at heavy cost: the higher pay levels established at trial sites would have to remain; these would serve as new datum points for the unions in their demands for higher pay; the increases would have to be conceded — with delays — on the grounds of parity, and there would be no offsetting changes in work practice, none of the benefits of MUPS. (In 1965 the personnel director had presciently pointed out that trials offered a one-way option).

The questions that the committee had to consider were therefore severely practical:

* What good features were revealed by the trials that ought to be retained, and vice versa?
* What were the inducements towards and obstacles inhibiting more rapid progress? How could lessons from this sort of analysis be built into company policy?
* Were any major changes in the salary scales indicated?
* How could the unions' — particularly the AUEW's — confidence be restored, or rather obtained?
* Could anything be done about the Wilton problem?

This comprised the rational-economic core* of the committee's work. It is worth noting that it served an almost equally important teaching purpose — as did all discussions in the course of MUPS/WSA. By exposing a group of directors to intensive examination of the MUPS trials, a larger, more informed group was formed within the Board which extended the MUPS power base in the boardroom. Up to that point, probably only Peter Allen and Rowland Wright were able, or cared, to adopt a knowledgeable and committed stand in Board discussions. The committee was a device — although it was not consciously contrived as such — by which this number was trebled.

A number of papers were prepared by CPD and provided the basis for much of the committee's discussions. One of them, 'The significance of MUPS in corporate strategy', was circulated to the divisions and responses invited to questions raised under four broad headings: the strategy — was it right? Progress — what savings were expected? How could the process be speeded up? Negotiation — what was the optimal balance between central control and divisional or works autonomy? Pay — should the offer be increased? If so, by how much?

The responses to these questions were divergent, but predictably so. More important — although perhaps this should be seen in the context of the Board's own commit-

---

* It is important to bear in mind the distinction between the overt and traditional purposes of much management activity and the more covert, unrecognised 'process' problems which underlie them.

ment to MUPS — there was unanimous support for the MUPS
strategy and the view that no alternative strategy was
feasible. With the exception of HOC Division (still seeking a
solution to its problems at Wilton) the balance between
centre and periphery was felt to be 'about right'. Over the
question of pay increases, the divisions were evenly split for
and against (5:4) offering an increase in the pay scale to
make MUPS more attractive. These issues were talked
through in a series of meetings between the committee and
individual division chairmen and personnel directors. From
this job of data collection emerged the consensual view that
the MUPS trials should be built upon and extended. Whatever
the private reservations — and there were many, amounting in
some cases to a hearty lack of enthusiasm* — there was a
public willingness to go ahead. Only HOC emerged as a
special case for which special treatment would be needed.

The other main focus of analysis was pay. The MUPS
scales were close to the levels of earnings with overtime for
general workers; with shift allowances they were above actual
earnings. For tradesmen, the MUPS scales were in many
divisions below the earnings. As I shall show in the next part,
the comparison is unfair but realistic. People do not make
elaborate calculations about the effect of overtime on their
pay packets (apart from anything else, overtime was a target
for reduction under MUPS). The natural instinct is to
compare the basic rates with weekly earnings. And in this
light, the MUPS scales were arguably inadequate. More
damaging was the detailed analysis of distributions of
earnings. Thus, a shift fitter (AUEW member) on grade 7
could expect to collect a basic of £28.65p per week. But at
Wilton, 352 of the 1,159 fitters were already earning more
than £29 per week; 208 of them earning more than £35 per
week — all of them on very heavy overtime. Such pockets of
highly-paid men could not be averaged away: they were in a
position, simply by refusing to accept the agreement, to bring
progress to a halt across the site.

In fact, the estimation of earnings *with* overtime was not
as unattractive as this account suggests. And the experience
of Hillhouse, where the key to change had been the

* Hearty lack was never allowed into the files — in which are to be found only
bland assurances of loyal support.

circulation of detailed estimates of earnings, demonstrated that employees could be made sensitive to the real benefits from MUPS scales — if they could be presented in some more concrete form. An analysis of the distribution of earnings was carried out among tradesmen at Wilton and Billingham — the most sensitive of the company's locations, employing 40% of the company's tradesmen and with the highest levels of overtime. The charts below show that with existing overtime, 5% of the workforce would lose money under MUPS and 57% would gain more than £3 per week. However, with a 50% reduction in overtime (from 18.7% to 9.4%), the positions were reversed: 47% would be losing money and only 7% would gain more than £3 per week. Taking the view that an incentive of at least £2 per week above current earnings would be appropriate, there was a strong case for increasing the offer.

Assuming savings on manpower of 18% (an estimate based on divisional returns), the following Table was prepared:

	At present level of MUPS salaries	MUPS + 5%	MUPS + 7½%
Cost	£10.3m	£13.7m	£15.3m
Gross Savings	£16.9m	£16.9m	£16.9m
Net Savings	£6.6m	£3.2m	£1.6m

The reader will probably remember that the first calculations of the Rutherford Panel recommended that direct savings should be split between the company and workforce 1:2, roughly the situation in the first column. The Callard Committee now accepted that it would be both possible and desirable to hand over all direct savings, keeping the indirect savings — efficiency improvements and administrative backup plus the indefinable benefits from changes in attitudes — for the company's portion.

The main recommendation followed, that up to £5m should be added to the pay scale, equivalent to a 7½% increase in the MUPS rates. This would meet the requirement for the extra incentive which the committee felt to be necessary. Where it could not supply the £2-3 per week above existing earnings, the shortfall could be taken up with overtime, which would be progressively reduced. (One of the main outside criticisms of MUPS and WSA was precisely this: that neither got away from the use of systematic overtime as a way of making up earnings. Against this, the ICI managers could demonstrate that overtime was better controlled than, say, at Fawley.) Other recommendations were made to meet the need to overcome obstacles identified in the review:

* Division chairmen were to give guarantees of 'no redundancy directly attributable to WSA' when it was permitted by local conditions. This was to quieten the fears of unions that there would be wholesale sackings.
* Lack of management preparedness had been identified as the crucial weakness of the MUPS trials. The committee therefore placed great emphasis on the need to train managers and to develop a deep understanding of the meaning and intent of MUPS. CPD was to coordinate the exercise, providing help for the divisions where needed.
* Relations with the trade unions were to receive the closest attention at local and national levels. There should be a review of the functions and training offered to shop stewards.

The Wilton situation stood rather apart from these recommendations. Basically a problem for management, it did not have much to do with the agreement although the problem was a crucial weakness. The committee therefore recommended that the management of Wilton should be returned to a state that lay somewhere between the old Wilton Council situation and the current one. HOC Division was still to have responsibility for the site, but with more power and particularly strengthened by having a more powerful personnel department. A Wilton coordinating committee was set up, with deputy chairmen of divisions involved on the site as ex-officio members; a personnel committee, with divisional personnel directors similarly, was to oversee the troublesome labour side. John Harvey-Jones was appointed as a deputy chairman of HOC to take the responsibility for the site.

These recommendations were important at a detailed level. More important was the function of the committee in 'getting the power and authority part of the strategy right'. It placed the Board firmly behind the extension of MUPS, provided the resources for the agreement to be pushed ahead and identified the CPD as the main centre of authority in what was to follow. The next step was to put the case to the unions.

Participation in re-negotiating MUPS

The process of re-negotiating MUPS stretched from mid-September 1968, when the unions formally requested a 'detailed revision' of MUPS, to the signature of the Weekly Staff Agreement on 10 June 1969.

It fell into three well-designed phases: information gathering, negotiation and consultation. In every way, it was a different process from the one which had led to MUPS. There was now knowledge of the problems and ways of dealing with them where there had only been guesswork and the paper studies. No less important, the whole process was built around the principle, held both by management and unions, that every opportunity should be given for people to make their views known.

This process started with more than two months of information gathering on union and management sides. The unions arranged meetings of shop stewards whose views were passed up to be considered by a union drafting committee in November. On the management side, a brief went from Central Personnel to all works managers and division personnel offices and the reactions collated at the centre. It is interesting but would probably be beside the point to present the two and make comparisons. The main issue was a process one: that the people affected by re-negotiation were now to be given an opportunity to take part in it. Also the negotiating teams on the two sides were to be supplied with the sense of what their constituents wanted from the new agreement. The basic area of union/management agreement was considerable: most fundamentally, that the idea of MUPS should be developed and continued and that it should be based in job assessment. The stark MUPS 'principles' on flexibility were muffled.

In addition there were a number of new demands of which the major ones were:

Higher salaries
No enforced redundancy
100% union membership
Safeguards — or rather union power — over flexibilities

There ensued a month of drafting by CPD, carried out in close consultation with divisional personnel staff who were involved in a phrase-by-phrase analysis of the CPD draft — looking for potential sources of mischief. The new draft was presented to, and worked through with, the unions in a joint committee meeting at the end of January. Major problems were discussed, of which the knottiest was, as it had always been, inter-union flexibilities: the craft unions pressing for more control over what work was to be handed over; the management pressing for a process that was itself flexible, and to a degree controlled by management. This is worth considering briefly since it conveys some of the flavour of these negotiations.

The point of difference between the two sides boiled down to the procedure for recording changes in work. Len Edmonson, the AUEW representative, held that changes should be recorded, signed and copies lodged with shop stewards and local officials; the company maintained that there was already a record of flexibilities in the job descriptions. The difference in emphasis was significant. A job description is a static record of a state of affairs and contains no information about what the situation was beforehand. A list of transferred work focusses attention on the fact of change: it becomes potentially a list of issues for dispute. A union defending its members' work against erosion is more interested in identifying areas of change. The company, wanting change, was anxious to place the emphasis on the whole job — in which small details of change are de-emphasised and their value as possible bargaining counters weakened. (A list of proposed flexibilities could easily be used as a 'shopping-list' for bargaining: a return to a Fawley-style approach which had been already explicitly rejected.) The issue was not resolved until the end of the negotiating process when its resolution marked the AUEW's willingness to support the new agreement.

The process continued but with the company and unions

joining in a joint drafting committee for another month. The draft was provisionally approved in early March. A massive communication and consultation programme was launched on 25 March. This was a calculated risk since it offered a visible target for the active opponents to any form of accommodation with the company. But the experience with MUPS had shown how essential it was to provide the people most affected by the agreement — management as well as unions — with the chance to react to the final product. An elaborate series of meetings and discussions was held throughout the company; members of the joint committee held meetings at works all over the country; shop stewards discussed it with their constituents. As in the previous consultation exercise, the results of this massive exercise were fed back to the centre — where they showed that there was broad support for the agreement. Where there were disagreements, these tended to be at the fringe of conditions and payments details; the major recommendations were accepted. And this was, of course, what it was hoped that the calculated risk would achieve, partly by demonstrating that the new agreement was not as threatening as rumour would inevitably have made it and partly by dangling the bait of substantial (average 22%) pay increases. After the relatively minor adjustments needed to assimilate the effects of the feedback exercise, the new Weekly Staff Agreement was approved by the joint committee on 25 May, signed by the signatory unions on 10 June and ratified by individual unions within the next month.

Apart from the extensive consultation, the re-negotiation was far closer to traditional bargaining than the MUPS negotiations had been. And this was later true of the differences between WSA and MUPS introductions through the company. MUPS had been put together by the joint committee in 1965 in a process of discovery and learning: it represented a major step forward in the company's labour policies; it was a fresh response to an urgent problem. Similarly, the MUPS trials were all of them voyages of discovery, both in learning about the agreement and in learning how to make it work. But there was none of this element of discovery in the re-negotiation. And by the time WSA was being introduced, the techniques of introduction, the skills needed and the ways around expected obstacles had all been pretty well charted. There were improvements to be made, but the process was much more one of making a well-designed system work.

The agreement

The Weekly Staff Agreement differs from MUPS in a number of substantive ways; but it differs more than anything in tone. In aims and the means proposed, it was the same agreement. But it had been 'repackaged' (see Appendix IV).

The substantive changes were:

1. *Money*. The new scale ranged from £850 for Grade 1 to £1,550 for Specialist and Technical Grade, in steps of £100. This was equivalent to a 22% increase on existing pay scales and was 7½% more than the MUPS scale. It was costly to the company, adding £5m to the MUPS level wages bill, but the need for it had been accepted by the Callard Committee, although not — or only unwillingly — by the divisions on whose books the extra costs would appear. 'A high price to pay for mismanagement at Wilton' was one bitter comment. But the result was to offer a considerable financial inducement for change generally; to meet the craft union demand, 'we're not being paid enough for the changes we're being asked to make'; and to raise the offer to levels that would be attractive in the Northeast (to this extent, at least, the jibe was accurate).

2. *Union membership*. ICI accepted the principle of the closed shop: ' . . . that weekly staff employees should undertake to join an appropriate signatory union'. This was obviously an attractive feature for the unions. Both CPD and division management had for some time accepted that it might have to throw the concession into the balance pan. The company had never been anti-union, so that the change did not offend established principle. However, in practical terms, the potential for setting up closed shops was likely to lead to trouble for local managers who had expressed worries during the consultations.

3. *Redundancy*. 'That there will be no enforced redun-

dancy at any location as a direct result of this agreement . . .'
was an essential safeguard for unions. However, it was not as
straightforward as it seemed and gave rise to problems when
there were redundancies, as at Doncaster, which the company
maintained had nothing to do with WSA.

4. *Union control.* As we saw in the previous section, the
unions pressed hard to get control over the process of
introducing flexibilities. In the event this emerged in WSA as
three clauses:

(a) 'only the signatory union in possession of the work can
agree to any other trade or grade performing that work.

(b) Each signatory union reserves the right as to whether or
not to accept any particular work from any other trade
or grade.

(c) The flexibilities agreed in each workplace will be
recorded in the job descriptions, jointly signed copies of
which will be given to shop stewards and Local Officials
concerned.'

In negotiating terms, it was a necessary concession to gain the
support of the AUEW. (The words of the clauses are, in fact,
Len Edmonson's own). But such formalisation introduced
further rigidities into a process which was intended to be
flexible and responsive and it remains symptomatic of a
deep-seated suspicion of management's intentions. The
copious references to the need for agreement and discussion
between management and workers would have covered this
need, if it had really been believed that management would
not abuse the system.

The repackaging of MUPS is evident from comparison of
the two texts. The most important change was away from the
starkness of MUPS towards something more discursive and
explanatory. MUPS had started off, without preamble: '. . . to
achieve optimum utilisation of manpower, the following will
be implemented . . .' and then listed the so-called 'five
principles' of flexibility. These were in themselves a blow at
precious tradition; presented in the weighty and unlovely
language of traditional management/union agreements, the
effect was deeply threatening.

WSA took a more oblique approach, starting with a
preamble in which the aims were laid out ('. . . maximum
efficiency . . . more effective use of people . . . improve the
rewards . . . eliminating unnecessary and wasteful practices
. . .'); followed by a description of the means for achieving
them ('. . . employees have knowledge and skills . . . understand the management point of view . . . joint discussion and
agreement . . .'). Only then did WSA get down to the
nitty-gritty, starting with the company offer and then,
cushioned in careful prose, the unions' concessions in the
agreement — in MUPS it had been the other way round.

It was a carefully-worded document and presented the
necessary information in ways that were unthreatening and in
a sequence that was logical. For the purposes of extending
the agreement alone, this would have been necessary. The
re-making of MUPS served an altogether more urgent political
purpose: where MUPS had become a focus for opposition, it
had to be visibly swept away and replaced with a completely
different agreement with a different title. Only then could
unions which had nailed their colours to the mast of
unalterable opposition be expected to lend their support.

But the message of MUPS was still there, although
muffled. And the five principles were there too, in a different
order. It was to this I was referring at the beginning of the
section when suggesting that not much had changed. But
clearly a good deal *had* changed. The MUPS message was still
there but it had lost its urgency and clarity; by becoming
persuasive it had also become more permissive than prescrip-
tive. The emphasis had been adjusted, pointing to the need
for management to change as well as the workforce; but so
had the balance of power, giving the unions a crucially, and
negatively, controlling role. These were the lessons from
MUPS; less was being attempted but with a greater chance of
success. And the door was left open for the process to be
built upon: 'In the future a continuous programme of
examination and change will be required because technological and social change will continue . . .' This open-
endedness was the key to WSA's long-term success: it would
stand or fall on whether or not management was able to keep
the agreement alive and working.

Postscript: Adjustment at the interface

Although WSA was designed only to bring about changes in working conditions of payroll employees, it was not to be expected that the changes could be isolated. Both by long tradition and by conscious policy, the payroll and monthly staff, in a ratio of 2:1 of ICI's employees, were separated (or linked) by differentials in pay and conditions. To bring about massive changes in one group was to change these relationships in ways that were bound to cause trouble among staff who saw their position in the company eroded. 'The day MUPS started, even if it was a failure', said one manager in CPD, 'a development programme for staff was a foregone conclusion. MUPS was a change programme for the total system.' The loyalty and commitment of monthly staff could be — and, as we saw with the supervisors, was — taken for granted up to the point where their own position was threatened. Thereafter, they began to press for improvements. It was a problem that only concerned the junior staff at or near the interface with payroll: and taking a leading part in the introduction of the agreement; technicians in laboratories and drawing offices working side by side with and often doing the same jobs as people who, for lack of suitable paper qualifications, were defined as payroll; office workers — clerks and typists — whose pay scales overlapped those of the payroll.

There was a confused and murky region where the two groups joined. At the extremes — between managers and shop-floor workers — there was a clear separation in types of work, responsibility and prospects. In the middle, the different categories were sometimes arbitrarily assigned and had all the more importance for that reason. In Chapter 4, I quoted from a paper written as far back as 1942 which confronted this confusion and concluded that it was inequitable and should be progressively abandoned. But it was built too deeply into the structure of the company to be easily legislated away. Moreover, it had real value in personnel management: staff status and associated fringe benefits were a form of non-financial reward and 'staff attitudes' (which MUPS and WSA were in part designed to foster more widely) had real meaning in terms of company loyalties and commitment. If these advantages were not to be lost, it was important to keep in touch with the way in which MUPS was changing the relative positions of monthly and payroll ('Weekly' after WSA) staff.

In November 1967, Donald Mumford — staff manager in CPD — had set up a panel of senior managers to look at this problem. The panel reported in March 1968 and recommended, in effect, a holding policy. They found some anxieties among junior monthly staff. They found numbers of cases where the MUPS increases had taken payroll rates past monthly staff rates for equivalent jobs. They suggested some minor increases — at a cost to the company of £1.5m a year — to restore staff/payroll differentials, some changes in the structure to eliminate particular inequities and a programme of improving staff effectiveness.

At this time, however, it was becoming clear that MUPS was going to enter a period of re-negotiation. The Wilton crisis was nearing its climax and the future of MUPS was uncertain. The company decided, therefore, to wait and see what would transpire. The recommendations of the Callard Committee, which included a 7½% increase over MUPS rates, demonstrated that MUPS still lived and revived the issue. The panel was re-convened to examine the new circumstances and a committee subsequently set up under Agricultural Division chairman, Ray Pennock, to make recommendations to the Board.

The Pennock Committee concluded that action was needed. The new rates would affect differentials drastically:

(*a*) Under WSA and other negotiated settlements, increases of 30-40% would be awarded some weekly staff while supervisors would receive increases of 6-15%. As a result, a typical process supervisor's differential would drop from 33% to 3% and a maintenance supervisor's from 39% to 6½%. Yet '. . . a differential of at least 20% is necessary to encourage and reward . . . the added responsibilities of supervision . . .'

(*b*) Some staff were working side-by-side with weekly staff, had the same origins or were involved in the introduction of MUPS and would be left behind by the new rates. Thus, 'a detail draughtsman with HOC (drawn from an intake of craft apprentices) will earn £1,285 at the age of 23 against the fitter's likely £1,450 at 21. A laboratory assistant . . . will earn £1,030 compared with £1,250 he would earn were he weekly paid and doing the same job . . .' At first look the differences arose mainly from different methods of assessment. Staff were assessed on ICI's Haslam scale; if junior technical staff were assessed by the MUPS method, the committee reported, they would be paid an average of 12% more. A later report — the Roden Report — concluded that the two systems were much more in line: it was not the method of assessment but the WSA rates that caused the trouble.

(*c*) Other junior staff would also suffer in comparison with WSA rates. The panel had earlier reported (on the basis of the MUPS scale) that '12.5% of our male staff clerks are on a maximum which is only £15 higher than the MUPS grade allocated to the most routine clerical work . . .' and 'many women staff, with maxima of £795 and £875, compare with some women payroll, carrying out very routine production work, on a maximum of £945.' Moreover, it would be hard to increase the scales of supervisory and junior technical workers without adjusting other junior staff rates.

In addition, the committee reported that the shift in differentials would affect staff attitudes. Managers were worried about the effect on morale of the company's apparently taking the staff so much for granted. Staff discontent was reported from MUPS sites — but there were hopeful signs that staff were anxious for the same sorts of opportunities to increase their earnings as MUPS had provided payroll. (That is, '. . . there is no evidence that the staff want something for nothing . . .') Lastly, if the company was not prepared to look after the interests of junior staff, there were staff unions only too prepared to do so instead.

The conclusion was that pay rates would have to be increased. This could either be done conventionally or by the route offered in MUPS, an increase '. . . conditional upon and which follows a planned company-wide exercise to obtain exceptional and demonstrable gains in organisational effectiveness . . .'

The trials had demonstrated the opportunity MUPS provided '. ... to make fundamental changes in working arrangements and the exceptional results that can be obtained when all the employees in a given unit are involved in the effort to make that unit more effective'. And the committee recommended a Staff Development Programme (SDP), modelled on the techniques developed in MUPS and extended on a company-wide basis in WSA, should be designed to garner similar benefits from a substantial increase in pay. Apart from anything else, the then Prices and Incomes Act made it necessary for the company to get a clear *quid pro quo* for any pay increases.

A more detailed account of the SDP programme is unfortunately outside the scope of this story although the changes are clearly part of the same picture. There seem to be two generally-accepted conclusions about the exercise: that it was a success and that the success was achieved at a low level of energy. SDP was introduced within nine months of its having been launched – a remarkable, but not unexpected, contrast with the difficulties of introducing MUPS. Everything in the package of 'staff attitudes' conduced to an easy ride. By analogy with Newton's Second Law of Motion we might predict that the amount of change achieved is proportional to the effort required to achieve it. A crude simplification – leaving out of account the question of where the change is achieved* – but probably valid in this context.

Many other cases were reported, mostly at this sort of level. The exercise broke down – or rather stumbled – when it came to looking at more routine office work. The problem here was the difficulty of measuring effective working. Apart from general indicators – such as numbers of staff required for a particular function – it was all but impossible to arrive at any measure of an office worker's performance. As a result, the sorts of progress achieved seem to have been variable and the efforts to achieve it have been quietly dropped.

* That is, in attitude or in the organisation. A great deal of the effort of MUPS went into changing attitudes. But an organisation which is already prepared for change may need no more than a small nudge in the right direction, a slight shift in the environment, to set it on the road to considerable organisational change.

We should note, in ending this section, that the question of comparability at the interface between monthly and weekly staff is still very much alive. How necessary it is and how much it is a product of the British obsession with class distinction is something for outsiders to guess. However, the motivation has not been strong enough to suppress a proletarian wish for membership of unions. A study carried out in 1973/4 at the behest of the now-defunct Industrial Relations Court found a quite lively interest among some groups for union representation. This was a marked shift from the attitudes reported by the Tavistock Institute in a similar report in 1971 — when unionisation had been decisively rejected. It is not hard to provide reasons for the shift. Most particularly, the intervening period saw the sharpest cuts in numbers. Supervisors had seen their numbers drop by twice as much, proportionately, as the weekly staff in the period 1965-73. Such an experience could well have instilled a widespread desire for the sort of security that unions exist to provide for their members. But the relevance to WSA and SDP is obscure.

11

Introducing WSA

The signature of WSA was the signal for a rush to get the agreement accepted across the full range of ICI's works. The programme was given a high priority by the Main Board; division boards, whatever their private reservations (and some had many) put their considerable weight behind it and a degree of competition to see which would be first began to develop. A target was set, of 40,000 to be working under WSA conditions by the end of 1970. It was up to the management of the works — with supporting help and guidance from CPD and the divisional personnel offices — to achieve this. The process of introducing WSA, covering 50,000 people in 2½ years (80% of them in the first year and a half) was quite a different one from that of the MUPS trials, in which 5,000 people had been covered in the 3¾ years to WSA's signature, and for three main reasons:

1. The two phases had different objectives. The trials had been tentative, a learning experience which had provided the opportunity to discover the problems of making organisation change, to develop the techniques for handling them and at the same time to familiarise all employees of the company with some radically new ideas. In the introduction of WSA across the company it was possible to put these lessons and techniques into effect and to build on the foundation of understanding — or just of familiarity with the ideas.

2. The dynamics of the two processes were different. In a learning situation, much of the official company/union interaction could take the form of uncommitted problem-solving discussion, while introducing an official company-wide agreement (as had been the process of agreeing it) had more of the features of traditional bargaining.

3. The scale of the two processes required different forms of control. The introduction of WSA across the company dwarfed the capacity of the CPD to control it in the detailed way the trials had been controlled. The role of the centre, therefore, changed and detailed control of the process was devolved to the division personnel offices.

At the end of September 1969, 11,700 men at 13 works were working under WSA conditions and 3,500 at another 6 works were at or near the stage of job assessment. For the most part, these represented the final working-through of the last MUPS trial sites. (A dozen or so works had volunteered as trial sites up to the point in September 1968 when re-negotiation got under way, and the books were closed.) Thereafter, numbers built up rapidly, as will be seen from the chart which shows the progress of the company through the WSA process. By the end of March 1970, 14,600 employees in 18 works were covered and a further 22 works had reached the job assessment stage. This period marked the peak of discussion and analysis activity in the company: between September and March, 21 works had made their way through to the assessment stage. By end-May 19,200 employees at 20 works were on the agreement and another 29 works were nearly there; at end-September 24,900 employees were covered in 41 works and another 18 works were near the end. By the end of the year, 49,000 employees — just over 90% of the total payroll — were covered, handsomely meeting the target. As we might expect, the rate of increase now levelled off. The more resistant works were left and these were to take far more effort. In November 1971, there were still 5,600 employees not covered by WSA, of which the greater part was at two works — 3,600 at the explosives works at Ardeer and 1,200 AEF members at Wilton.

It was, for the most part, a story of hard work and success; the lessons learned during the trials were used by a management that now understood what was intended in WSA and had been trained in how to achieve it. However, there was wide variation in the results achieved: a number of the introductions were highly successful; most were competent; a few were no more than perfunctory.* Naturally enough, the successes achieved in individual works attract most attention. One example was the extremely difficult job of introducing WSA to the complex Castner-Kellner works in Cheshire — one of the biggest works in the company with perhaps the most mixed technology. But I shall argue later in the book that some of the most important changes were much lower-key changes in structure, organisation, bargaining relationships with unions and the beginnings of new methods of problem-solving.

The chart of progress (Fig. 8) on to the agreement gives a vivid picture of the activity within the company — and also of its diversity. No narrative 'told from the centre' can adequately describe this process.

Action at the periphery

It was necessary to collect power at the centre in order to shift the massive bulk of ICI. But the work of shifting, the action, took place at the many sites strung round the periphery of the organisation: not just in divisions and works, but in the hundreds of plants and, within them, the thousands of joint discussion groups where job descriptions were worked out and agreed. Short of cataloguing the events in exhaustive (and exhausting) detail it is impossible to convey the immensity and diversity of such an effort. We can look, and shall be looking, at some 'results' — aggregated statistics which conceal under their bland surfaces more than they reveal. I have described, and shall some more, something of the strategies; and then the attacks and skirmishes; the pacts, treaties and other successes. But even these can tell us little of the quickening that went with the discovery of common interests between ancient foes; the grand cooperative efforts; the individual acts of courage. And of this I have myself only been able to discover a small part in my travels around the company, some time after the events — tales from

---

* The story is told of one works manager — of the old school — who had watched the 'behavioural' antics of the trials with unconcealed contempt. He knew how to manage. 'Just tell me when you want it in', he grunted, 'and I'll give it to you in two weeks.' He did — but how much organisation change resulted is another matter.

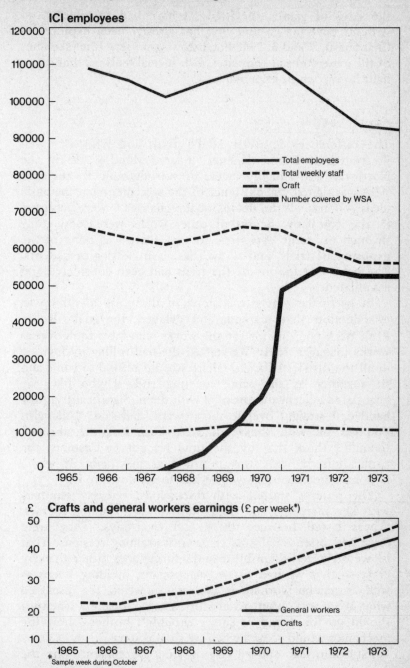

Fig.8 ICI employees and earnings

ICI employees

Total employees
Total weekly staff
Craft
Number covered by WSA

Crafts and general workers earnings (£ per week*)

General workers
Crafts

*Sample week during October

the days of giants. Inevitably, I have had to select. And without covering ground that has already been explored in Chapters 6, 7 and 8, I include below some very brief sketches of the experience at four sites with special features that cast a light on the whole experience.

1. *Castner-Kellner*

The differences between MUPS trials and WSA was well illustrated at Castner-Kellner, a large Mond works in the Northwest and a highly successful introduction. By the time WSA was signed, the existence of the agreement and the basic ideas — if not all the details of the changes — were accepted in the company. Scores of other works were soon going through the same processes, so that there was none of the exposure of trials, and no worries about setting precedents. The hard-won lessons of the trials had been considered and assimilated.

In particular, there was none of the political run-up to introduction that marked, and delayed, the trials. Robin Paul, WSA coordinator for the works who later took over as works manager, said: 'We started the ball rolling by inviting in all the district officials. There was no refusal to come and sit together at the same meeting and, if you like, we negotiated a licence to proceed with them. Significantly, they handed it straight over to the stewards and said: "All right, you get on with them and we'll keep in touch through them." I think that by the time we got to Castners, the application of WSA was regarded as inevitable. It was a national agreement and we just had to get down to it.'

The process started with discussions: one-day seminars with key managers and then shop steward training courses. 'These lasted between three and five days. They were organised intentionally as cross-craft training sessions. That is, we organised them by manufacturing area rather than by craft so that we had fitters, electricians, building trades as well as general workers at the same meeting. We discussed what WSA was about, what work sharing meant — when we should go for it and when we shouldn't bother — how the mechanics would go and when we should start.'

Paul himself started by getting agreement on the

mechanics of introduction. 'The mechanics of application required the understanding and cooperation of the stewards at every stage: if they wouldn't cooperate in the mechanics, we'd never get through to the principles.' So he prepared a crude arrow diagram, 'a sort of critical path programme without strict timings which I could discuss with the shop stewards — there were more than sixty of them — to see if they accepted the logic. This included the training requirements, the gathering of information, where and how the information was studied. Very important, it had several break-points where approval from both sides was required before we could move to the next stage. Shop stewards who were worried about moving into an uncertain area and losing their control at least knew that we had to pass through another decision node before getting jobs written up or having them assessed, or whatever it might have been. This gave them a lot of confidence that they could retain their grasp of the situation. I think that getting acceptance of that arrow diagram was the first stage to opening up discussions in different areas.'

Having gained acceptance of the approach and the sequence of activities, they got down to the business of analysing the work, which at Castner started by cataloguing all the work in a reference period. 'The problem was to eliminate unnecessary work. Under the old bonus system there was a tremendous amount of automatic work to build up units and justify bonuses. All this rubbish was swept out under WSA. We got at it by taking three-month reference periods, asking if it was really needed in making, for example, chlorine . . . A lot of assistance was given by estimators and work study officers and at the end of the period the work would be summarised and organised systematically. This allowed the working study group — which consisted of the operators themselves, the shop steward, foreman and management — to go through it and say what still needs to stay in and what could be done better . . .' This was unusual because most of the works started their analysis with management teams. Paul commented, 'I was particularly worried about the risk of any phoney involvement of the troops, about having discussions to make them comply with plans already worked out by methods study by management. The plan in the bottom left-hand drawer was often referred to and I used to open the drawer to show there wasn't a plan in it.'

Also, the fragmented, 'bottom up' approach was to some degree enforced by the nature of the site. Castner-Kellner is a factory with a long history, the original site for chlorine manufacture on Merseyside in 1895. It has been re-built three or four times in that period so that it has some of the most modern plant in the world next door to some that has survived for thirty years and more. 'One is a plant we call Aladdin's Cave, where hydrogen chloride is made by burning hydrogen and chlorine together in big glass vessels. It really looks like something from the industrial revolution . . . The point is that you get quite different groups of employees working in the old and the new so that you can't get a strong site-wide weekly staff push on anything but you do get a very strong local identity on a given plant. This was an advantage for us since we'd meet with opposition on a point of principle in one plant but had the ability to continue with discussions with groups that were interested and wanted to push ahead.' In all, there were some 20 different applications.

The cooperation of the unions was important. Unusually again, compared with other works, the AUEW was not a source of opposition. 'The district committee never tried to hold up the whole site, although they were obviously difficult about specific issues. So we could apply WSA package by package as each group professed themselves ready. The first group, the cell-room, went on in March 1970 and in October 1971 we were still negotiating with the carbide plant . . .' On a number of plants it was the general workers holding impatient craftsmen back. One case was carbide. As at Hillhouse, the carbide plant presented special problems because of the conditions — heavy and dirty work which attracted a high Abnormal Conditions Bonus. 'There was a ceiling on conditions payments under WSA which hardly covered what the men were already getting. I must pay a tribute to Bill Bradley, the regional officer of the G&MWU, who saw that not having carbide on with the rest of the works was bound to be a source of friction — both for him and the company. We persuaded the general workers to accept a lump sum buy-out of some of the more peculiar features of their bonus system. At the same time the jobs were considerably modified and improved under WSA. It was all pretty back-breaking work with enormous multiple layers of supervision. Bringing WSA in to such a place looked pretty difficult but the men responded well to the chance to get away from it all so that a lot of the improvement came through the enrichment of their jobs and re-structuring.'

The sequence of work moved outwards from the initial analysis of work in plants during the reference periods. 'It moved on to discussions with neighbouring groups on flexibilities, relationships, the throwing up of any proposals for eliminating work by capital expenditure.' (There was quite a lot of consequential capital investment.) 'From these we moved to the drafting of job descriptions and getting approval of the descriptions from the whole group involved. Then we moved forward to assessment, re-cycling back to the discussion table if the results of the assessment weren't satisfactory. And finally ratification of the application. In all of this build-up of the job, the involvement of weekly staff was genuine. Obviously, management had to have its own view — they had to be ahead of the game to know when to be able to close the discussion and say "Yes, we can go to assessment now . . ." or whether the improvements were inadequate and were not going to make a self-financing application. For we did try to have each of the 20 applications self-financing in its own right . . .'

For the most part, the groups went on as wholes. 'But this became difficult towards the end because we couldn't hold the craftsmen back. This was bound to happen in a works of Castner's size. Obviously the first group to go would be a process group, with the craftsmen hanging on as hard as they can. But once some craftsmen were on, all the craftsmen wanted to be on — but we had hardly started discussions with some of the groups . . .'

The Castner-Kellner introduction of WSA is generally accepted to be among the most successful in the company. Taxed with this, Paul said: 'If this is true I think that the particular merits are that it was fair and it was systematic. It was considered a good application by the shop stewards. They had worked hard at it and although there had been a lot of difficult negotiations, they were up against a management that was determined to make improvements in the factory and determined to give everybody a chance to better themselves ... The main achievement has been in the change of relationships with shop stewards and weekly staff in general ... The main social advantages ... or management relationship advantages ... were twofold. First, it was the most splendid training exercise for our operators that had ever been devised. A lot of them didn't know precisely what the important parts of their jobs were. WSA, by going through it systematically, getting them to learn the job they were supposed to be doing and getting it clearly laid out, for the very first time gave many of them a clear picture of what they were being paid for! The competence of the factory in emergency situations — which is where you notice how well a team is working — was noticeably greater after WSA than it was before. Secondly, the huge benefit on the management side was of forcing a complete change in the relationship with work people. They were no longer standing back passing out requests — tonnages and outputs — and expecting them to be carried out; they had a dialogue and a day-to-day relationship with their weekly staff in which the comments on the job and problems were flowing up just as naturally as down ... so that the habit of questioning whether something was necessary, or whether the right instruction had been given, was established in the factory. Out of this we led into the regular communications meetings where every operator has the opportunity to discuss his work with management and supervision in regular meetings ... I don't want to give you the impression that it is all very cosy and clubby. It is still very gritty. But the issues are properly and reasonably discussed; they are opened up and dealt with, on the whole, much earlier; and it is now natural for the weekly staff to be involved in the forward thinking of their areas ...'

2. *Nylon VIII: The Green Field Far Away*

The only works in ICI which was able to introduce WSA without the distraction of dealing with existing practices was the Nylon Works at Ardeer in Ayrshire. When ICI's Board decided in 1964 that a new nylon salt plant was needed, it could have been built at any of a dozen sites in Europe. Nylon salt — the production stage before making the poly-

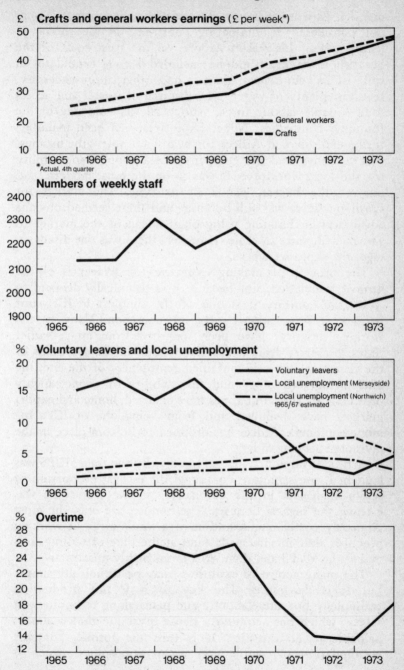

Fig.9 Castner-Kellner: indicators of change

Crafts and general workers earnings (£ per week*)

£

*Actual, 4th quarter

Legend:
— General workers
--- Crafts

Numbers of weekly staff

Voluntary leavers and local unemployment

%

Legend:
— Voluntary leavers
--- Local unemployment (Merseyside)
—·— Local unemployment (Northwich)
1965/67 estimated

Overtime

%

mer — is expensive; transport costs although substantial were not considered a dominating constraint in the choice of location. For this reason Ardeer, on the West coast of the Scottish lowlands, could be included among candidates in spite of its remoteness, since it had other, more necessary, features: plenty of water, easy disposal of wastes and access to a suitable labour force. Above all, ICI and one of the founding companies, Nobel Explosives, had been manufacturing explosives at Ardeer for nearly a century; the business was declining; and the company felt a strong responsibility for the local workforce. It was to be the most modern, and one of the largest, plants of its type. The market for synthetic fibres was still booming and there seemed obvious advantages in building a big plant ahead of the market to garner economies of scale. However, there was one disadvantage: the explosive works.

The process of making explosives at Ardeer is of the utmost fascination, not because it is technically demanding — on the contrary it is one of the simplest in ICI — but because it is a unique social phenomenon. Many of the working practices have been inherited from much earlier times, preserved from decay like a body in the dry sands of the desert by the self-contained remoteness of the site, the unchanging technology and the stability of a once highly profitable market. But times have changed, home and export markets have dwindled and from being one of ICI's big money spinners, Ardeer has dropped to bottom place in the divisional pecking order.

Attitudes do not change so rapidly. By the time MUPS was launched, the structure contained the highest proportion of senior managers in the company and the workforce was earning the highest bonuses. The bonuses are only the most obviously costly manifestation of a whole array of working practices that in sum made (and at the time of writing, still make) the MUPS and then WSA terms highly unattractive.

The manufacture of explosives may be technically simple but it is dangerous. The key to it is not production technology but the elaborate and painstaking technology of safety, which has acquired a dense mystique that is almost palpable to an outsider. It is this, the formal, complex accumulation of simple acts in an atmosphere which is fraught with the potential for terrifying accidents,* that makes Ardeer unique — and has perhaps helped to embalm past working practices so effectively.

I have dwelt on this at some length because it formed the environment in which the new plant was to be built. And ICI's managers were keenly aware of the potential dangers. As a result, the first condition for building a new factory was that the working practices of Ardeer should not be used as a model. The point was made to the Scottish Trades Union Council (STUC) and was, the need for the extra jobs being accepted as paramount, accepted. But the STUC had some difficulty in persuading the local unions to accept this, particularly (quite the opposite to the normal pattern in ICI's experience) the T&GWU, whose members comprised 90% of Ardeer's workforce and benefited more than anyone else from Ardeer's labour practices. At about the same time, in the last half of 1965, the signature of MUPS seemed to offer the opportunity for introducing new practices.

The interest in MUPS was not just negative: a device for excluding bad practices from Ardeer. Building a new and very modern plant threw up the issue of ideal manning in an acute form. An internal report on the Nylon VIII exercise, says:

> 'The principal objection [to conventional patterns of management] was the existence, side by side, of technically qualified managers and unqualified foremen and assistant foremen. Modern plants like Nylon VIII needed technically knowledgeable management at every level, dealing directly with small groups of highly trained operators.'

There was a more general worry about the effect on operating modern plants of the traditional hostility between unions and management '. . . a total anachronism in a capital intensive industry of this sort in which the potential dividends of collaboration were great'. And there was the conviction — strongly held by Sandy Morrison, who was to become the works manager — that the present payment

---

* Explosives manufacture is in fact less dangerous than a number of other industries — for example, trawling and mining. But, as one manager said, 'The difference is probably that we are making something that is *meant* to explode.'

scheme was not just inefficient but positively harmful. A contract that laid down a fixed amount of work, carefully measured, for a sum of money was too rigid for the sort of working appropriate to large process plants: '. . . incompatible with the idea of a workforce sharing responsibility as members of a unified team.'

These ideas coalesced in two important decisions about manning which could only have been taken for a new plant:

1. They would not recruit for foremen or assistant foremen. The most junior manager was to be the technically-qualified shift manager (formerly called shift superintendent). The aim was to improve the quality of management and remove some of the ambiguities of the existing structure.

2. At the same time, this change would require greater personal responsibility from the payroll. This coincided with the second decision, to recruit a higher calibre of worker — the need for which had been learned at other large, sophisticated units.

A number of other decisions were taken at this time: to keep the number of unions represented on the site down to three — T&GWU, ETU and AUEW — in order to simplify the negotiation; to abolish clocking-in; to pay the workers by crediting their bank accounts every two weeks. The last two decisions were less practical than symbolic of the desire of management to improve the status of employees.

The mechanics of introduction need not concern us here, except for three aspects: recruitment, training and the design of jobs. The works advertised widely, well outside the catchment area for Ardeer. Indeed, it was policy not to take anyone from ICI's explosives plant within six months of their having left it. The official reason was to avoid drawing off the best of Ardeer's workers. Recruiting started at the end of 1968. Over the following year 5,000 men applied for jobs and 500 were taken on. This gave the management plenty of scope for selecting men who (as the advertisements had stressed) were not just intelligent but were also looking for opportunities to work independently and take responsibility. We shall see that this policy produced its own, not altogether unwelcome, problems when it came to designing the jobs and, later, running the plant.

Training was given a high priority by Sandy Morrison as the essential preparation for running the plants at the highest pitch. First, the managers went on, and then ran, courses in 'MUPS appreciation'; outsiders (from the nearby University of Strathclyde) gave courses on group dynamics to more senior managers — courses aiming at some of the same sort of skills training as the 'Coverdale' or 'Blake Grid' courses used by other works. All new recruits were, and still are, put through a course designed around the question (to which people were encouraged to provide their own answers): What makes a good job? The training for the specific jobs that followed was extremely thorough. 'It has to be' said Morrison. 'There is no point in getting in highly intelligent men and then putting them in the hands of supervisors who tell them what to do, down to the smallest detail. But if they are going to work without supervision, they must know the job really well.'

Lastly, the *design* of jobs became a more taxing and crucial business than had been expected. 'At the beginning,' said Morrison, 'we placed considerable emphasis on the negative aspects of MUPS — the elimination of demarcation and reducing the size of the workforce. The concept of job enrichment had not been discussed. And the first job descriptions tended to reflect this. But we soon learned that discussions over demarcation would quickly degenerate into acrimonious negotiating sessions. And also that there were more positive benefits. In time, jobs became progressively enriched, usually through the efforts of the worker himself.'

The main result for the works, as elsewhere in the company, was the saving in manpower on one side and the higher pay and more complete jobs on the other. When Nylon VIII had started up, the WSA scale was considerably higher than those offered by comparable employers — other chemical companies in the region. But the rapid wage inflation has reduced this differential. However, the WSA scales still represent a premium over other employers. (Direct comparisons with the explosives factory are not meaningful because of the special features I have already described.)

For ICI the overt benefits have appeared in numbers. The

numbers of payroll to be employed was predicted in 1965, when the scheme was first sanctioned, at 1,164. This was reduced when assumptions changed to allow the use of contractors for certain types of sporadic maintenance to 1,063. In the event, the numbers employed by October 1972 had come down further to 878 — a reduction of 18%.

Savings like this are significant. But, Morrison says, 'the real savings are to be found in the quality of work'. And he quoted the conclusions of a report from the division safety officer:

'In the absence of lower levels of supervision (foremen and A/Fs) tradesmen are directly responsible to the Junior Engineers. As a consequence much more responsibility than is usual on the works of Petrochemicals Division is placed on the individual tradesman. The responsibility appears to be accepted with enthusiasm by the tradesmen and has led to a much greater pride in their work than is seen elsewhere: it is, in the opinion of the author, the reason for the very high standard of electrical and instrument maintenance on the works.'

Comparison with Wilton
I have briefly indicated how different these ways of working are from the explosives factory next door, drawing from the same labour pool. But the technologies are so totally dissimilar that we would expect such differences for this reason alone. A more interesting question might be: How does Nylon VIII — manning methods introduced, free of the constraints imposed by existing activities, on a greenfield site — compare with a similar plant elsewhere? Such a plant exists, the almost identical (but larger) Nylon VII Works on the Wilton site. And the main differences, as one might have expected, derive from the initial freedom to alter the basic decision-making structure. The differences in manning ratios, if they exist, are obscured by other factors. Thus, in changing a catalyst cartridge, the process operators are not involved at Wilton as they are at Ardeer. The reason is not demarcation (although these *are* more apparent at Wilton) but the fact that, on a larger plant, there is other work for process operators to do whereas at Ardeer there is only the one unit,

which shuts down during a change. Plant-by-plant, the numbers are virtually the same; works-by-works comparisons are not meaningful because Ardeer generates its own electricity and employs contractors for maintenance and Wilton does neither of these things.

Once more, we are left with the rather unsatisfactory — but highly important — qualitative measure of differences. E.A. Turrill — who has worked at both plants — says: 'You won't find any important differences in manning. The real difference is in speed of reaction and simple efficiency.' The main conclusion from a comparison appears to be that the advantages for Ardeer arose from the fresh start it was able to make. Within the framework provided by MUPS and WSA, much else became possible: there were no limits to the enrichment of jobs imposed by existing practice.

3. *The anhydrite mine*

A curious episode bridged the gap between MUPS and WSA at Billingham: a spontaneous surge of enthusiasm for MUPS which had the workers in the anhydrite mine prepared for the agreement two years before they were allowed it. The movement started in 1967, as the ideas from the MUPS trials began to percolate through the site. The first step was taken by shop stewards, asking the mine management if they could become a trial site. It was not possible then — nor later, even when trials became more widespread, because of the deadlock in the existing Billingham trial. However, it was agreed that the mine should prepare itself by unofficially going through the MUPS hoops — much as Gloucester and Stowmarket had — and by cutting back on the workforce by not replacing 'natural wastage', people who left.

The entirely voluntary programme was so successful that, when the stewards again approached the site management for permission to become a trial site, in October the next year (1968), they could report a 14% reduction in numbers, from 416 to 358. (Staff, from 35 to 26; payroll, from 381 to 332.) Moreover, 16 of the 28 job descriptions had been assessed, covering 78% of the workforce. By July 1969 they had been ready for some months, but had had to wait for the new agreement, and were straining to start with WSA. But in

August the local District Committee of the AEF, which had a blanket ban on WSA negotiations, refused to allow the mine to go on to the agreement. It was not until October 1970, when all the surrounding problems had finally been settled, that the mine was allowed to do what it had been prepared for a year and a half before. Why the mine should have provided conditions in which this spontaneous movement arose has a lot to do with the nature of mining; but it also sheds a light on the nature of site dynamics and the behaviour of individuals alone and in group situations. For a start, 'mining is a rum business'. Studies into the patterns of work underground have stressed the high degree of inter-dependence and team work shown by men in these uncertain and often dangerous conditions. Or, as a Billingham worker put it to me, 'I hadn't heard of flexibility until I came to Billingham. I worked in the Cleveland ironstone mines before they were closed down, and flexibility was the natural way of working. If a bloke needed help, you gave it to him; if a wagon came off the rails, everyone around set to to put it straight again. But here ... it was a question of waiting until the right bloke happened past — and God help you if you did someone else's job, even though you could do it perfectly well *and* not doing it meant hanging around and plant downtime.'

But the mine was a rum place, and separate from all that. The men were a little community underground, completely shut off from the influences above. Their loyalties were to each other and to the mine and not, it seems, to anything or anybody in that remote world above ground. Moreover, they saw that MUPS was no more than the way they were used to working, only more systematically worked out. And, the final motivator, they knew that the mine's existence was at risk. Knowing this, the shop stewards had taken a policy decision as early as 1964 to cooperate with the management in productivity-improving changes. MUPS fitted the mine tradition and the circumstances equally well. How well this was accepted was demonstrated by the fact that, at a vote on whether or not to go forward for WSA (when the local union was opposed), only one AEF member out of 49 voted against.

It is as though the anhydrite mine repeated on a smaller scale the circumstances of small and remote works like

Stowmarket where the problems arising at the big sites in old industrial regions were simply not encountered. We may speculate about the causes of these differences with the small and remote sites. With the mine, operating in the same environment as the rest of Billingham, we have a case where a group felt free to make up its own mind, unconstrained by political influences or worries about how they would look to their peers elsewhere: they were invisible and behaved as men concerned for their jobs might be expected to. In a far more extreme form, an analogous difference was — and in factories always is — noticeable between the behaviour of individuals and of groups. An illustrative case was the final vote by AEU members at Billingham on WSA, in October 1970. At a mass meeting the voting was on two similar motions, both militant, one slightly more so than the other but both amounting, in effect, to rejection of the agreement. Ten days later in a secret ballot, the voting was three to one in favour of accepting. The point does not need to be stressed: the anhydrite mine, in site terms, was always running on a 'secret' ballot. The story does not have a happy ending. 'It was heartbreaking', said Jim Bell, personnel director at Billingham from 1972. 'It was the best introduction we had and the boys were fantastically cooperative. And then we kicked them in the teeth: we shut the place down. We had to! We had no alternative. We'd have been bankrupted if we'd gone on making sulphuric acid from anhydrite. They understood. But it was bitter.' The excellence of the mine operation and the cooperativeness of the men was no defense against the high costs of the process of which they were a part.

4. *Doncaster: The dark twin of Gloucester*

In many ways, the account of Doncaster's WSA experience belongs with Wilton, Billingham and the other works in the Northeast. And as such, it would not rate a separate mention except that it is so close to Gloucester in technical ways and yielded such different results. The works came on to the agreement in November 1970, with none of the enthusiasm of Gloucester. Morale was low and the results were disappointing. Although nominally working to WSA standards,

manning ratios hardly changed. It was a period of near-crisis
in the fibres industry but the numbers employed had
dropped only by 108, or 4%. Partly in response to that
experience, partly because of the continuing fibres crisis and
partly in the course of a re-organisation of business areas in
the division, a massive redundancy was declared which bore
particularly heavily on Doncaster. 569 men left the works. If
any 'spirit of WSA' had survived through these unpromising
conditions, it was speedily extinguished. The bad relations
between the two sides were demonstrated in a damaging
strike of fitters lasting more than a month at the end of
1971, called over the somewhat legalistic — but in its
implications quite real and politically charged — issue of the
management's right to make changes between shift and day
workers and the unions' right to consultation over such
changes.

Yet in formal ways, Doncaster and Gloucester are very
similar. The range of products is different, Doncaster
concentrating on the heavy denier yarns — for example
carpet yarn — and Gloucester on textile grades, but the
processes are virtually identical. Although Doncaster is larger
than Gloucester, with weekly staff of 2,120 comparing with
Gloucester's 1,700, the difference would not mark the
transition into 'big site' dynamics.

Doncaster has the characteristics of an old industrial area.
The main source of employment has been coal mining, with
its long history of strikes and more recent history of steep
decline. Among other major local employers, the town
suffered from two major shutdowns less than ten years
before the MUPS agreement. As on Teesside, local union
attitudes are dominated by the need to defend jobs;
management/union relations are characterised by a high
degree of militancy. In the long debate over union policies
towards MUPS, it was not surprising that shop stewards at
Doncaster should have found common cause with their
counterparts at Wilton.

But even before MUPS was thought of, 'Doncaster was
always a most unhappy factory', as one Fibres Division
manager put it to me. The difference with Gloucester is
striking, and although this reflects differences in local
culture they are all part of the environment within which the

company has to work. In the seven years after British Nylon Spinners merged with ICI, Doncaster recorded an average of 1% per year time lost in strikes compared with none lost at Gloucester. Sickness and absenteeism rates are higher; overtime rates — which reflect the push from the unions (whose members want overtime) and the ability of managers to hold systematic overtime at a minimum — are also higher.

Given the local environment, management would have had difficulties at the best of times in gaining enough trust from the unions to begin talks on a change so radical as that contained in WSA. But to the local conditions was added the inheritance of years of management which had not taken the problems of man management seriously. In the words of another manager: ' . . . the incentive scheme became a farce . . . There was serious overmanning in many areas . . . Manning standards became negotiated rather than work study figures. It was the attempt to get back to realistic manning standards which caused many of the subsequent problems.' It was very much a part of this picture that relations within the works — between managers and workers and between the works manager and managers — were characterised by secrecy and mistrust, which only confirmed the local tendency to treat all exchanges with managers as battles with an ancient and implacable foe.

That the introduction of WSA at Doncaster had many of the same features as at Wilton is not surprising, since the two works experience many of the same local environmental pressures. Moreover, the engineering shop stewards maintained close contact and, with Huddersfield, supported each other in their opposition first to MUPS and then, but decreasingly, to WSA. The main opposition came from the AUEW: 'We refused to talk', Brian Day, the senior AUEW shop steward said later: 'MUPS meant handing over all control to the management.' Most specifically, this meant control over the bonus incentive scheme — which had been the province of the shop stewards. And in the same way, the main support for the new agreement has come from general workers — who saw the agreement as offering a way out of the rigid union caste system.

The sequence of events — the meetings to gain interest in the agreement; the study groups formed to analyse the work;

the attempted involvement of people at all levels — followed the pattern of other works. But, in the face of the unions' determined opposition the campaign would have got nowhere without two important changes. The first was the appointment of Alan Turner as works manager; the second was the revelation of ICI's power to take work away from Doncaster.

Turner, who came after a year as assistant works manager to Harry Penny at Gloucester, was able to bring with him an experience of what could be achieved in an almost identical factory but in more favourable conditions. With his encouragement, managers were able to make strenuous efforts, mainly through a hierarchy of discussion groups similar to that used in other works, to communicate with the workforce. For a time, according to Ray Ashmore — the WSA co-ordinator — there was high enthusiasm, as men discussed their jobs and ways of improving them, increasing the 'content', and changing the level of supervision. But this waned with the introduction of work study methods — an old bogey — in studying the jobs and re-establishment of shop stewards, at their own insistence, as the main channel of communication between managers and men.

Probably most crucial of all, however, was the change in the climate that came as the Fibres Division management revealed their trump card: that Doncaster was only one among four ICI nylon factories — the others being at Gloucester, Pontypool and Oestringen in Germany; orders could always be channelled to the plants with the lowest costs; and new investment would be made in the most attractive site. Doncaster had no pre-emptive claim on the company's resources and attempts to hold out for more money than other works could only harm the workers there. The message was doubtless put across with more subtlety than this statement of it, but it was effective. The AUEW shop steward, Brian Day, claims that 'we were manoeuvred into the agreement by the threat of redundancy'. Later, in November 1971, the AUEW called their strike. They received no support from the T&GWU, because according to two T&GWU stewards, Joe Blackham and Joe Daniels, the members were frightened for their jobs — although the stewards thought the strike deserved support. The workers had already been through a period of short-time working

(which had double force to shock in a factory with a
reputation locally for steady employment and high overtime
rates) and had just experienced the heavy redundancies of the
mid-year.

This situation deserves some examination since it raises in
stark form the very circumstances and attitudes which WSA
was designed to supersede. On one side were the unions, the
stubborn defenders of their members' right to work; acutely
suspicious of anything that might infringe their 'birthright' or
'immemorial privileges'; with some ideological stiffening —
how much it is impossible to say — in the opposition to any
attempt to bridge the gulf fixed between employer and
employee, to compromise in the war between capital and
labour. On the other side were the company and its
managers, the inheritors of the right to exploit and make
decisions about other people's lives. Both sides had a long
history as intransigent opponents: a remote and authoritarian
management facing a group of militant unions. Each side's
behaviour provided fresh support for the other's assumptions,
and justification for the other's attitudes. The result was an
acutely wary and suspicious relationship. That something
better was possible was demonstrated by the brief period of
'WSA enthusiasm' soon after the discussions properly got
under way; its fragility was demonstrated by the speed with
which it disappeared in the face of small setbacks. The
situation demanded a sensitivity and tact which the management could not command — and an almost heroic forbear-
ance.

Even if these qualities had been displayed, it is doubtful
whether a breakthrough into the unions' trust could have
been quickly achieved. I would be tempted to call this
impossible, circular, self-confirming situation tragic if it was
not so common. To bring about change has to be a
cooperative effort; both sides must want it. When the
attitudes on one side are embedded in a long history of
unemployment and privation, more must change than just
what is found within the works' boundaries. On the other
side, a long experience of technical problem-solving is not an
adequate training for bringing about such changes in sensitive
circumstances.

A last point. I have drawn the picture in rather dark

colours not in order deliberately to falsify the situation, but
to point up the contrasts between Doncaster and Gloucester.
But it would be wrong to leave the impression that nothing
has been achieved. Although progress in finding a new
balance of power, based in trust, received a sharp setback
with the 1971 redundancies, there has been real progress at
the level of re-organising work. As at Gloucester,
many of the old limitations and heavy supervision have been
eliminated; jobs have been enriched; the new pay structure
guarantees a regular wage. Workers I spoke to (in 1972)
seemed generally satisfied with the new arrangement, giving
them more money for more work. The responsibility for the
large parts of the job that had been so rigorously supervised
was a source of satisfaction. There were also positive
comments among shopfloor workers — but not among the
stewards — about the more objective basis of job grading
under WSA and the elimination of the arbitrary differences in
take-home pay that resulted from the old bonus incentives.

Control from the centre

To the end of 1968, the CPD had taken a dominating role in
the detailed management of the trials. After MUPS had been
re-negotiated, the role progressively changed. The main
change was the shift of the detailed, day-by-day monitoring
of individual works from CPD to the divisions. Something
more routine, less geared to learning from a new experience
and to dealing with crises and exceptions was indicated. The
role for the new exercise can be put under three headings:
policy-formation and management; relations with unions at
national level; provision of services and expertise. The means
used were the same as for the trials.

The primary role of the centre was still to inject urgency
and vitality into the programme and to maintain consistency
of application, so that individual works did not wander too
far away from the intentions of the agreement. This last was
a real danger when managers were faced with difficulties and
were tempted to buy union agreement by relaxing some of
the rules. The main controls were exercised from divisional
personnel offices but CPD received copious reports on the
progress of each works. The three liaison officers travelled

around the country more or less constantly, keeping in touch with what was happening. An important way of pooling information was to hold regular meetings of division labour officers, who were able to discuss their problems with others having the same experience.

The role of the joint committee now changed. It had come into existence as the continuation of the joint committee which had put MUPS together and played an important part in the trials, providing a non-negotiating, problem-solving arena for company/union discussions.* But once WSA had been agreed, the focus of interest began to swing back to negotiating issues at the fringes of WSA — a more traditional relationship. The change was analogous to that in the processes by which MUPS and WSA were agreed: MUPS as a joint, participative exercise, although agreed within the highly unfamiliar framework of consultation, more of a negotiation leading to a firm, new agreement on pay and conditions.

The committee met less frequently as the action was dispersed to the increasingly confident divisional centres and the main purpose, of joint central problem-solving, diminished. Thirty meetings had been held in the three years to the end of 1968, when they were stopped as company/union relations moved on to the more formal plane, of negotiating the new agreement. The committee was revived at the end of October 1969 and met half a dozen times in the following year, when it was agreed that it should meet four times a year thereafter.

As an introduction became more routine, other company/union institutions became more important — for example, the disputes procedure which was used to iron out local problems of introducing WSA, most particularly disputed assessments. And the training and other services provided by CPD (of which more in the next section) were part of CPD's continuing function in the company. Of those, the management of the job assessment scheme was crucial to the

* An internal CPD paper, written in November 1969, described setting up the joint committee as an attempt: '. . . to bring divisional thinking (but not divisional representation as such) more directly into national discussions . . . and to establish an atmosphere of exchange of views, investigation and problem-solving — rather than avoiding commitment because of negotiation implications . . .'

successful control of WSA — which could all too easily have got completely out of control. It was in CPD, under Frank Roden, that the training of assessors and maintenance of company standards was located.

Status of WSA

By the end of 1971, all but 9% of the company's weekly staff were covered by the new agreement. The programme had gone through periods of intense experimentation and learning and into the development of specialised expertise. The management had acquired enough professionalism to enable it to handle the problems of organisational change on a more routine (that is, less of a crisis) basis. And the ideas behind organisational development were if not widely understood certainly familiar among the workforce. We have seen how this change in the way in which problems arising from MUPS/WSA were handled were reflected in the agenda of the joint committee and management's advisory committee. As the 'one-off' aspects of WSA were absorbed into a more on-going routine programme, the negotiating energies of the unions flowed again into fringe issues from which small improvements in their members' pay could be obtained.

Two changes resulted from this:

1. The energy level of the programme ran down. Interest flagged once the first discussions were completed. Managers having satisfied the requirements of their superiors in introducing the programme turned their interest back to the day-to-day problems of management; unions turned their energies to issues where further concrete benefits could be obtained.

2. An increasing part of the negotiating activity between company and unions went into exegesis of the WSA text. Not all problems could have been foreseen when it was originally drafted: these had to be cleared up (for example, the payment of juveniles and part-timers). Other issues had been left purposely vague. In one way and another, these were opportunities for the unions to squeeze more out of the agreement (no bad thing), which became increasingly elaborate.

Once the agreement was 'in' throughout the company, the question of how to keep it alive became a subject of concern in CPD. A conference was held with the unions at the beginning of 1972, the 'Windermere Conference', for which a good deal of information was gathered in CPD. Among the papers prepared for internal use was one by Derek Holbrook which provides a fitting end-piece to this chapter.

'1. At the limit, if the broad WSA approach is eroded too far by too many special or different things, job evaluation itself becomes an irrelevance. That would be the end of our salary control system and that would be costly and disruptive.

'2. We need a system that is both clearly recognisable and reasonably simple. Without that management cannot defend the structure except by intricate negotiation and then inadequately. Intricate negotiation has an appeal to both managers and union representatives because some problems otherwise seem stark and unresolvable. Beyond the parties principally involved however intricacy creates only uncomprehension and mistrust . . .

'3. Union leaders might see the creation of intricacy and exceptions as their classic role, because it breaks the management front and secures benefits for their members. In fact they are driven to it, just like the management, as victims, because they are trying to do a job. As the process goes on the intricacies themselves create endless additional work and problems for the unions and can sour relationships among and inside unions.

'4. Intricacy includes some cost risks for management, but is not necessarily an overall gain to union members. It can be a major distraction from thinking about policies, and pressures that could produce much bigger gains in the really big basic areas. That is why management is relatively easily tempted into intricacy. The cost for management arises instead from the loss of control, the mistrust, and having to respond to bargaining attitudes and all the argument and disruption when it tries to get things done.

'5. After WSA we have recognised a number of extra-WSA pay headings as legitimate. These include overtime, call-out, temporary shift payments, conditions payments and deputising payments. We have recognised them as genuinely necessary, because these situations arise differently as between different people ... If they had more collective power the groups most affected by different situations would in fact force us to be more precise and less broad: the unions are really forcing us to be more just in a short-term calculable way. We want to be just however only where the case is distinct and abundant, because almost nothing is quite the same for everybody ...

'6. Monthly staff by and large understand, welcome and respond to the broad approach. We are going to acknowledge this in the type of conditions we provide for them and therefore there could be differences between them and weekly staff for a long time. These will not be differences between first and second class citizens, but between groups who regard management and their jobs in different ways and who put different priorities to the Company. It is up to the unions to a great extent to influence how things go, as long as ... we are convinced that their members in general fully understand and accept the implications of their policies.'

12
Beyond WSA

The key feature of WSA, and what sets it apart from many other change programmes, is that it is not a one-off productivity deal but a blueprint for new working relationships and of a *continuing* process for looking at and thinking about work. But the dynamics of introducing such an agreement and those of keeping it on the move are very different. The task of introduction had all the energy and excitement that comes from trying out a new and hopeful answer to old problems; it was finite, limited, precisely determinable; and it had the highly visible and concrete objective for management and workers alike of agreeing the local terms for acceptance. In contrast, building new methods into the on-going job of running (or working in) a plant is an altogether more diffuse activity, with no end-point, no easy source of energy and no clear objective. It is no wonder that WSA is in constant danger of running down and that it has had to be kept on the move, watched over and guarded against decay or diversion into the reedy swamps of ever more detailed bargaining on marginal issues.

A number of solid changes have been made and are now a part of the working scene. (These are looked at in the next part.) Some, such as more 'authentic' communication between managers and shop stewards, are new habits learned in the process of introduction. Others, such as the elimination of the institutional aspects (e.g. separate pay structures) of craft/non-craft demarcations, were among the aims of the agreements. Still others, such as problem-solving in work group discussions, have emerged informally and even spontaneously in some parts of the company. But the advances are unevenly distributed and do not yet add up to 'WSA working' (somehow defined) throughout the company.

Indeed, at the time I was collecting information in the company there was a distinct sense that WSA working was on the decline; the Goths were hammering on the gates and the managers were sitting around, like the senators of ancient Rome, dismally waiting to have their throats cut. This was probably a temporary lull; nothing to do with Goths but the product of exhaustion (a sort of post-puerperal depression) and the difficulties of managing with the new agreement in a combination of high unemployment and poor business.

In addition, we might have expected a decay of the WSA spirit with time. The bad old environment, and the attitudes it supported, was waiting outside for any opportunity to break back in to the (for a time) charmed world of a WSA introduction. All the works I have described have reported a stiffening of attitudes and a reversion; change has become harder to bring about.

The Nylon VIII plant at Ardeer provided a particularly interesting case — and one that is, in many ways, representative.

Nylon VIII could not isolate itself from its environment although it managed to introduce some barriers between itself and the explosives works. The environment was merely put at a greater distance and it is now creeping back in. Partly, this is a function of settling down to 'steady state' operation. Anyone who has taken part in commissioning a new plant knows how the sense of potential crisis, almost of pioneering, does extraordinary things to the people who become totally involved in the need to make the new plant work. In this atmosphere, divisions and demarcations disappear; rank has far less meaning than expertise; decisions are made cooperatively — all happening quite naturally in a situation dominated by the urgent task. (At a more commonplace level, something of the sort is summed up in the expression 'night shift spirit'.) But it only lasts as long as the crisis and when that is over the old ways tend to return.

The start-up period at Nylon VIII was highly successful; relations were very good; the introduction of WSA was greatly helped by these circumstances. Now? At the time of writing, managers were saying, 'Nothing has changed for some time and they (the process operators) are reverting to old attitudes.' Many managers spoke of the growing difficulty of introducing any further changes. 'Why should we change?' a T&GWU shop steward asked. 'If it won't make any difference to the job grade, what is the point in agreeing any more changes?' (An unforeseen consequence of the large steps in the grade structure.) And, as in other locations, the job descriptions have become new sources of demarcations: their existence makes flexible change difficult.

Sandy Morrison admits, 'I was too starry-eyed and optimistic about the chances of changing attitudes.' Old attitudes although modified have, after all, persisted; shop stewards tend to adopt a bargaining stance wherever change is discussed; the workers generally tend to assume a continuing relationship of conflict with the managers. A vivid illustration was provided by the withdrawal of the T&GWU from joint consultation – the communication system, described later in this chapter, that has followed the works council scheme. As a result, the regular meetings of work groups came to a halt and this important part of the process of keeping WSA alive was temporarily lost.

But for a manager faced with the apparent failure of WSA styles, it is difficult to see a way forward; just as, for the shop steward, there seem to be obvious advantages to a reversion to the old bargaining habits. Morrison said that he was not finding it easy to persuade his managers to continue to play the game within the WSA rules: faced with a difficult situation, the temptation to slip back into something more authoritarian was strong. Each side reinforces the other's determination to dominate the situation, in what the anthropologists call 'schismogenesis'. To this extent, WSA – or any agreement which must exist in an unchanged environment – is fragile, precariously balanced, levitated almost, over the bogs of indifference on one side and ancient habit on the other.

The effort of keeping it levitated is considerable. And, as I have said, it can draw on none of the energy released by introduction. It is not surprising, therefore, that an altern- ative way should seem attractive, epitomised in the vigorous query, 'Where is the next WSA?' A number of the more energetic managers and union leaders, having seen the way in which the introduction of WSA galvanised the company, have concluded that a further new deal is needed. But this is to misunderstand the dynamics of different modes of change and assumes that the shock of newness is necessary to achieve change at all. It is tactical thinking and runs the risk of tossing WSA out of the window before its full value had been gained — and of getting caught up in a frantic pursuit of new ideas to launch at shorter intervals for diminishing returns. There has to be a limit to the number of times the trick of energising a system with a radically new initiative can be pulled. (There is a limit to the number of 'radically new' initiatives.) And the values of shock in 'unfreezing' a social system belong at the beginning of a long period of change. The objective, then, would be to make the most of WSA, not seeing it as a gimmick but as a long-lived framework for change. The bonus incentive scheme that preceded WSA lasted for fifteen years: things change more quickly now, but this would be a more appropriate time scale.

Two routes are available for the company: taking action within the existing framework and/or, having identified key blockages, making appropriate changes to the framework to facilitate for the change. We can consider these blockages under a number of headings: attitudes; communications; political and institutional relationships; reward and control systems.

1. Many managers achieved the clear objective of introducing WSA in their works but subsequently lacked the energy and enthusiasm needed to keep up the pressure in the interests of less obvious gains. Others had no will to do so since they could not accept the reality of union 'ownership' of work, still clung to the illusion of total managerial authority and therefore saw no point in the exercise. Against these blocks, should be set the experience of those managers, in works and at division level, who systematically kept up the processes started in WSA, with steadily improving results in terms of manpower utilisation and labour relations. Even the dissatisfaction has a positive side: Dick Beckhard commented on the improvements in managers' awareness that the complaints revealed: 'They were worrying about things they wouldn't have noticed or acknowledged five years ago.'

The cost-cutting and redundancies of the two years of industry recession, 1970-2, left an aftermath of bitterness and insecurity with shopfloor workers and managers. Among the former, in some areas, it made attempts to extend WSA difficult. Among the latter, the supervisors who played a leading part in the WSA exercise found themselves among the prime targets for cost-cutting; their enthusiasm was noticeably impaired.

2. Communications between management and shopfloor greatly improved, but they remained 'inauthentic' within the management structure. Whether through a basic lack of trust (between divisions or between divisions and the centre) or through a cautious British respect for hierarchy (which restricts direct and open expression of views) the consequence remained as a seizing-up of the managerial information system.

3. The new role of the shop stewards has still not been worked through. By role they are — and their unions are at national level — committed to opposing managerial will. Thus, as a matter of principle, change without pay (that is, changes to a job description which does not, on assessment, change the grade) is becoming increasingly difficult in some areas — which is against the spirit of the agreement and the basis of job evaluation. More generally, at national level, the relations between company and signatory unions was bound to be confused by the polarisation of political attitudes brought about by the Conservative government's anti-inflation (some would call it an anti-union) policy.

4. The job evaluation system made comparability between jobs and parity of reward a reality across the company wages structure. This had the virtues of fairness and of virtually stopping wage drift. But, by creating a rigid structure, it removed from local management any element of flexibility in the payments area — which affected both management and union ability to bargain. At the same time union interest and energies migrated to bargaining over such marginal intricacies as conditions payments.

5. In the first flush of enthusiasm over WSA, there was a tendency to forget, or ignore, many of the control systems based in work measurement in which ICI management had become expert. The need for it was felt as soon as working

reverted to something more like normal patterns.

Unblocking attitudes

Of these blockages, the first — attitudes — has most affected
the way in which WSA was being pressed forward within the
existing framework; the others all indicated policy changes
which could be made to 'unblock' progress. And there were
vigorous efforts made early on to keep the effort of WSA
alive and active.

This effort was, in the first instance, up to local managers
entirely. In the first statement of aims in WSA, it said:

'In the future a continuous programme of examination and
change will be required because technological and social
change will continue. The benefits of such change carried
out in the spirit of this Agreement will be that the
Company will be able to provide a more secure and more
rewarding future for its employees and be better able to
maintain its competitive position in world markets.'

But it could not say how the progress could be made to
continue beyond what was required to start the agreement
off.

In travels around the works, it became obvious that
this — largely voluntary — effort was unevenly distributed. At
a crude guess, it seemed that no more than half of the works
were, in any systematic way, attempting to maintain the
open-ended nature of the agreement. Basically, this meant
continuing the processes of building up informal work
groups* by arranging regular meetings to discuss problems
arising within their work area. At longer intervals the groups
would meet with more senior managers to receive information about their performance and the prospects for the
works as a whole.

---

* The informal work group is no more than a recognition of a working reality: a
team of people, with interdependent roles, in one work area — a process plant
shift team, a group of canteen workers, workers in a section of an engineering
workshop. They work together, usually grouped under a supervisor, and are
concerned with the same problems. It was the basic working and discussion unit
for WSA introduction.

This method of communicating had been established in Gloucester well before MUPS. Regular 'gen' sessions had become the practice at Hillhouse and, it later transpired, throughout Mond Division. Where they were imaginatively used, they were found valuable for solving problems in ways that could draw upon the experience of the people concerned – and involve them in the solution. Where they were not used, I found a distinct sense of disappointment among shopfloor workers: expectations had been built up during the introduction of WSA, a new way of working had been tried which, it seems, managers abandoned as soon as it had served their purposes. This may only rarely have been the case (one manager was proud of having taken facilities – an office and a telephone – away from his shop stewards when the discussions had been completed); more commonly, the managers were re-absorbed into their day-to-day problems and could not find the energy for anything that was not immediate and vital.

To make the most out of the opportunity offered by WSA, a campaign was mounted by CPD in 1972 to draw the divisions together and alert them to the need to 'intensify WSA', which meant making the works management aware of the ways in which WSA methods could be used. In March 1972, a memorandum went out to division personnel managers in which were discussed ways of keeping WSA moving forward. It was the result of a sequence of events which had included the joint union/company conference at Windermere. The conference had been inconclusive, but pointed to the possibilities of further management effort.

This initiative elicited a number of replies from divisions who were already set upon this road – notably Mond, which had instituted periodic audits as a way of building upon the start made in WSA. Later, some divisions reported that they had used the memo as a starting point for 'events', involving works management in discussions about how they could make further progress. One report, from the Dumfries factory of Plastics Division, described a series of discussions that had been built on an opinion survey, designed and circulated by the management. Another report, from the plastics works at Hillhouse, listed as characteristic successes that had been achieved using the WSA-derived problem-solving discussion group. These ranged from radical changes in the work of a laboratory to handling crisis situations in new ways at useful cost savings.

These changes appeared to be moving towards two goals: the primary company goal of improving the use of people on a continuing basis; and developing new systems of problem-solving and decision-making. The first has been the more difficult, held back by environmental factors (particularly unemployment) that have limited change. The second appears to be a more spontaneous result of the way in which WSA was introduced. Informal work groups have meaning to the individual members who welcome the opportunity to raise problems for discussion with other interested people. For the manager, they provide a route for passing down information about plant operation — information that had previously been jealously guarded at the supervisory level, or higher. Probably more important, they provide a means whereby changes — shutdowns, crises or the installation of new plant — can be discussed with the people concerned and difficulties fully aired. Several works managers have told me that this has been an invaluable way of anticipating change so that it does not come as a shock — and provoke resistance. Paul Marsden, the site manager at Billingham, said that, in his opinion, the development of problem-solving in informal work groups is one of the two most important changes that WSA brought about. Billingham was one of the places where it was not methodically introduced but arose, modelled on WSA discussions, to meet the needs of the moment, specifically of plant closures and redundancies.

To sum up this section, there are two main routes through which attitudes favourable to change can be encouraged: through management and shopfloor. In the first, continuing training and development is needed to keep the ideas of WSA in the front of managers' minds. This can range from works initiatives — the Coverdale training programme arranged at Hillhouse, and the 'grid' training programme at Grangemouth — to division-arranged seminars and conferences, like the Plastics Division 'events', and the continuing training effort of CPD. On the shopfloor, one of the unexpected benefits of WSA has been the growth of a new form of decision-making based in work group discussion. The model was established during WSA discussions and it has been spreading: 'We must protect them,' said a CPD manager, 'for they are absolutely fundamental problem-solving units and one of the best of the ways we have of integrating people into the system.'

Joint consultation

Opportunities for taking new initiatives still remained which fell a long way short of replacing WSA. It was necessary to continue to explore and experiment with new techniques in order to maintain the company's 'OD technology' in a state of readiness. And there remained much to be done in tidying up the formal structure of industrial relations. The poor communications among management have been mentioned early in the book. Quite a different anomaly, and one more easily dealt with, was the form of the works council scheme.

It was anomalous because adding a third, quite distinct, form of representation and communication to the irreducible necessities of the management and union structures. The jealous watchfulness of the unions had ensured that the area of discussion left to the councils — basically welfare issues (health, safety, pensions) — was so limited as to rob them of the power to change things, and so of interest too. The councils had been appropriate to the times in which they had been started: forty years before, when the unions were weak and there was a need to set up channels of communication with the workforce. But those times had passed.

However, the need remained to communicate in more formal ways than, for example, the work group discussions could provide. And the obvious channel of communication was one that would not have been considered when the councils were set up: the shop stewards. The unions had been suspicious of the council scheme from the beginning and in some places stewards had refused to take part. Yet they are the natural representatives of the union members. As a result of their refusal to play a part (and the company's unwillingness to give them one) another block had been introduced in to the communications system. Over time, the role of stewards has changed: they had been recognised for bargaining purposes; the balance of power between informal and formal union structures had shifted, putting more power into their hands. And in the introduction of WSA they were necessarily given a central role. It was this last point that focussed attention on the most constructive possibility that a revision of the works council scheme could offer.

A new scheme was agreed with the unions in July 1970 called 'joint consultation'. The purpose was fundamentally the same as the scheme it replaced, with the difference that shop stewards were to be the members' representatives and since the new system officially involved union represent-atives, there were no bars on subjects for discussion. As with work group discussion, the emphasis was placed on problem-solving discussion; if an issue moved into the negotiating stage, it can always be — and indeed must be — put into the company's formal procedures.

The basic unit of discussion is the plant committee, to which shop stewards are elected annually as representatives. Management representatives are appointed by the company, and include the plant manager. The committee meets every month and is a forum in which are discussed the affairs of the plant — progress, problems, changes and suggestions; infor-mation from the company; issues from representatives. And from it are elected representatives to sit on a works committee, which has a similar constitution and function, only covering the larger works area. It is a formal consultative arrangement. Indeed, 'one of the reasons why we were able to gain acceptance', the manager responsible for the system said afterwards, 'is that after WSA people were thoroughly familiar with the meaning and the uses of consultation. The distinction between problem-solving discussion and bargaining was now clearly established in everybody's mind.'

Even so, there were problems in introducing the new system, ironically enough, because it had become a bargain-ing issue. By a curious reversal of the intentions of joint consultation, having been identified as something the management wanted, was re-defined as a management 'demand' — for whose acceptance the local unions felt able to demand concessions in other areas. It is rather — the analogy is chosen for vividness, and not to be insulting — as the realities of a situation like mother-feeding-baby can be reversed (if the mother allows) so that the baby assumes a position of power, 'making Mummy happy' by eating.

Joint consultation was introduced slowly and with considerable difficulties in some works. At Nylon Ardeer, for example, the T&GWU broke off all negotiations with management so that even work group discussions — which had been proceeding as a natural follow-on of a highly successful WSA introduction — were brought to a halt, with dire effects. But every works in the company had agreed to the new system by spring 1973. The next step, which is being taken cautiously, is to extend the system upwards until something analogous to the old central council results. But it is by no means certain that this is an inevitable result; there may be no urgent need for a consultative 'superstructure'.

Joint consultation has been a necessary adjustment to bring the realities of local union (i.e. shop steward) and management structures more into line with each other. But there are no completely logical solutions to the anomalies which exist within complex social systems. Clearly, the new formal machinery for consultation overlaps with, and could be in danger of smothering, the nascent informal work groups — which are in some ways more fundamental and more closely related to the necessities of work. But so long as they are not thought to be competing with each other, there is no reason why they should not co-exist.

Emerging problems

WSA was an adjustment made to bring ICI back into harmony with an environment — social and commercial — which had evolved away from the stable, self-perpetuating internal systems of the company. These still reflected the vanished conditions in which they had been formed; a conscious effort was needed to assess the new conditions and to devise ways of making appropriate changes to the company's internal arrangement. Clearly, the environment continues to change and the immense stability of a large organisation like ICI guarantees that the pace of its own evolution is going to lag behind these changes. And this raises the questions: When will some further major adjustment be called for? What problems will they centre on? Is it necessary to wait for a crisis to energise the system again before the necessary, large, internal changes can be made?

These questions cannot be answered by analogy with the circumstances that led to WSA; the events surrounding the agreement had changed too much. The agreement has changed the awareness within ICI of the ways the external social environment impinges on it. A new expertise for analysing organisations and changing them has been developed and its uses are now widely understood. And a process for continuously monitoring the need for change has been built in, however imperfectly, to the management of the company. In times of rapid social change, organisations must increasingly have the capacity to learn and consciously adapt themselves.

None the less, a number of potential challenges to existing assumptions and ways of doing things can already be seen. For one thing, the 'existing ways' are not so very different from old ways: the changes in attitudes brought about by WSA are by no means complete; they can only be a beginning. Many if not most senior managers acquired their experience and formed many of their attitudes in times so different from the present that the ideas in WSA still seem outrageous. Unions, even more, are not likely to relinquish their ideas about an eternal and uncompromising war on their members' behalf against capital: for, if they did, they could not continue in their present form. These attitudes on both sides will take a long time to change.

More to the point, the expectations of the workforce are continuing to evolve in directions that will threaten traditional assumptions about ICI's role as employer and the constraints on efficiency that will be imposed by employees' demands.

This issue was raised in a report prepared in 1972, a summary of the views of outside experts on ICI's personnel policy. It raised questions about the fundamental assumption inherited from the earliest days of the company, that ICI should provide a complete working environment and a career for life. The assumption emerges in the strong emphasis of the payment system on internal comparability and fairness – an emphasis that has meaning when the employees are comparing themselves with others within the system but not so much when their standard of comparison is with the outside

world. It is one of the starting-points of this book that a
major force for change has been the *choice* that affluence has
put in the hands of an increasing number of people. In a full
employment economy, an important element of choice is
exercised between jobs. This must diminish the loyalty a
company can command by virtue of its simply offering
secure employment; long-term career expectations can be
realised between a number of employers — and there are a
thousand reasons why a man could prefer to work within a
larger, rather than a more limited, set of job possibilities.
Such a line of reasoning poses a threat to the job evaluation
basis of WSA. It may be premature: a very experienced
personnel manager referred to the 'immense value that there
still is in belonging to a club like ICI'. In another sense, it has
already happened. Shopfloor workers are already far more
used to moving around between jobs, in search of variety as
much as of advancement.

But the problem may arise in acute form among management, now dominated at senior levels by men who joined ICI
on graduation for a 'career for life', but being replenished by
men who may have quite different views. The change in view
may not be altogether a loss to the company. In a stable
management structure, in which appointments are always
made from within, the more volatile elements are lost to the
market and impurities — less marketable people — build up;
lacking a fresh view from new entrants, the higher levels of
management become too sensitively attuned to ICI ways and
may miss opportunities that lie outside the familiar routines.
If a more open policy of recruitment was enforced by the
conditions I have described, it could be to the advantage of
the company.

One way of looking at a diminution of the importance of
the organisation is to suggest that workers move around to
assert their need for greater autonomy. This should not
surprise us, since we have seen that a large part of WSA
focussed on precisely this issue. But it has implications that
go beyond the shopfloor. The needs that are resulting in the
formation of work groups as important problem-solving
centres are felt throughout the company. But they are quite
inconsistent with the huge size of many modern cor-
porations, a size which has some — but not compelling —

economic justifications and no justifications in human terms. And this raises questions about the extent to which power can, or should, be devolved from the centre. What benefits can that achieve and at what costs? The question has arisen in small ways, as in the freedom (or lack of it) that local managers have to reward workers outside the job evaluation scheme. There may be questions to ask about the need to break the company structure into smaller units which can provide a setting for workers and managers whose scale is something more nearly human.

The same argument applies, and the same forces are evident, in the unions. The split between informal — local and formal — national organisations reflects a need among union members for a system that more directly and visibly serves their purpose. At the same time, the unions are growing larger and more powerful.

Both sorts of development point to the importance of an organisation providing settings for its members in which they can satisfy their needs for autonomy while performing their tasks. WSA in ICI, and other programmes elsewhere, are only the beginnings of a process of change that will have transformed people's working lives before the end of this century. They will have given to everyone who wants it some of the freedom, satisfaction and self-respect that have been the prerogative of the professional middle classes.

Rather than finish on that millennial note without qualification, we should realise that there are several ways of achieving this end. Job enrichment and other techniques based on the assumption that all workers seek satisfaction in their work, offers the most obviously attractive way (it is the most middle-class way since it is 'moral' — in encouraging the urge to work — and it assuages guilt about gaps in life-styles), but it is also possible to design organisations around the assumption that work is a necessary evil, boring and to be endured in the interests of the satisfactions it — or rather the income from it — makes possible. Even in the solutions they propose, companies must be flexible.

PART V

Results,
Analysis and Speculations

A standing temptation offered by any change is that of losing the real purpose of the exercise – the content – in the excitement of the process of bringing it about. This is not unique to organisational change. It is an inescapable part of journalism, for example, that the business of informing readers is lost in the self-justifying excitement of meeting deadlines and beating competitors, and the real pleasures of draping a glittering surface over a few drab facts. The excitement of reporting events becomes the enemy of understanding and analysis of the underlying issues – and may be quite inconsistent with the needs of readers.

In the last two parts of the book, we have been dealing in a world of events. In this part, I shall look at the results ICI achieved in its enormous effort of organisational change. WSA did not exist for its own sake – although, while its introduction dominated other activities in the company, one might have thought so. An important feature of this period was the way in which the difficulties encountered generated a new set of goals (getting the agreement accepted) much as a rose will break into new growth from a point of stress. But underlying the excitement and frustrations, the satisfactions of achievement and the despair of endless delay, was the slow and steady purpose of the agreement: for the company, to improve its use of people and, more specifically, get labour costs down; for the unions to improve the pay and conditions of their members while defending their ancient rights. These are the subject of Chapter 13.

The goals merged, for there were managers in the company who were quite as enthusiastic as anyone in the union movement about the welfare of the individual; and there were (fewer) members of unions who saw their self-interest as tied up with the well-being of the company. And, of course, on both sides there were many who opposed anything that so radically challenged familiar ways of doing things. A third set of goals emerged which was not logically the property of any sectional interest. This was the goal of changing the web of internal relationships within the company, the assumptions about roles that determined how managers and managed got on together. It was not articulated as a goal but it was implicit in both MUPS and WSA, if only because the process of arriving at job descriptions was to be cooperative. And this goal was also to create a state of affairs that would make further change more possible. These unquantifiable changes — which I have called the 'soft face of WSA' — are the subject of Chapter 14.

All reasonable men hope to learn from experience. And in Chapter 15 I attempt to draw some specific lessons from the introduction of WSA, a number of points where different decisions should arguably have been made and issues which are best left as questions, for there are no unamibuous answers in a situation of this complexity; moreover, many of the problems within the company arose for reasons outside the discretion of the personnel group largely responsible for managing the change and many more had — and have — their roots outside the organisation, in the fabric of our society. I raise some of these questions in Part VI, when we look outside the company to see the agreement in a broader context.

13

Results 1.
The Hard Face of WSA

When we first looked at MUPS, in Chapter 5, I suggested that
there were several levels of analysis. The most obvious,
conspicuous and in some ways the crudest level was that of
the straight productivity bargain, the trading of benefits:
inefficient practices and demarcations for money; better pay
and conditions for the workers and more efficient working
and lower labour costs for the company. And this is the right
place to start looking for the results of WSA. For if the
company had not seen the possibility of hard, cash benefits
in the sort of changes proposed in MUPS, it would not have
chosen that way out of the commercial crisis that threatened.
Nor, by a similar logic, would the unions have agreed unless
there had been benefits for their members.

I shall concentrate in this chapter on costs and benefits for
the company. Quantifiable benefits to weekly staff are
unambiguously reflected in the increases in earnings; costs are
reflected in the decrease in numbers — although it was more
of a cost to the unions, who saw it as a loss of job
opportunities for their members, than it was for those
remaining in ICI's employment. Indeed, how far this is a
genuine loss at all depends on the view one takes of the
effects on the total system. A 'zero sum game' view would
start from the proposition that any agreement, even one so
complex as WSA, is merely part of a bargaining process which
determines how the company's surpluses shall be allocated.
But the basis of MUPS and WSA was an attempt to increase
the total surpluses so that there would be more for all. The
loss of jobs could be seen as part of a process which was to
the net benefit of the worker/company system.

The benefits to the company are much harder to identify.
Ideally, we should look at the company as a whole, the

ultimate standard of judgment since the agreement was decided at a company level to achieve company-wide results. But there are problems. For a start, it is not enough to look at labour productivity although it is tempting, since the use of labour was the focus of the exercise; still less to use the measure of numbers of men through the gate, which was the measure the company found itself left with. There was a great deal else going on before, during and after the introduction of WSA.

The point is easily grasped. As a useful simplification, the company is a system with inputs, outputs and, between them, a transformation process. The ratio of outputs to inputs is a measure of the system's efficiency: if it increases while the transformation process remains the same, efficiency has increased. But if the processes change − which they do, constantly − it may be hard to know what happened. And if the composition of inputs and outputs change − as they do − comparisons become meaningless. Old plants are closed down and new ones built. In response to market forces, new products are introduced and old ones improved: it is possible to halve the apparent productivity of a spinning factory, for example, by doubling the denier of yarn spun; output of plastics is crucially affected by the grades being made. Production technology is constantly being improved and there is an unremitting pressure in a continuous process industry to build larger units: doubling the size of a plant can reduce costs by up to 40%; if manning for the new plant is increased, say by one man a shift, labour productivity will apparently have been increased by 60% but the work being done by individuals may not alter at all. Dominating these changes are the changes in the company's economic environment. The chemical industry is highly cyclical; production volume can change in response to demand by 25% in a four-year period. The plants must be run, whatever the volume, so that labour requirements are relatively inelastic − which means that when production drops by 25% labour productivity will also drop by 25%. Even if labour could be laid off so quickly and the plants still run, a drop in throughput increases the proportion of fixed costs in final costs − for a capital-intensive plant in which fixed costs were a half of final costs, a drop of 25% in volume of output would increase unit costs by 17%.

There is no need to labour the point. The introduction of WSA was only one of a whole set of changes taking place in that period — and more or less continuously — that affected ICI's results. Some were management initiatives designed to achieve parallel effects to WSA, notably capital investment; others were out of the company's control, in the environment, with more random effects. To take changes in labour productivity and attribute them to WSA is pointless; to try to extract from the closely intertwined and interdependent data that part of the changes which is due to WSA is mathematically impossible. The only way into the problem is through the question, 'What would have happened without WSA?' But it is logically impossible to answer, for it cannot be assumed that nothing else would have been done. On the contrary; companies respond in dynamic ways to changes and challenges: if the challenge of ICI's commercial crisis had not been met by WSA, it would have been met in some other way.

None the less, the exercise had to be monitored. To do this ICI chose the simple measure of numbers. Targets were set and performance measured by reference to manning data. It was in some ways an unfortunate choice. Units of measure are tools, but all tools impose themselves, getting between the user and his intentions. And while to set objectives and monitor performance by reference to manning was in the right direction — for at one level WSA was a de-manning exercise and to reduce manning would push labour productivity in the desired direction — it was also bound to have a distorting effect. At the least, it was inconsistent to measure progress by numbers saved within the framework of an agreement that aimed to get away from a straight productivity bargain. But nothing else was available and there had to be some system of objectives that was clear and unambiguous.

In time, the company collected data about the progress of WSA that allowed a more penetrating look into what was happening. Plant-by-plant analyses were sorted under three headings: stopped, continuing and new work. But even here it was not possible to draw firm conclusions relating manpower to output, which requires constant conditions. To have the stopped and new work identified was a great advance, but the continuing work itself rarely provided a stable base for productivity comparison: in addition to the volume effects fed in from the market, product mix is constantly being changed and the plant technically adjusted. The only firm basis for comparison was, once again, numbers; and this was only meaningful on a disaggregated basis, plant-by-plant. Yet the seeker after truth is in a double bind because individual cases are all, by definition, special cases. Having found data from which to make a comparison, it is impossible to generalise.

With all these reservations, I shall attempt to draw some conclusions about the quantifiable effects of WSA.

Works — brief notes

Some broad conclusions about results achieved at the works are summarised in Figs. 4, 5, 6, 7 and 9. The picture they convey is valid, with local variations, through the company: substantial increases in earnings for the weekly staff; reductions in the workforce, in the proportion of voluntary leavers and in overtime. I have chosen these last three indicators of WSA results because, in the absence of a satisfactory analysis of productivity, they illuminate relevant aspects of working. The numbers employed needs no comment: it was one of the aims of the exercise to bring the manning of ICI more in line with its international competitors; a reduction in crude numbers is a measure of success in achieving this. Turnover, the numbers of voluntary leavers, is a sensitive measure of workforce morale. On the whole, workers satisfied with their jobs are not as footloose as those who are bored and fed up — with the work or with the way they are managed. Other things being equal, we can take a reduction in turnover to indicate an improvement in working conditions. However, other things are rarely equal and turnover is more sensitive to the availability locally of other jobs. I have therefore included data about local unemployment to set movement in the turnover figures in perspective. Overtime can be taken as a measure of the success with which management control systems are working. The problem of 'systematic overtime' — the use of overtime to make up earnings — has not been a major concern of ICI's management. It never reached the levels, for example, of the Fawley refinery — levels that made its elimination a high priority in the Fawley agreement. And the company has accepted that the need for overtime is inescapable in a maintenance function whose workload can fluctuate widely with periodic overhauls, emergencies and commissioning new plant. However, the importance of controlling overtime is no less important as a measure of the success with which management systems work. We have already seen that one of the spin-off effects of introducing WSA was to provide a framework and an occasion to re-think management systems, which is reflected (among other things) in the overtime data. We can see these changes demonstrated in some more detailed points about individual works.

1. *Gloucester**

The most striking measure of the effects of the changes brought about within WSA is given in the estimate of the works manager, already quoted, that twice as many people would be needed to achieve current (1973) rates of production. It can only be an estimate, since there were a number of major changes in the factory during the period under study: a new activity (warp-knit beaming) was installed; changes in the product mix resulted in a shift toward the finer deniers of yarn; and there were 'learning' changes in methods of working that are an inescapable part of any factory operation. For these reasons, the effects are most clearly reflected in the simplest available measure, numbers of people.

From a managerial point of view, possibly the most extraordinary feature of the Gloucester results is the fact that — unlike nearly all works and indeed the company as a whole — there was a net cash benefit from MUPS from the beginning. Moreover, the savings at Gloucester consistently exceeded the planned savings. Thus, in 1968, the first full year of MUPS working, the total manpower was 2,369 compared with 2,974 in September 1966 (pre-MUPS) — a saving in numbers of 23%. The labour costs went down from

---

* Only early trial works were studied in this depth. Once the process of introducing the agreements seemed to be underway, this sort of detailed interest lapsed.

£3.7m to £3.5m, a saving of 5.5%. And the 2,369 employees compared with a planned MUPS target of 2,435. In the next year there were still further savings: against a planned 2,503, the average number employed was 2,365, taking the savings up to 25.5%. However, the new WSA rates applied that year and labour costs went up to £3.9m so that notional savings against a pre-WSA cost adjusted for increased volume of production were 13%. During this time, the average cost per head had been rising steeply: £1,230 in September 1966; an average of £1,460 in 1968 and £1,640 in 1969; to £1,830 in May 1970 — an increase of 57% which, by 1970, had eliminated any direct savings on MUPS.

These figures can only be indications; the datum points have had to include adjustments for inflation and changes in work patterns and capacity utilisation. Moreover, they obscure some important points of detail. More was lost from the payroll than from monthly staff: of the 756 in numbers saved by 1969, 139 were monthly staff, representing a 22% reduction in staff numbers, compared with 26 per cent savings in weekly staff numbers. But those 139 were predominantly supervisors and represented the highest rate of rundown in numbers of any group in the works, 40%. Of the 617 savings in weekly staff, process workers showed the' highest rate: 546 fewer, representing 27% savings, compared with 57 (22%) on the craft side. This fact demonstrated that the craft unions were not the most threatened.

Table 3 Manpower Savings at Gloucester

	Sept. '66 (pre MUPS)	1968 Average	1969 Average	May 1970
Manpower:				
Actual	2,974	2,369	2,365	
— Monthly	624		474	
— Weekly	2,350		1,891	1,931
Adjusted plan		2,435	2,503	
Savings*	—	23%	25.5%	
Costs:				
Actual	£3,671,340	£3,483,616	£3,897,598	
Savings*	—	10%	13%	12%
Average pay per head	£1,230	£1,460 (+ 19%)	£1,640 (+ 33%)	£1,830

* Against adjusted datum line, taking into account new work and levels of working.

In real terms, however, these numbers cannot reflect more than a small part — the productivity bargain or rational-economic aspects — of the changes, which are also to be found in methods of work and such morale indicators as turnover (below 5%) and labour troubles (nil). Almost more significant than these, the management has been able to keep the agreement open-ended: a process of review allows a continuing enlargement of jobs and further savings in manpower. Thus, by 1972 savings in manpower, allowing for new work in the factory, were up to 37%; output per man had increased by approximately 40%.

But by then there were signs of resistance among the unions, the reasons for which are worth examining since they illuminate the basic paradox of the unions' position, whether they cooperate with or resist changes. By 1972, two things were happening: unemployment was high throughout the country and the excitement had drained away from the WSA exercise, leaving its operation in the open. As a result of the first there was a generalised feeling among shop stewards that they had a duty to hold on to all jobs and resist further encroachments into the precious pool of employment available to their members. In some unions, this took the form of an instruction from headquarters. At the same time, the atmosphere created by the Conservative government's Industrial Relations Act made any cooperation with management something like high treason.

2. *Hillhouse*

The works passed the first test, of being self-supporting in terms of savings from improved manning against costs of increases in salaries. Strict comparisons are difficult to make since, in the time since the agreement was introduced, a number of smaller plants and one major plant (the carbide furnace) were closed down; others, including a complete vinyl chloride unit, were started up. Nor are statistical morale indicators very significant. The plant has had only strike in its history — the one-day national strike called by the AUEW in protest against the Industrial Relations Bill in 1971; overtime was well-controlled even before the agreement and has fluctuated with the commissioning of new plants more than with changes introduced by the agreement. Voluntary turnover shows a drop from 10% in 1965 to under 2% in 1971 — but 1971 was a time of high unemployment. Total time lost through sickness, absenteeism and other causes, fell from an average of 6.1% in 1965 to 5% in 1971. None of these statistics provides a conclusive argument about the effectiveness of the agreement. A more convincing 'managerial' measure — although cruder, because of the changes listed above — is in the reductions in people employed through improved manning. On the Mond site, 109 people were saved out of 853, allowing for extra staff required in the commissioning of new plant. (Overall, between 1965 and 1972, the numbers of monthly staff dropped by 20% and of weekly staff by 18%, to 558 and 2,034 respectively.) The result of this was a saving of £10,000 per year which was turned, at the higher WSA rates, into a loss of £65,000. However, including savings in staff — mainly managerial and supervisory staff — the net result has been break-even.

The basis of WSA was to be that the company would hand over all savings in improvements in manning to the unions in the form of higher wages, keeping indirect savings as their part of the deal. These too have been relatively small at Hillhouse. An example of indirect savings is the improved efficiency in the operations of the cells attained by making 'on shift adjustments'. These have resulted in £20,000 a year savings in electricity — but such savings have to be related to Hillhouse total costs of about £12½m a year. Other savings are so indirect as to be difficult to see, let alone to quantify.

3. Billingham

The introduction of WSA coincided with two major changes in Billingham's working environment: the rise in unemployment through 1970-2; and a large number of redundancies from plant closures. The first hardened the unions' attitudes against any changes which would reduce the number of jobs available to their members. The second cast a blight over the site and further reduced any willingness to cooperate — although, ironically, the greatly improved communications that resulted from WSA made the redundancies easier to manage.

In terms of numbers, the drop was substantial, from 10,649 payroll and 3,579 staff in the first quarter of 1965 to 7,187 and 2,487 in the second quarter of 1973 — a drop of 33% and 30% respectively. However, the plant closures accounted for 2,000 payroll and 230 supervisors in that period — excluding managers and indirect staff (i.e. associated central services such as personnel and accounts). Of the 3,462 reduction in payroll, therefore, 1,462 could be attributed to improvements in working (through WSA), minor closures and reductions in service jobs. Paul Marsden, general manager of the site, points out that it is 'fairly fruitless' to try and allocate these jobs to different categories, since they are not as separate as they seem. Moreover, some genuine WSA savings were made in plants that later closed down.

Productivity undoubtedly increased during the period. For example, while numbers were being run down production of two main and fairly representative Agricultural Division products, ammonia and methanol, increased by 25% and 875% respectively. But much of this productivity was also due to changes in technology and new investment: between 1963 and 1972, £77.6m was spent on new plant by Agricultural division, but because of the shutdowns the division's assets actually dropped between 1966 and 1972, from £112m to £103m.

On the other side of the picture, the workforce benefited substantially. The average earnings of all Billingham site workers (in a sample week) went from £20.20 in 1965 to £41.20 in 1972. (In Agricultural Division, general workers earnings went from £19.25 to £40.45 and engineering craftsmen went from £22.75 to £43.05; craft day workers, who gather plentiful overtime, did best as a group with an increase from £22.60 to £47.80).As a result, even with the manpower reductions, the Billingham site annual manpower bill increased, from £11 million in 1965 to £16 million in 1972.

The effects on workforce morale and behaviour are, to some extent, reflected in the figures for labour turnover, which dropped from 14.5% to 8% between 1965 and 1972, and for sickness and strikes. A less ambiguous measure of achievement in the turbulent conditions is shown in overtime, which was 11% in 1965 and 4% in 1972. This too needs a gloss — since the high levels of 1965-70 to some extent reflect the high level of construction and maintenance activity due to new investment. Re-thinking the work also provided opportunities for introducing planning control systems in other works. Overtime is more strictly controlled now than it was because there are better systems and because, for example, managers have computer programs available which carry out instant cost-benefit studies which can tell whether overtime is justified.

At a more detailed level, changes have been brought about both within management and in the workforce. Enriching jobs has inevitably reduced the amount of supervision needed. In the Product Works, a management structure which had seven steps between works manager and assistant foreman has been reduced to one with four — with a saving of 88 supervisors out of 250.

4. Nylon Ardeer

We should note briefly that although there was no 'before' situation for comparison, there were substantial notional savings. When the new works was sanctioned, in 1965, it was estimated that the payroll would be 1,164. This was reduced to 1,063 when assumptions were changed to allow the use of contractors for certain types of sporadic maintenance. In the event, the numbers employed by October 1972 had come down still further, to 878 — a reduction of 18 per cent on the revised figure.

ICI's progress*

In common with all other major chemical companies, ICI went through a complete trade cycle (usually between four and five years) during the introduction of WSA. Trading profit went from a low of £61m in 1966 to a peak of £100m in 1968 and £97m in 1969 and dropped back to £64m in 1971. This was reflected in the return on funds employed, which went from 8.1% in 1966 to 11.4% in 1968 and back to

* The data in this section refer to ICI Ltd — a larger population, because including subsidiaries like Imperial Metal Industries Ltd, than the so-called 'CPD population'. Conclusions cannot be more than indicative of trends.

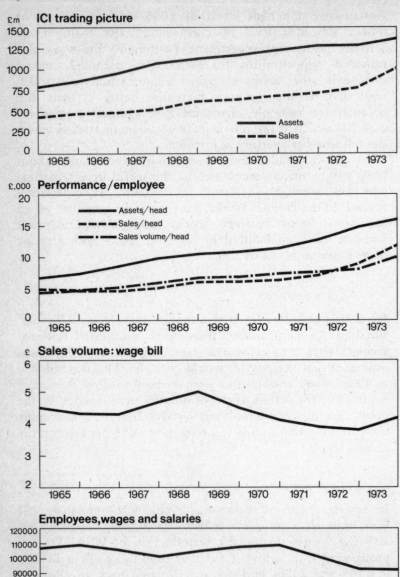

Fig.10 ICI Limited

ICI trading picture

£m, vertical axis: 0, 250, 500, 750, 1000, 1250, 1500

Years: 1965, 1966, 1967, 1968, 1969, 1970, 1971, 1972, 1973

— Assets
- - - Sales

Performance/employee

£,000, vertical axis: 0, 5, 10, 15, 20

Years: 1965, 1966, 1967, 1968, 1969, 1970, 1971, 1972, 1973

— Assets/head
- - - Sales/head
-·-· Sales volume/head

Sales volume: wage bill

£, vertical axis: 2, 3, 4, 5, 6

Years: 1965, 1966, 1967, 1968, 1969, 1970, 1971, 1972, 1973

Employees, wages and salaries

vertical axis: 90000, 100000, 110000, 120000

— Total employees

£m, vertical axis: 100, 150, 200, 250

Years: 1965, 1966, 1967, 1968, 1969, 1970, 1971, 1972, 1973

- - - Wages and salaries

7.3% in 1971. The cycle is important for two reasons:
providing the economic setting within which WSA was
introduced and demonstrating the extraordinarily unfortunate timing of the introduction. For, in order to produce
the extra chemicals to meet market demand, the number of
ICI's employees was increased by 5,700 between 1967 and
1970 to 102,500. Demand fell and unemployment rose in the
1970-2 period. As a result WSA was introduced, from
end-1969 onward, both from a high platform of manning and
in a climate peculiarly unfriendly to job reductions. A large
part of the manpower reductions that were so expensively
bought merely took ICI back to a level of manning
appropriate to the low point of the cycle.

However, labour productivity certainly increased substantially. Sales and production volume per employee increases as
below (annual rates):

	Sales/employee	Change in ICI Price Index	Production vol/employee
1963-72	8.5%	-1%	8.5%
1969-70	5.7	0	5.7
1970-1	10.4	3	7.4
1971-2	18.2	1	17.2

At the same time, the average cost per employee increased by
two-thirds, to £2,700 per head, between 1968 (the WSA base
year) and 1973. Numbers employed dropped by 7,000 in
that period, to 89,600 — having reached 102,500 in 1970.
By themselves, these figures suggest a crude cost-benefit
trade-off: higher salaries, fewer people and greater productivity. But much else was happening.

1. *Capital investment.* In the period 1968-72, ICI Ltd
invested £473m in fixed assets. Gross fixed assets increased
by 30%, to £1,330m. Fixed assets per employee increased by
40%, which is to say that the plant available to each
employee, his productive hardware, increased by that
amount: even without WSA, 'productivity' would have been
strongly affected. And this understates the effect of capital
investment quite considerably. For at the time that MUPS
was introduced, ICI plunged into a massive capital investment

program designed to bring ICI's plant up to the competitive mark, just as MUPS was designed to reform its use of people. In 1965 and 1966, ICI Ltd spend £123m and £138m on capital plant; the full effects of this expenditure were not felt for some years because of technical problems and other delays in commissioning to full capacity. It would therefore be more realistic to take 1965 as a base year for capital employed: *in that period 1965/72 gross fixed assets per employee exactly doubled.*

2. *Product mix.* The composition of both inputs and outputs is highly dynamic, responding to changes in production technology, the development of new products and prices and demand in both consuming and supplying markets. Factories are constantly adjusting to these changes, which have marked effects on productivity.

3. *Capacity effects.* Probably most important of all is the effect on productivity of level of demand, and so of production. In large chemical plants, labour costs are partially fixed costs: the scope for changing them in concert with levels of production is limited. It is vividly illustrated by the sharp increase in ICI's profits in 1973, a year in which many factors (including devaluation) came together and all indices of performance rose sharply. The investments of 1965-71 and changes in manpower utilisation provided a setting in which a high level of demand produced ICI's best year. How much of this improvement was due to the gains of WSA is a question that cannot be answered.

What we can do, however, is to set ICI in its international context. Many of the same market factors provided a setting for all the large international chemical companies. ICI can be usefully compared to its main European and American competitors over the 1968-72 period in terms of those statistics. The absolute figures are of little value for comparative purposes, since they reflect large differences between the companies in capitalisation, in product mix and in structure. These differences are illustrated in Table 4.

However, the comparisons are more meaningful when looked at in terms of annual rates of change. Over the years 1969 to 1972 the average annual increase in ICI sales value

Table 4 *(£000's)*

	Dow	Du Pont	BASF	Hoechst	ICI
Sales value per employee 1972	21.2	17.1	16.0	12.5	8.8
Fixed assets per employee 1972	25.1	21.5	–	–	14.8

per employee was 11½%, a higher figure than any of its main competitors, whose annual rates of increase ranged between about 4% and 9½%. Over that period also ICI did better than its competitors in added value per employee. On the other hand, the percentage of the employee costs to sales relationship rose somewhat more in ICI than in most of its European competitors – but all the European companies did less well than their American counterparts in this respect, probably reflecting a lesser ability to absorb this element of increased cost through capital and scale. These comparisons suggest some relative increase in ICI productivity over the period, although the improvement in added value is open to question in its end effects, remembering that employee cost is a component. However the data can only be taken as broadly indicative, since there is the obvious shortcoming that they do not reflect changes in the value of money in a period in which inflation has had such a marked and varied effect upon costs and prices both at home and abroad.

Bearing all these reservations in mind, a number of internal estimates were made to try to assess the effects of WSA in isolation from the other factors. These have involved heroic assumptions about 'what would have happened without WSA': essentially they have been based on the known decline in numbers over the 1968-70 period, adjusted to take account of the plant closures and new plants, adjusted also by estimates of savings generated by the application of WSA principles in the new plants. They have necessarily produced ranges of effects rather than precise numbers, and they range from a high end-1972 'loss' of £34m to a low of £3m. If the low figure is nearer the truth, as in my view it is, the company should have broken even on the deal some time in 1973. This view is supported by discussions around the company with works managers who, on the whole, agree that 'break-even' is the best approximation of WSA's effects. In the next chapter we shall look further into the implications of this conclusion, for it is by no means the last word — it is, in fact, only the beginning of an attempt to map the achievements of WSA.

14
Results 2.
The Soft Face of WSA

Asked to assess the consequences of a major policy decision, a manager versed in the quantitative arts might be expected to start with the assumption that if the effects do not appear in the profit and loss accounts they do not exist. We have seen that the best guess at the financial results of WSA indicates a break-even situation. Would we be right in concluding, therefore, that battle between costs and benefits for the company has ended in a draw? That nothing significant has changed? On the contrary, I shall argue that the most important changes would not by their nature appear in the accounts immediately. The benefits from them have been considerable, bringing ICI more into tune with its social environment; they will be more so, laying the foundations for continuing change and improvement.

The amount of work involved was colossal in total, but detailed in application. It is this aspect that it is so important to grasp when looking at the changes achieved. For the basic unit of change was the individual job. And this involved an enormous amount of hard-slogging, detailed, but, to an outside observer, largely invisible work. Many of the most important changes have been similarly low-key, but of fundamental importance in determining how the organisation was to work in the future. The NBPI Report of 1969 had this to say:

'In order to introduce the scheme in a particular works and to take full advantage of it, it has been necessary to examine every operation of every process, to identify all the tasks necessary in carrying out any particular operation, to determine the manning necessary and the number of tasks formerly the prerogative of craftsmen that by agreement could be performed by operators, as and when necessary, and vice versa. This has been completely worked out after full discussion and by agreement at all levels and at all stages, fully written up and formally agreed. This has involved a massive exercise in communications since every worker involved has attended very often several discussion meetings before agreement relating to his own particular sphere of activity has been reached . . .'

If we had no other measure, the amount of work done in analysing work and agreeing job descriptions would be some indication of the extent of change brought about in the company. It is as if the only measure of the amount of work done cutting metal in a machine shop was the wear on the tools and consumption of electricity. In fact, engineering outputs are easily defined and measured; in a programme of organisational change they are neither, and we can only infer the amount of change from the amount of work that went into it, and by description. But if agreeing job descriptions was the main 'output' of the exercise, the effort required was grossly disproportionate. The changes went much further. The re-design of every shopfloor job in the company enforced re-thinking the jobs further up in the structure. The primary result was a substantial amount of enrichment and enlargement of — or merely the unaccustomed exercise of thinking imaginatively about — jobs. But because the process of doing this was cooperative, with shop stewards and workers closely involved in erstwhile 'management' decisions, much more was called into question and re-examined: assumptions about roles and relationships; who is to be involved in decision-making and where the information relevant to decisions is to be found. It was also an essential starting-point for the whole exercise that management should get its own house in order, so that the process of introducing WSA enforced a re-think of management systems of planning and control throughout the company. In all the introduction of WSA was a gigantic task, far greater than its originators and the Board members who let it through can have realised. Although its results fell well short of the apocalyptic expectations of its more enthusiastic supporters, to have achieved so much, to leave the ground so well-prepared for further change and to have done it, in effect, at nil financial cost was in any terms remarkable.

Asked to sum up the changes brought about by WSA, a senior manager said: 'I can put it in one word, cooperation.' Which is to say, as he went on to point out, that relationships between managers and managed based on authority and one-way communication had been replaced by something more open, still far from equal but allowing more interaction and participation: and that a basic assumption of endless conflict between unions (defenders of their members' rights) and managers (servants of capital) was being challenged by the discovery of areas of common interest. More practically, managing could no longer be a matter of technical problem-solving — in theory leading to a set of unilateral commands and prescriptions, but in practice often leading to negotiating situations with the unions that basically took the form, 'You tell us what you want and we'll tell you what we agree to — and for how much.' Instead, there was the beginning of a more open, joint problem-solving approach of which the spontaneous growth in some places of work groups was an expression — of need and usefulness. It was quite as much a question of the managers' willingness to share some of their power, or just information, as of the shop stewards' willingness to listen. The channels of communication opened up during the process of introduction were being used: by the shop stewards to sort problems out before they became serious; and by managers to keep people informed about results, problems and likely changes.

This is the best face of change: it is not typical of the company as a whole. We have seen how some works have made strenuous and imaginative attempts to keep the ideas of WSA a continuing part of their activities. But other works, for reasons that will be obvious from the accounts of individual experiences, quickly reverted: an exhausted management slumped back, having achieved their 'target'; the unchanged external environment came sweeping in, having been kept back by the excitement of introduction, to wash away any changes in attitudes in the workforce. But it is to the best we should be looking for signs of what can be achieved. The regular meetings of the work groups in which information is passed both ways: the now-established custom of informing the stewards and work groups concerned of any major changes well before they take place and to invite their help in dealing with problems that might arise — to the point of deciding not to go ahead with some changes. The result is a more cooperative method of working. I shall start by looking at the changes in attitude that are the ultimate measure of organisation change.

Attitudes

The only generalisation possible is that, inasmuch as there was a consistent direction of attitude change throughout the company as a result of WSA, it was towards cooperation. But local variations were acute, from 'no change' at the more obdurate sites of the Northeast to the quite startling changes at other sites. As a first approximation, we can draw a naive distinction between the attitudes of managers and of union members, and I shall look at attitudes I observed under these headings. But it is naive because it has to be seen in the light of another marked split, between local and national groupings. Management and unions, in some circumstances, had more in common with each other — as it were, laterally — at the national and local levels than they had vertically, within their own structures. That is, it was possible for ICI and the signatory unions to reach an agreement centrally since both shared a 'national' vantage-point from which to survey company and union problems and both reached the same main conclusions. But they could not convince their own people at the local level, who shared very different perceptions of the situation and the effects on it — or, more to the point, on their own lives — of the new agreement. The split appeared more overtly between local and national union organisations than within the management structure, which could command power (in particular, power over the reward system) not available to the unions. However, opposition to MUPS/WSA was never a strong overt bond between local unions and management — except at Wilton, where they found common cause in 1968 when trying to gain acceptance of a special deal. But it did, and does, emerge in such ways as the collusion between management and shop stewards to pack job descriptions to gain as favourable an assessment as possible, an odd sort of activity for a manager but understandable in terms of the problems he might be facing locally — and of a desire to do the best for the people under his command.

1. *Shopfloor*

It is tempting to view the shopfloor as a single body of people with relatively homogeneous attitudes and behaviour. As I have already pointed out, there is immense variety between locations and, within a location, between union groups. I found a sharper distinction between the union members and their shop stewards, whom I shall therefore deal with separately.

There was a striking similarity of views between people I spoke to at shopfloor level. The answer to my usual starting question, 'Would you want to return to pre-WSA pay structure and conditions?', was *unanimously* negative. The main reason was, of course the higher WSA rates, closely followed by the stability of the annual salary as a basis for payment. Many pronounced themselves heartily glad to be free of the old bonus incentive and the endless aggravations it gave rise to. But it did not take much questioning to get deeper, into the area of job satisfaction where there was a wider range of response.

The most positive reactions came from workers in works which had the most outstanding WSA successes: the new system had been imaginatively introduced, there was still some of the enthusiasm left and a cooperative spirit permeated the works. I am talking of such works as Gloucester, Castner-Kellner, Hillhouse, and even at Nylon Ardeer where the 'spirit of WSA' was under heavy pressure from the works environment. It is dangerous to generalise from such particularities, but these cases do mark one extreme of the responses to the agreement.

The middle of the distribution — perhaps over half the people I spoke to — was marked by indifference to the motivational aspects of job enrichment, although not to such other changes as work group discussions and regular information sessions with management. The indifference took in some cases a form — 'I do what I'm told. I mean, you only work for money, don't you?' — so elaborate as to tempt me to look for other reasons: for example, defensiveness (against the unfamiliar idea of being involved with hated work) or disappointment.

Indeed, the only strongly negative shopfloor reactions I encountered were centred on frustration at the lack of progress along the path laid down in WSA. This was widespread. Where management was criticised, it was not for change so much as for lack of it. ('We had all this stuff about job enrichment. Well, where is it?') It was an ironic reversal of my first expectations. But these may have been naive. For it seems likely that, once given reassurances about job security, there is little reason (among general workers anyway) to cling to existing ways of doing things. This has obviously been less true of the craft unions, who benefited considerably from their protected status. In contrast, it should be obvious that no group of individuals has a larger long-term personal investment in the status quo than management. What started as a management-led campaign, aimed at shopfloor, to change working practices, has become in some places a shopfloor-led, management-resisted move to take the changes further. A more usual view of industrial change might be one in which managers are proposing imaginative and far-sighted courses of action which are opposed by the workforce. In fact, once a worker is convinced that a change is in his interest — and particularly in his financial interest — there is very little reason for him to oppose it so long as his needs for security are met. It is the systems that surround him, unions and management with their heavy investment in and commitment to the existing ways of working, existing values and relationships, who are ultimately the obstacle to movement.

2. *Shop stewards*

The reactions of shop stewards must be charted on a different map. Not just because they are, by observation, different; but because the steward is himself in a different relationship with a project like WSA. As representatives of his union's members and guardian of its long-term interests, his is a political role. He must want to perform it, since he offers himself for the job, and this again marks him out as different: more politically-aware (in the usual sense) and presumably with abilities and power needs that can only find outlets in such a role. The unions' position *vis à vis* management is almost entirely a defensive one: partly by choice and partly because it is the only role the companies will allow. For these reasons, the stewards are built in as an opposition to managerial will — with the added frustration of being an opposition that is permanently out of power.

The attitudes of stewards, none the less, span a wider range than those of the shopfloor workers: from the extremely positive attitudes of some stewards at Gloucester ('I've never come across a place like this before. The stewards talk like managers and the managers talk like stewards') to the negative — and, in my view, tragically destructive — attitudes in the Northeast. The TUC report on shop stewards' attitudes to WSA (Roberts and Wedderburn) is a compilation of this sort of response. 'A con trick . . .', 'All drivel . . .', 'Brain-washing . . .' — and a far more complete account than I can attempt. These reactions express quite fundamental resistances to changes that have complex roots: they might upset the power balance: the company might succeed in putting across a view of the industrial situation that would change and limit the role of the unions. The TUC report reflects a strong feeling among stewards that the company was somehow dishonourably using the higher pay of WSA as a bribe to the workers, who could not be trusted to safeguard their own interests against such a temptation. The stewards were there to defend their unions' job opportunities and to look after the defences accumulated over years of union activity against the managers' unfettered use of their power. More specifically, the craft unions (particularly the AUEW) were not likely to relinquish their demarcations — of which, again, the craft stewards were the first line of defence. Where this attitude could not be dented by managerial blandishment — or dissolved away in an atmosphere of trust — the traditional bargaining stance dominated all proceedings: 'How little do we have to give away to get the money?' (And the answer was, at a site like Wilton where the management had exhausted itself, very little.) It is entirely consistent with this approach that the behavioural aspects of WSA should be ripely scorned as irrelevant and fancy additions to the real issues.

Lastly, WSA hit more directly at the personal basis of a steward's power by replacing a negotiable bonus incentive with an impartial method of assessment. 'We have nothing left to play with', one Wilton steward said, with remarkable frankness. The agreement had, at a stroke, cut away a large part of his role. (Not necessarily a wise move.) The net result, at a meeting with the Wilton senior stewards, was a unanimous, 'Yes!' in answer to my lead question, 'Would you like to go back . . .?' But it became apparent on the same day that this was the stewards' view alone, and in no way representative of the men they were representing.

It is worth considering this paradox for a moment, for the reply was a *group* answer and would probably have been (and, on occasion, was) contradicted in private conversation. Public votes are an affirmation of publicly-held principles; a private vote may come closer to the individual's needs. But stewards are, within their works, public men.

3. *The managers*

For my evidence on the manager's view, some of the same rules apply. Speaking for the record — for example, to a visiting writer — a disaffected, or merely disillusioned, manager is likely to support a company policy that he will attack the same night, after a good dinner.* It will not be surprising that I received very mixed signals. Rational doubts were expressed by a few managers who, while conceding the WSA was in tune with the changing social environment, maintained that it had come too soon and without enough preparation.

The enthusiasts for WSA were almost entirely to be found, as with shopfloor workers, where it had worked. Which came first, the success or the enthusiasm, is a moot point. Lack of enthusiasm was to be found where the agreement had not achieved what had been hoped. This was truer in works where the technology was seen to be

---

* One senior manager took the trouble to write to me and deny the things he'd said a couple of days previously. I'd make the mistake of continuing what had seemed a valuable discussion by letter and he had to 'put the record straight . . .'

inappropriate, or where commercial circumstances imposed tight constraints and any 'softening' towards the workforce increased costs in ways that seemed senseless. On a site like Wilton, where the technology was appropriate but the constraints were political, the managers were more sympathetic — they could see the point of the exercise even if reaching the objective was going to be a long slog.

One exception to the generally positive — or, at worst, neutral — response was a senior manager who spoke of the whole exercise with scathing contempt. His own works had encountered nearly insuperable problems and he was not prepared to admit any success at other works: if there was an apparent success it was entirely due to special factors (which is, of course, at least partly true). It is not belittling the rational content of his criticisms to suggest that the need to come to terms with a sense of failure lies at the roots of much of the reported cynicism and disillusion about the agreement. The experience of introducing WSA demonstrated that there was no simple rule, no *complete* explanation in terms of technology and local factors for the variations between works that could absolve managers from their responsibility for the outcome.

A more thoughtful, less defensive response came from an engineer who wrote to me in 1973: 'I find the ideals and values expressed in WSA to be wholly acceptable and in line with my own . . . But I don't think that we were ready for it. I don't think we are ready now: not management, supervision, weekly staff nor the unions. I believe that an analysis of the needs of the site would probably produce something more like a Scanlon scheme (a straight incentive scheme linked to productivity increases) than an open-ended scheme like WSA.' In other words, he rejected the most innovative feature of WSA as being too ambitious. He also felt that the greatest benefits were the result of purely management initiatives, by way of improving planning and control systems, for which a major behavioural change programme was, strictly speaking, unnecessary. But whether such changes would have been made so widely without the stimulus of WSA is another question.

The best picture of what works managers in the company felt they had got out of the agreement is to be found in nearly fifty reports prepared at the end of 1971 for the joint company/union conference held at Windermere in January 1972. Some items were almost universal in these reports. The most common comment — not much to do with WSA — was that further change had come almost to a halt in the climate of high unemployment then prevailing. But, given that, among the benefits listed were:

— Getting away from 'interminable bonus disputes'.
— The integration of engineering and process workers that the re-thinking process made possible. Also, improvements in planning systems.
— Improving the relations between managers, supervisors and the shopfloor.
— Setting the stage for future improvements in results (although this was clearly seen as resting on management initiative).

Among the disadvantages, or costs, were:

— Rising sickness absence.
— Lack of fundamental change in attitudes.
— New demarcations in the job descriptions.
— Disproportion between efforts and results.

Among problems foreseen for the future:

— Constraints imposed by lack of promotion prospects at the top of the scale.
— Difficulty in getting further change given large steps in pay structure.
— Interest in negotiation migrating to conditions payments and other variables not covered in the agreement.

Some of the managers felt that the benefits were not specific to WSA, summed up in one comment: 'Savings have been hard work and are due to management effort rather than to any built-in blessings associated with WSA. It could be argued that most of our savings could and should have been made without WSA . . .'

More telling were the worries about making the new style and the easier rules work in an unchanged environment. 'The basic attitude changes we all talked about so glibly during pre-WSA discussions have been very slow to arrive . . . [There is] no doubt that everyone does extremely well when an emergency situation declares itself. It is in these times one sees the real potential . . . and receives heart to continue with the struggle for further improvement.' But in one works where 40% of the general workers were on manual and repetitive jobs, the manager commented fatalistically, 'To payroll WSA was nothing more or less than a straight productivity deal, a means by which they got higher earnings . . . the general workers' work is very boring . . . it is not surprising that the men . . . tend to be uncooperative and extremely rigid in their attitudes . . .' It was a rigidity that was confirmed by the lack of change elsewhere. Another manager said: 'The craftsmen gave away virtually nothing . . . feeling among the general workers that they've been conned . . . hardening attitudes . . .' To attempt to bring about change in a community within a much larger unchanged community is to see how difficult and ambitious the job was in the first place.

Lastly, there should be no doubt that the managers felt extremely exposed and vulnerable without the traditional sanctions, specifically the bonus incentive scheme. This belonged to the old untrusting days, when everything that moved was measured. Were the old sanctions thrown out too blithely? ICI had acquired a great expertise in their use and the managers felt the ease and confidence of familiarity. To relax the rules when many of the attitudes remained unchanged was to invite abuse. But it is an irresolvable paradox, for unless they were relaxed there would be no change of attitude. One manager commented on the need for middle-class attitudes if the new arrangements were to work and concluded that 'it would take several generations to breed out the old attitudes . . .' If this is true, it is not a truth confined to the shopfloor. Another manager gave his opinion that it would need at least 15 years before the attitudes of managers would have changed enough for WSA working to become an intrinsic part of working life. Management attitudes have been a key determinant of the progress of

WSA, not just on to but through WSA.

Participation

The introduction of participative decision-making was not one of the overt objectives of — or, so far as I know, even articulated by — the original designers of the agreement. But it was at the heart of the *process* of introduction and, inasmuch as job enrichment yields more control within the boundaries of a job, it was one of the considerations in job design. More fundamentally, if the purpose of WSA — and its main achievement — was to shift the company towards a more cooperative way of working, it is hard to think of a more suitable area for cooperation than in the decisions that affect people's working lives. I have looked at this in Chapter 12, when discussing the growth of work groups and work group discussions and do not propose to cover the same ground. To be consulted about his own job was a totally new experience for most workers and allowed the process of introduction to tap into a great source of the energy for change. Moreover, once started, the process could not be stopped without incurring a heavy cost in terms of people's attitudes. (This happened in some places.) Given the taste of participation, it appears that workers will insist on having their say and are prepared to be constructive about it. Three examples will illustrate this:

— The works manager at Castner-Kellner told senior shop stewards, in a regular meeting, that a new cell-room was to be built. (Brine is split into chlorine and sodium in electrolytic cells, an important Mond Division process.) It emerged in discussion that the previous cell-room, although technically advanced, presented some difficulties in maintenance. The fitters said that they could suggest ways around these problems. As a result, they became involved in the design of the new plant: a model cell was built which enabled them to try out their jobs and suggest modifications to cope with problems that the engineer designing the unit could not possibly have foreseen. It was a way of bringing relevant information and experience into the decisions.

— At Gloucester, the works manager has been in the habit of signalling changes long before they appear and finds the response of the people involved invariably helpful. He told me of a new machine being introduced into one of the areas which would have effects on manning. The matter was put in front of the plant committee before the decision to invest had been made. By the time the machine appeared, some months later, everything to do with it had been exhaustively discussed; the people likely to be affected had all had chances to make their views known. When the machine came, there were no problems about the change, which was fully understood. Another Gloucester example concerned a new method of working, 'random' doffing, which had been worked out by a plant engineer and seemed to offer some theoretical advantages. It was known that it would probably be more difficult to operate but it might lead to significant savings in conversion. There was some head-shaking when the idea was brought up at the plant committee and prophecies that the techniques would not work for all sorts of un-theoretical reasons. None the less, one of the doffing teams willingly tried it experimentally. When they reported that the technique didn't work — that is, that the practical difficulties outweighed the benefits — their view was accepted by the management, although with some grumbling.

— A manager at Nylon Ardeer, whom I was questioning about the difference between that works and the similar one at Wilton, said: 'You won't find any important differences in manning. The real difference is in speed of reaction and simple efficiency. At Wilton you have to go through the system; the management structure is traditional* so that decisions involve managers at a higher level than we find necessary. We try and make sure that they are taken straight away at the level where relevant knowledge and experience is found.' And he mentioned a problem that had arisen the previous year, when a unit broke down at Wilton. Could the Ardeer unit operate at higher levels of production? The problem was given to the plant manager (the second of four tiers in the structure) and the answer was provided by the

* It has changed since he left the works but his point still stands.

shift teams. They ran the unit at 40% above rated capacity
for a month: At Wilton the problem would probably have
been given to the top level of management and solved within
the management structure, quite possibly less well (in the
manager's view) than was possible at Ardeer, because the
relevant knowledge would not have been so readily available.
'This sort of swift and flexible response would not have been
possible.'

Specific examples like these could be multiplied to fill a
book by themselves. The point is made: that assumptions
about who takes decisions have been successfully challenged
and that new ways of working are being explored. Even at
Wilton, where the introduction of WSA has achieved less than
elsewhere in the company, both managers and shop stewards
agreed to me that communication had not so much improved
as become possible as a result of the exercise of introduction
and at nearby Billingham, the extremely difficult problem of
contraction, and its implications for the workforce, could
only have been solved without disruption within the framework of communication WSA established. Jim Bell, personnel
director at the time said: 'Once we had analysed the
situation, I immediately told the conveners. There was some
grumbling but only a couple of threats to strike in protest.
The more experienced conveners soon put an end to that by
pointing out that strikes would only make the commercial
position of the site more dicey still and would imperil such
jobs that were left. Once the basic information was communicated, joint working parties were set up to organise the
run-down. It had to be done in the best interests of the
company, the community and the workers'. This comment
contains much about the meaning of participation. The
problem was not kept within the management camp and a
'solution' handed down, it was openly communicated and a
solution jointly arrived at. Almost certainly, the solution —
rate of run-down; people affected by redundancy; terms —
was not what the managers would have wanted if left to
themselves, but it was effective because it was in the
ownership of the people affected.

This is a very impressive achievement, taken across the
company, but it raises a number of questions which
stubbornly refuse to go away: about power, objectives,

stereotypes and manipulation. Participation, which has become something of a political buzzword, flatters the humane parts of all of us, but is riddled with logical inconsistencies which are not resolved by men of goodwill mumbling polite clichés at each other.

(*a*) If decision-making is genuinely participative, who is in charge? What is the job of a manager? Where does the power lie? In fact, what I have been discussing is only rarely participation: mostly, it has been a matter of consultation and discussion, mobilising the information (human as well as technical) in the system for the attention of the decision-maker. It is questionable whether group decision-making is possible at the present: a number of people told me that, where shopfloor workers and stewards were given the opportunity to take decisions, it was explicitly rejected; discussion was fine, but decision-making was not — perhaps because it implies not just responsibility (which people learn to enjoy) but commitment and, so, confusion of roles. In a number of works, there are attempts now being made to move toward 'autonomous group' working, on the model of the Norsk Hydro experiment. This may be the logical next step for the processes of change I have been describing.

(*b*) What is the objective of any decision-making process to be? Is the group to act in the interests of the company or of themselves? On a larger platform, this is the issue raised by the move to appoint worker-directors. A director has a function which he cannot perform if he is a representative, since decisions enforced by the rational-economic logic of maintaining the company's health may be inconsistent with the interests (narrowly defined) of sub-groups. Similarly, a work group may be forced by the logic of a situation to accept a decision which is against their own interest. If they refuse to take the 'right' decision is it the moment for the manager to reveal his hand, step forward and declare the company's interest? What is the reality of participation then? The issue does not arise yet, since the processes I have described are more consultative. But the paradox is waiting, like some shark of logic, underneath the peaceful waters of humane industrial policies. It can only be resolved when the objectives of the group coincide with those of the company.

One of the aims of WSA was to bring about such an alignment, but it takes time.

(c) Who is in the group? By which I do not just mean, Which individuals? (which answers itself) but, What roles? How long will the stereotypes of manager, shop steward, supervisor and worker persist? Communication between individuals is seriously hindered by their need to play out roles and their stereotypes of other people — and both are resistant to change. The paradox is that the roles are important organisationally, although they may be dysfunctional for group working.

(d) Whose interests are being served? What is the fundamental reality of openness and warmth in human relations when it is for some harder end than merely better relationships? This is a knotty question which I only want to raise: to the 'paradox of sincerity' there is no satisfying answer this side of Utopia.

Job enrichment

Re-structuring work was the means by which the changes of WSA were introduced and the central activity around which much else revolved. It cannot be said to dominate and lead the three headings under which I have chosen to examine the unquantifiable benefits of WSA; these are interdependent. However, the analysis of work, re-design of jobs, agreement of job descriptions and their assessment were by a long way the most concrete tasks in the process, the structure within which everything else happened, and the most solid and visible achievement.

MUPS did not start with a full-scale programme of job enrichment. The ideas about re-design of jobs started with the ideal manning studies which, the reader may remember, identified demarcations as the main obstacle to more efficient and productive organisation of work. I have described in Chapter 9 how the ideas of job enrichment were accepted and finally supplied the framework for a more systematic approach to the design of jobs than the agreement's *ad hoc* beginnings could provide. Looked at across the span of ICI activities, the resulting grades structure (Fig.11)

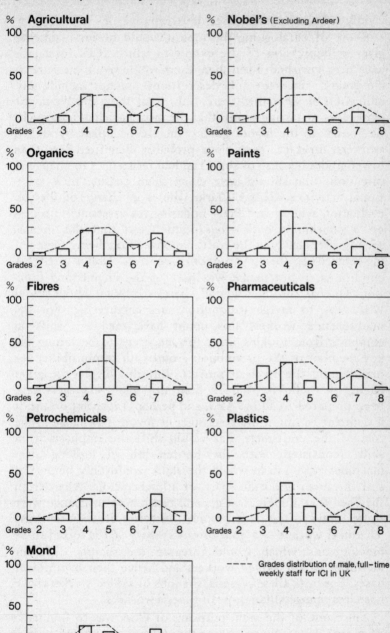

Fig.11 Grade profiles by division

vividly reflects the differences between divisions.

Short of cataloguing the jobs it would be impossible to give an impression of the extent to which ICI's total jobs have been enriched. Even then, there would be no measure of movement, since the job descriptions did not include any indication of what they were, only what they are. We might expect, as a starting point, that the most enriched jobs might be found at the higher grades, mostly occupied by skilled workers. In fact, they have probably benefited less than lower grades because of some residual resistances to change in directions that should have taken them outside their traditional activities. George Clark, who is in charge of the job evaluation scheme in CPD — updating the assessment process on a continuing basis — has pointed out that this means, specifically, changing the craftsman's role from being engineering-centred to being production-centred. Under pre-WSA conditions, maintenance was part of the engineering function. One of the 'managerial' changes brought about under WSA was to merge production and engineering. For the maintenance worker, this could have meant a shift in emphasis from looking after the *machines* to becoming the key member of the production group with responsibility for maintaining the level of *output*. But this involves a larger change in methods of work than most plant managers have been prepared to allow. Also, and perhaps more important, it is a threat to union interests since it involves a change in the role of the craftsmen that would shift the emphasis from skills (consistent with the limited job of looking after machines) to a job in which the skills would only be part, if still the most important part, of a larger whole. Apart from the fact that the greatest general resistances to change were to be found in the craft unions, this raises the spectre of the 'chemical worker' — a goal towards which ICI is feared to be moving, and which would threaten the sharply different identities of the skilled workers and hence their own power bases. For both these reasons, the jobs of skilled workers have been less changed than those of general workers.

Since one of the main purposes of WSA was to find ways of more adequately rewarding the skills of general workers, it is to be expected that a great deal was achieved in the process plants. This has involved some elements of inter-union flexibilities, but it has been more important to reorganise the work within teams, training people to do a range of jobs, encouraging movement within the teams and giving process workers many of the routine decisions that were formerly taken by assistant foremen.

However, these changes have been subject to the overriding constraint of management interest. According to Clark, the willingness of managers to encourage the radical re-design of jobs was far more important than the grade structure. 'Some of the most enriched jobs I have seen were amongst the lowest grades' he said, and cited the case of the lavatory attendant at one works. To his basic job of cleaning were added elements that gave him complete autonomy in his area of work: he was given the responsibility for ordering his cleaning materials and the paper and soap needed in the lavatories; he was given the job of making minor running repairs — replacing tap washers and repairing the 'furniture' — and trained to carry them out. I mention this in some ways absurd example because it illustrates well the detailed ways that jobs can be enriched — ways that owe nothing to the complexity of the technology but have much more to do with the completeness of the resulting job and the freedom given to the worker in carrying it out. According to Clark, the result was a far more satisfying job for the lavatory attendant, who is now a man with complete autonomy in his own work area.

'The main limiting factor to job enrichment is the imagination of the manager', Clark says, and points out that it required constant vigilance and an ability to ask the right questions to identify those pieces of a job that belong together and that have been separated in the past for reasons that are no longer good. 'We express our need as a company for fully-trained people, and then we supervise them to a point where no training is needed. There are many cases where, through long tradition, supervisors are involved in decisions that do not directly concern them. It is the worker on the job, for example, who must decide when more materials are needed. But he must get the supervisor to sign his requisition before he can collect them from the stores: Why?' The answer to that is probably something to do with assumptions about what people are capable of deciding for themselves. But we saw how, at Nylon Ardeer, it was possible to leave out the whole supervisory layer — reflected in the difference between the grade profiles of Ardeer and Wilton. It is an important part of the Ardeer picture that, in order to carry a degree of self-supervision, a higher class of worker was recruited — all of which emphasised the constraints on other works, which might have been tempted along the same path 'We couldn't abolish our supervisors even if we wanted to', the Nylon Works manager at Wilton said. 'We have to conform to the practice of the site and we simply cannot make changes like that by ourselves.' Moreover, 'We would have to develop a different standard of operator, with different skills, attention, understanding of his work . . .'

But, as we have seen, the most successful enrichment was not necessarily at the top of the grade scale. At Gloucester a notable example of changing the system of working in the Drawtwist area — banks of machines which take reels of yarn which they stretch, twist and wind up on to bobbins of specified weights, when the machine stops and the bobbin is doffed by a team which then sets it up for the next bobbin. A team of four men will handle banks of 8 to 20 machines, depending on the type of yarn. But the work does not appear in such a way that it can be smoothly spread over the available manpower and machines. The length of time taken to wind up a bobbin varies and the resulting pattern of doffing is irregular and bunching is unavoidable. To achieve maximum utilisation of the machines, the bobbins should be doffed as soon as they are filled. To get close to this ideal, a great deal of sophisticated mathematical analysis has gone into devising the optimum compromise. This went a good deal further than merely fixing manning levels; elaborate schedules were printed out by the computer every day, by which the doffing teams were strictly controlled. But this too was suboptimal, since it was based on rigid assumptions about the times needed to doff.

When the Drawtwist area came up for discussion in the MUPS trial, it emerged that there were all sorts of ways in which the teams could 'bend' their mode of operation to cope with bunching which could not be programmed on to a computer. It was decided to give the teams the chance to draw up their own schedules and make many of the running decisions by themselves, taking advantage of these flexibilities in practice. This eliminated many of the delays of the old system under which, for example, the operator had to tell a supervisor about a breakdown before the maintenance staff was informed; or make some simple adjustments — speed checking and cam setting. More unexpected, for amateurs of scientific management, was the improvement in operation resulting from having the teams schedule their own time. There was an immediate gain in machine efficiency of 5%, and the staffing was much reduced — on one bank from 50 to 35 men while the same work was done by 38 instead of 40 machines. Morale and satisfaction in the work greatly improved: 'Now we can plan our own work' — to the level of deciding when to take their breaks, previously part of the foreman's job.

Two other examples where a more complete view of the job led to greater freedom and autonomy among the workers were given me at Nylon Ardeer. Shortly before I visited the works, there had been an accident in the railway yard: a man had been injured. Following the normal procedure, a committee was swiftly convened to investigate the accident and met the same day. As a first action, the chairman of the committee said that, until they found out what had happened, all traffic should be banned from that section of the line. He was told by the senior operator in the works team that *he* had already given the order on his own authority. Another illustration from Nylon Ardeer was given to me of how the teams have learned to act more efficiently because autonomously. There had been an early morning failure at the power generating plant — which always causes an immediate crisis in a chemical factory where reactions are in progress. However, in this case the emergency lighting supply failed too and with it the telephones. But the elaborate series of controlled changes for shut-down was gone through quite smoothly, without supervision from the managers who had rushed to the plant (as it were in their pyjamas) to oversee it and then found themselves superfluous to the operation and sitting helplessly in a darkened office.

Demarcations were not the obstacles to such changes that they had appeared at the beginning of the exercise. First, because many parts of the company were already working flexibly, but informally. As a T&G steward said at Rock Savage Works: 'We were doing things that were unheard of in the Northeast.' At another works, a process worker in a shift team I spoke with said: 'There is no demarcation here.' The shift fitter added, 'We don't mind them using tools. If they can do the work, it's not skilled.' And this seemed an accepted, if informal, definition of allowable flexibilities.

It might be possible to say that, where flexibilities were a real problem, it was never overcome — as at Wilton and Doncaster. In any case, the changes made possible by flexible working lay more in the area of job enlargement than enrichment — horizontal rather than vertical extension. Thus, at Hillhouse, an outstandingly successful example of flexible working was the 'composite building worker'. A complex web of demarcations had grown up between the different skills of the building trade which cut across the natural unity of individual jobs. Painter, joiner, bricklayer — all had their spheres of influence, and a job which overlapped any of these territories had to wait for the appropriate skill to come along. To knock all the jobs into one was no more than a return to a method of working generally accepted in the building industry. It also meant that building workers, initially assessed at Grade 6, were put on Grade 7. The change, according to the senior shop steward at Hillhouse, 'was highly unpopular with the unions concerned but extremely popular with the men'.

I should point out, for the sake of completeness, that this account of job enrichment does not accord with that of the shop stewards, described in the TUC report. Many of them were very dismissive of the whole process. And, as I commented in Section 1 of this chapter, a number of workers took to the view that the whole business was an elaborate charade. However, such attitudes reveal a circular sort of logic: initially cooperative attitudes made possible the sort of changes in working that arguably elicit more cooperative attitudes. I say 'arguably' because, of course, such initial cooperation was seen as a betrayal in some areas and by some unions. And the changes in working, the satisfactions from doing more complete jobs and the closer involvements in decision-making that resulted could all be — and were — interpreted as a sort of working-class Uncle Tomism.

Two residual problems remain, in particular, which are inherent in the process of job enrichment. As in the previous section, I shall pose these as questions:

(*a*) Is it inevitable that today's enrichment should become tomorrow's routine? I discussed in Chapter 12 the problem of rigidities that are bound up with written job descriptions. We are always looking forward from the narrow base of the present. We make what may appear to be huge changes, but in retrospect they can seem small and commonplace. Is this the fate of job enrichment too? The workers do not remain still but change, become more demanding and not just for money but for challenge and interest. This points to a need for a continuing process of analysis and enrichment if the same problems are not going to arise in the future.

(*b*) Who is being enriched? Is job enrichment for the sake of the company or does it enrich the worker's life? It is perhaps more of a moral paradox than a practical objection. We may accept that the enrichment of a worker's job — yielding more money and more satisfaction (if it does) — is in his interest. This is not vitiated if the change is also in the interest of the company — and indeed, it would not be made if it were not. But there remains the small, niggling worry which I earlier put under the heading of 'manipulation'. However, small and niggling it may only be, for the fact of greatly improved working conditions throughout the company can hardly be denied.

Structure

This does not complete the tally of unquantifiable changes brought about by the introduction of WSA. The changes fanned out into the company at a number of levels — of which I do not propose to make a catalogue, only to note some of the more important. In particular, WSA allowed (or forced) the company to make some relatively 'neutral' changes (that is, changes which were not obviously to the benefit of company or workers) which could have important long-term effects.

(*a*) *Job evaluation.* One of the most important effects of

the Prices and Incomes Policy — and particularly of the
NBPI — was the change brought about in the rationality of
the bargaining process. When any pay claim was likely to be
examined to see if the money offered bore any relation to
benefits from changes in working, the debate tended to be
conducted within that framework. In much the same way, the
process of working up a job description and assessing it gives
a rational basis for relating work to reward that could
profoundly influence the way people think about their work
and the bargaining process in the future.

(b) *Grade structure*. There remains a substantial gap
between the skilled tradesman and unskilled worker. But
where this was once institutionalised in separate bargaining
for separate basic pay scales, all workers are now on a single
scale. Moreover, this allows the principle of unskilled workers
getting more than skilled — as yet only a tiny splinter. The
effects of such a structural change are hard to foresee, but
they must in the long run close the gap and go some way
toward eliminating the class distinction. In time, such
changes could have their effects on the trade unions
themselves.

(c) *Systems*. It has been impossible to contain the changes
of WSA at the level intended. They popped up among
monthly staff in the form of the Staff Development
Programme. And a precondition for them to take place at all
was the complete analysis of the management systems in the
works. In some cases, this process yielded more benefits than
WSA itself; in all cases, it was a novel experience to look at
the total system, with valuable lessons for the future.

(d) *Looking ahead*. The whole process of introduction was
a valuable learning experience. Most managers in the company have now been through training that has changed their
view of their function. All employees have been through
discussion and analysis of their jobs. Whatever the situation
was before, this fact has changed it: the company is prepared
for more planned change, which has now entered the realm
of tools and techniques available for general use. There is a
central OD facility at Millbank and a group of trained
internal OD consultants — taken more seriously in some

divisions than others. One of the consultants said: 'The difference between our understanding of OD processes now and our ignorance of what was involved when we launched the MUPS trials is immense. If we had started from where we are now, everything would have been different.' This suggests that many of the delays and frustrations of the trials were an essential part of a learning process that brought the company to its 'now' position. It also suggests that it is ready to move on and build on the experience gained.

15

'If We Had It To Do Again...'

We have now completed our journey through MUPS and
WSA — although, as we have seen in Chapter 11, the
caravan is now moving on to other places. ICI did not end up
where it had hoped to get, largely because it could only guess
where it was going when it set off in 1965. There have been
successes, some of them remarkable by any measure. And if
the effort has seemed disproportionate, the difficulties have
been immense and the journey filled with frustration and
danger. Logic demands that, having completed the journey,
we should be able to look back and derive lessons, identify
the obvious, avoidable mistakes, pinpoint the traps and
pitfalls: answer the question 'If we had it to do again . . .'
with a programme of action that would take any future
traveller smoothly and efficiently to his journey's end,
skirting bogs, impassable mountain ranges and precipices on
the way.

There are two answers to this question, depending on the
definition of 'it', the objective. If *it* is merely to gain
acceptance of an agreement — which became the objective of
many exhausted managers during the last phases of WSA —
there are unquestionably many lessons to be learned which
can legitimately be used to improve the process the next time
round. There were great successes to be built on and failures
which, in retrospect, might have been avoided. And if the
objective was only to gain acceptance of the agreement, it
would not be difficult to devise a route which involved a
good deal less wasted effort.

But this is as one might say that the objective of getting
married is to have a wedding. The agreement was to be a
starting-point for a continuing, on-going, open-ended process
of organisational change; gaining acceptance for the agree-

ment was only part of that process to the extent that it
became, itself, an instrument of change. The second answer
to the question, therefore, is that there can be no way of
mapping out an elegant, waste-free programme of organisational change: the lessons of MUPS lay in the learning of
them; the outcome was inextricably tangled with the ways in
which it was achieved. It is a hard lesson to stomach since it
suggests that you always start from scratch and that there is
not much that can be done to control the process once
started. It even suggests — shades of Samuel Smiles — that
there may be virtue, or rather learning, in suffering. But in
the God-like position of having it all to do again, we would
no more want to design the delays and frustrations of the
MUPS trials into an ideal change programme than we would
choose to design suffering into man's life — however beneficial the results in terms of solidly achieved organisational
change on a well-formed character.

Specifically, it would not be helpful to try and cut out
from the MUPS trials the wastes and frustrations, since these
had a real utility. The two-year delay was a period in which
management and unions got to understand the logic of each
other's position; it was a bridge between the way in which
the agreement was launched (rooted in ICI's traditional
technical problem-solving management style) and the way in
which the problems encountered came to be solved, more
organically and participatively; and it was an arena on which
ancient battles were re-enacted in ritual form, watched by the
whole workforce, but focussing attention on MUPS.

Perhaps more to the point — since seen simply as a learning
experience, the trials could have been differently and more
consciously designed — it would not have been possible to
have mapped out a course so far in advance. The problems
were only dimly understood and only when they were
experienced would their reality be respected. To most
manager, the unions and shop stewards were dealt with as
infrequently as possible over a negotiating table; they were
not people or bodies with useful information, only with
power that had to be contained. To learn that this division
was a problem that was as much in management as in the
unions themselves was not something to be programmed,
only encountered.

Secondly, the techniques for organisational change available to the company were not, even if they had been understood, adequate to encompass problems which were not defined. They had to be developed in response to the demands of the situation. Nothing could demonstrate this better than the very different approaches adopted in the beginning by management at the many different sites in the company and the way a sort of professionalism began to emerge with experience.

Lastly, the amount of effort required to make even small changes was colossal. Consider how difficult it is to change one man's ideas; consider how much more difficult it is when he is joined with other men who hold the same ideas as himself, and when these ideas are supported and consolidated by the whole of his own society — with the values of the union movement and the working classes. This sort of change was being attempted for 66,000 people. The work done was to be measured in thousands of man-years and millions of pounds. And this too could not have been suspected when the company first embarked on the programme of change, since the change presented itself within a framework of received managerial practice which had yet to be shown to be irrelevant.

If we are to suggest better ways of introducing WSA, therefore, we have first to think ourselves back to 1965 and to consider the work to be done and the attitude change to be achieved. Whatever methods were chosen, there would still be a need for a period during which the problems were identified; to serve as a bridge between the old and new ways of bringing about change at the human level; and to serve as an arena for a conflict that would focus general attention on the real issues.

It is rather unsatisfactory to conclude that untidiness was unavoidable and that, even if we had the power to reshape events to avoid particular mistakes, they would crop up in another form elsewhere. The main work being done was that of learning about the problems and developing techniques, through trial and error, to handle them. However, we can also conclude that the processes of change should themselves be adaptive, capable of learning ways around new problems. In computer research, there is considerable emphasis on the development of 'artificial intelligence' and the reason is clear: it is no longer difficult to design computers and associated software to handle specific problems, but the result is limited to the problems for which it has been designed and therefore to the designer's definition of the problem. How much better to design machines that can *learn* to solve problems which have not yet been encountered!

The MUPS trials were intended, among other things, to discover what the problems were and to test out possible solutions. In practice, they produced a deadlock because there were no solutions available for the problems encountered nor, more fundamentally, were the problems understood. If there was a flaw in the grand design for MUPS it was that the fact of this ignorance was not explicitly acknowledged, nor were the techniques for change organised in a way that could handle the inevitable, unexpected discoveries. In other words, lack of preparation — the provision of central resources, the development of skills for handling organisational change, the lack of a strategy for dealing with the unknown — was the main flaw. And this in spite of the very careful studies that went into the Rutherford Report and the long discussions behind the MUPS agreement.

But this is asking for a great deal. We look into the future with eyes trained by the past. And in times of rapid social change — which are the changes WSA was designed for — the past is always out of date.

These sections will deal with the more satisfactory topic of what we *can* learn from the WSA experience that would help in some future exercise. In true organisation development style, I have divided this under 'content' and 'process' headings. The distinction has been made at several points already in the book so far — between *what* an event is intended to achieve and *how* it is being achieved. Under the heading of 'content' therefore we are concerned with the overt aims of WSA and the formal structure designed to achieve it — specifically, the provisions of the agreement.

'Content' lessons

1. *Salary inducements*
It is easy — with a complex agreement like WSA, all too

easy — to allow its assumed centre of gravity to shift over to the human relations aspects: job enrichment, staff status and participation. These issues attract a great deal of attention and interest. However, the elaborations of behavioural theorists may well be as much (if not more) projections of their middle-class professional values as they are objective conclusions based in scientific research. And, interested as we may be in the more complex benefits designed into WSA, the people whom it covers are more sensitive than anything else to the money it offers. This fact was no less frustrating to the union representatives than to the company. Shop stewards were frequently alarmed at the willingness of their members to trade away, as they saw it, for money, a precious heritage of carefully accumulated defences against the exercise of managerial prerogatives. Managers were no less frustrated at the unwillingness of workers to make changes that were, as *they* saw it, in their own (workers') interests except when they were paid to do so; willingness to change could be directly correlated with the inducements offered by higher salaries.

The initial offer in MUPS was the result of some thought: it was based on the broad principle that two-thirds of the money savings from the estimated 15% cut in numbers should go to the workforce as higher wages. This was a nice judgment between the need to sell the new agreement internally (there had to be something in it for the company) and the inducements needed to sell it to the workforce. Subsequently, in WSA, the rule of thumb was changed and all the direct savings were passed over as a 22% average pay increase, the company contenting itself with indirect savings.

It was a difficult calculation. The pay scale had to cover all the company's workers, at sites operating in very different labour markets. If it was pitched at a level which would be attractive to the works with the highest earnings, it would add very considerably to the costs of those works which — through effective management control of bonuses and over-time or as a result of local circumstances — had managed to hold earnings down. The company's reward system did not encourage division management to accept such cost penalties without protest. However, a pay scale pitched at any level below the top works' earnings rates would leave those parts of the company without any solid inducements to move towards the new agreement.

As it happened the most exposed works were in the Northeast. The need to attract and hold craftsmen in competition with local engineering and steel works; the problem of contractors' labour; the strength of the unions on the site — these generated pressures under which overtime was fixed at high levels and bonuses had drifted up toward 40%. As a result, the MUPS scale was in some cases below earnings even with maintained overtime; if, which was the intention, overtime was substantially reduced, more than half the craftsmen stood to lose. And, of course, much more than maintaining parity was needed to induce workers to make large changes in their patterns of work — however much management argued that it was in their own interest — still less to give up ancient union protection.

With the benefits of hindsight it is possible to see that the company's only chance for a speedy introduction on difficult sites was to fix salaries at levels sufficiently attractive to generate a grassroots interest which might in time be strong enough to overwhelm the largely political opposition of the shop stewards. Once that moment had passed and the opposition dug itself in, a war of attrition was inevitable. The contrast with the first successful trial sites is striking: at Hillhouse, Gloucester and Stowmarket the salaries offered were attractive to the payroll from the beginning; this fact provided the 'enabling' conditions within which the introduction could proceed.

2. *Rigidities — new demarcations*

Two substantial objections to the way WSA has worked arise from the very success of the agreement in laying down new ways of defining and assessing jobs. Both are the result of its rigour and explicitness which, firstly, can result in the replacement of old, informal flexibilities by new, complex demarcations and, secondly, has removed the small remaining degree of local autonomy from managers and shop stewards — with bad as well as good consequences.

In any working situation, informal methods of doing work are developed spontaneously; sometimes, these are also 'illegal' and infringe management or union working rules. For example, there was always a degree of informal flexibility in working the extent of which depended on the locality. This has been particularly true of shift work (often referred to as the 'night shift spirit') and most of all on the continuous process plants, where team working comes naturally and rules are not much considered during the frequent minor crises which theaten the efficient operation of a plant. But try and enshrine this state of affairs in black-and-white, explicit job descriptions and issues of 'ownership' of work were immediately raised, swiftly to be elevated into issues of principle — defence of the union members' jobs. So that as little as possible was conceded when it came to discussing job descriptions — which often contained less flexibility in working than had previously been the practice.

This effect varied according to region. Clearly, we would expect it in the more defensively militant areas; where work group discussions went well, as they did at Gloucester, Stowmarket, Billingham and other parts of the company, there was enough openness to get past the initial defensiveness. At Wilton, Doncaster and Huddersfield only the minimum was conceded.*

3. *Rigidities — managerial straitjacket*
The second unwelcome effect of the explicitness and completeness of the new wages structure was to remove from local management the small degrees of managerial flexibility possible under the old scheme. The small (10-point) steps up the ladder of job categories and local job appraisement provided scope for management to make small increases of

---

* Apropos these regional differences, Jack Lofthouse — whose working life was spent mainly in the Northeast — suggests that they may have been made *worse* by the work study and job appraisement introduced in 1954 and 1948 which 'attacked the ancient Teesside tradition of *de facto* flexibility, particularly between a craftsman and his mate'. At the best, they were an efficient working team. Work study raised questions about the definition of the mates' job and formalised the working relationship while, at the same time, the company was working to reduce the number of mates. Bonus incentives also struck at traditional ways of doing things, particularly the egalitarianism expressed in 'the rate for the job' (which had its helpful as well as its restrictive side). The net result was that 'the Teesside tradition of teamwork and flexibility was broken down to be replaced by rigid job definition and demarcation'. It is a refreshing insight into the problem of the Northeast which is too easily seen as being largely of the unions' making.

pay; the bonus incentive scheme could likewise be 'bent' to meet local needs – as witnessed by the high bonuses at Wilton. Such flexibility was bad for the company since it allowed room for retreat by weak management in the face of union pressures for more money; it was good in providing local management with a measure of visible and effective authority in an area that mattered to the workforce – money. More generally, managers are effective to the degree that they have the power to make the important decisions affecting their area of responsibility. (The only cogent objection to the development of 'siteliness' at Wilton was just this, that it forces works management to defer to site authority, e.g. in such matters as the timing of buses: a small detail but one of the pieces of which the visible authority of management is composed.) It seems quite likely, at the time of writing, that there will be a degree of devolvement of power over money decisions to meet this objection. And this suggests that the original agreements could have built into the pay structure small elements of local flexibility that would meet managers' need to have the power to bargain without imperilling the integrity of the whole structure.

This is a question of balance. At the time the agreements were being worked out, the need for control and comparability across the company had high priority – in reaction to the way earnings had drifted up under the old scheme. And the extent to which the job grading system has successfully achieved this end is remarkable. The main benefit has been to remove from the arena of local bargaining nearly all the residual powers over pay, a move that was aimed more at the shop stewards – whose main source of power this was – than anyone else. The change is measured not just by a central estimate that variance in job grading across the company is probably no more than 5% (probably optimistic but impossible to harden up without considerable research); it emerges also in the frequent complaint from shop stewards that they have nothing left to bargain over: all substantive bargaining has effectively been removed to the centre. We should note in conclusion that this cannot be a satisfactory answer. Apart from the needs of management, the shop stewards exist and have power needs which will be satisfied in one way or another. To remove from them one arena of action is to leave these power needs unsatisfied; other arenas exist outside managerial control and will be developed.

'Process' lessons

With the single exception of the first 'content' lesson — the level at which the initial pay offer was set — the main lessons from WSA are to be found in the *process* of introduction. But for the most part, they were learned by a process of trial-and-error while the company was encountering the disappointments and delays of the trials. I have argued that this was a necessary process. However, some of the errors were, in retrospect, avoidable.

1. *Movement*

A major mistake the company made, although it was inescapable at the then level of experience, was to allow the introduction of the agreement to lose momentum. Many other issues enter into this: most particularly, the money offer was not attractive enough to generate strong support at the grassroots. But the company was not adequately prepared, either in understanding the problems that would be encountered or with the training facilities and expert resources (e.g. internal consultants) to help to handle them. And once momentum was lost, the dynamics of the process were altered: the opportunity was created for opponents to dig themselves in; attitudes hardened. In a case like Wilton, this was doubly dangerous since the deadlock was political in nature and not likely to be resolved by 'problem-solving discussion': the only way around the Wilton road-blocks was a general tide of enthusiasm.*

It is not so mechanically simple as that. It may be possible to flood out the opposition with money, but it is expensive — and obliterates other changes. More is needed to keep the process of change moving along: money merely provides the enabling conditions. Here I am thinking of what is called 'skilled intervention' in OD jargon. It is the most important

---

* This is, of course, to see the situation entirely from the company's point of view. I hardly need to point out that the shop stewards feel their opposition prevented the company from taking their members for a ride and that they secured a considerable victory by getting the money for minimal change.

skill of the OD consultant, requiring sensitivity to those crucial moments when a system is at a point of balance and only a small push is needed to change its direction. (I once axed a large tree so carefully that I was able to push it with one hand to fall precisely where I wanted.) There is enormous energy latent at such moments and the skill lies in using it. And if we look back through the introduction of WSA, we can identify a number of key events where this happened, and some where it didn't.

— At Wilton, we saw the unleashing of this energy in the sequence of events that followed Jack Lofthouse's controversial speech (p.127). For a time, the solid resistance to any change was made fluid in the storm of rage that followed the speech. This was the opportunity that was used to set the local productivity talks in motion. The amount of energy around was demonstrated by the way the talks went — except where the process was opposed at individual works or, ultimately, by central management.

— A completely opposite example, and a much more crucially missed opportunity, was the refusal of the company to allow training sessions for Wilton shop stewards more generally to follow the highly successful training and discussion week at the ETU College at Esher (p. 125). It was a spontaneous surge forward, impelled by curiosity and interest, that did not recur. The reasons for not proceeding seemed good at the time, but unimaginative.

— A lesson in how much an opportunity can be taken was given by Harry Penny at Gloucester, who waited for a move from the local unions before he put MUPS in front of them (p. 111). It was not until the local T&GWU committee invited him to take part in a training session for shop stewards that he, as it were, 'made his pitch'. The approach had demonstrated that there was a readiness to change, and he took the opportunity.

— Similarly, at Billingham, after it had become obvious that the MUPS trial was not going to proceed the management consciously withdrew from the scene. It was after some six months of inactivity that they came together with the unions again in a meeting which unleashed a new surge of energy for change.

— We can generalise this more and consider the circumstances in which the whole process was set off: the Rutherford Panel, the Board decision to proceed, the MUPS negotiations and signature. The ideas had been around for some time, in some form. But the circumstances had to be right: there was an energising (or unfreezing) crisis; the answer which MUPS provided had to be seen to be relevant to the problem; but it had to be presented in a way (through trials) that was not too threatening to existing perceptions.

— A completely opposite case is the launching of joint consultation, to replace the works councils (p. 221). Here the change was presented as a management initiative and became identified with management interest. Local managers, given the job of introducing it, found that the unions used the dynamics of this situation in their own interest: 'You want it. What's it worth to you?'

Anybody who is trying to influence a group of people knows the importance of timing. He watches like a surfer for the breaking of the wave, the opportunity presented by a shift in mood. It needs sensitivity and the capacity to adapt to events as they occur. But the opportunities, if lost, may not recur and no one can afford to lose the impulse they provide for keeping change going. A river in flood can carry an enormous amount of material in suspension. Once it slows down, the silt drops to the bottom, where it will remain until the next spring floods, if not forever.

2. *It always costs more*

Part of thorough preparation should be to gain a realistic understanding of the amount of effort involved in order to have resources to match. At the beginning, it will be remembered, one estimate put the whole exercise at less than a year which, had it been a normal sort of management-led change in wages and conditions of work, could have been realistic. The disillusion of managers and workers was dangerous. First, sheer exhaustion and frustration led to the transformation of management's objectives. Secondly, some of the problems encountered with the unions were a direct result of disappointed expectations.

It is very likely that, had the Main Board even vaguely guessed the full extent of the work involved, the company

would never have attempted it. It is also likely that
something less ambitious would have been tried — and
perhaps more completely achieved — or that the attraction of
different approaches (as in the method of negotiation) would
have become more evident.

However, one conclusion is firm: that changing complex
organisations is very expensive in time, money and effort. It
will almost certainly be far more time-consuming than a
company expects or is prepared to accept; and it will achieve
less than hoped. This is by the nature of the process, which
to be effective must impinge on every individual in the
organisation and engage his attention at a most detailed level.
There are no short cuts to this sort of change.

3. *Supervisors*

A lesson from WSA which almost deserves a chapter on its
own is the involvement of supervisors. It has now become
part of the conventional OD wisdom that supervisors are
ignored and ought to be far more closely involved in change
programmes. The reasons are clear: supervisors are at the
interface between management and the shopfloor; their
understanding and commitment is essential to complex
management initiatives affecting detailed aspects of work
organisation. However, it is equally clear why they have
rarely been sufficiently — if at all — involved in exercises like
WSA. First, management attention was drawn to shop
stewards as the workers' representatives. This was both a
necessary part of the changes being planned, where union
approval had to be sought, and a result of a historical process
during which the supervisor's power has diminished and the
shop steward's increased. Secondly, given the opportunity,
the shop stewards did all they could to freeze the supervisors
out of discussions — fruits of an ancient enmity. This was
happening anyway because of management's tendency to
build bridges over the supervisors' heads and deal directly
with shop stewards. Lastly, the supervisors have traditionally
been among the most loyal of ICI's employees and their
compliance could be taken for granted.

But only up to a point. The whole focus of the job
enrichment aspects of the program was at the shopfloor;
but if jobs were to be enriched, it could only be, ultimately

at the expense of the next layer. Self-supervision, autonomous working: at first blink, these have to reduce the role
of the supervisor. And to loss of authority was added the
insecurity of severe redundancies: between 1965 and 1973, the
numbers of supervisors dropped by 28% while that of weekly
staff dropped by 14%, taking supervisory ratios down from
12.4:1 to 14.9:1. His enthusiasm was, understandably,
limited. And he was in a position to vitiate part of the
exercise by simply refusing to hand over his chain of office.
To paraphrase a shift fitter at Huddersfield:

> 'What I like is to be left to get on with my job. This is why
> I liked the idea of WSA. But they won't let it happen. I
> mean, take weekends. I'm supposed to come in, see what
> jobs are to be done, make my own decisions about which
> should be done and how. There isn't a foreman down for
> the shift. But Jim comes in anyway saying that he was
> passing by and thought he'd have a look in. He sticks his
> head around the corner and says: "Everything OK, Harry?
> Let me know if you have any problems". So what can I
> do? I don't even try now.'

This isn't direct opposition or open defiance. It is just one
of the small and detailed ways in which an attempt to bring
about change in an organisation can be stopped — probably
without consciously intending it. If one of the main
inducements to becoming a supervisor is the authority that
goes with the job, it is hardly to be expected that he will
voluntarily take part in handing it over.

A more constructive approach was illustrated in conversation with a foreman at Wilton. Working shifts on one of the
big process plants, he has five men in his team who now take
many of the decisions that were formerly his: mostly to do
with keeping the plant physically running:

> 'Now I no longer have to go around telling Frank or Jim to
> change this setting or watch that reading — and *then* come
> back to make sure they've done it. They get on with their
> own jobs and only come to me if there is a problem which
> they need help with. This leaves me free to get on with
> things I never had time for before: dealing with paperwork

and information in and out; making sure we have the supplies we want and are getting the help we need from the Works. . .'

. . . what the Tavistock Institute theorists call 'boundary control', and the proper job of the group leader. This supervisor had to discover this fact for himself and is much happier with his job than he was before WSA; many others, probably most, are still struggling with the threat to the traditional definition of their job, very much to the detriment of the agreement's working.

This suggests that a high priority should be given to involving supervisors at every stage of introducing a new agreement. They should be involved in early discussions with other managers. And there should be special training offered to provide them with the skills and understanding needed to perform their role in the change process. Many such training schemes were provided — for example in leading discussions. But if the end result was still seen as a threat, and if the supervisor was left out of many of the more important discussions affecting his area of authority, the skills are unlikely to be well used. More important, therefore, is the effort to help the supervisor place himself in the changed organisation.

4. Not invented here

The immediate reaction of many people presented with MUPS was, 'What's this got to do with me?' MUPS was an alien artefact which was not immediately relevant to any of the different circumstances it was designed to cover. The involvement and agreement of national union officers was not by itself sufficiently influential: shop stewards are used to standing up for local rights which their national offices have overlooked. And the local managers — one of whom told me he greeted his meeting of angry shop stewards with, 'I only got it myself half-an-hour ago . . .' — felt much the same way, although for them opposition (not one of a manager's roles) took the more covert form of lack of enthusiasm.

This problem had been partly foreseen and a way round it designed into the agreement with the 'central agreement/local introduction' format. It was intended to provide a framework within which diverse local conditions could be accommodated. But it was not foreseen that the framework itself, with all the solid authority of Millbank and national union offices behind it, would be rejected.

The answer lay in ownership — or rather the lack of it. If ICI had finally been able to reach agreement with the signatory unions over this important change, it was only after months of detailed discussion during which every aspect of the change was exhaustively debated. And in the course of those discussions both sides had formulated to their own private satisfaction radical ideas which were incorporated into MUPS, ideas which challenged the basic assumptions that ruled the working contract in the company. They had reached those ideas through a great deal of hard work and had ownership of them. Simply to pass on the fruits of those long discussions was tantamount to giving advice to someone else: however penetrating and deeply-rooted in experience, it was ignored as irrelevant.

Of course, this greatly simplifies a complex situation in which political relationships (within and between unions as much as against management) played a major part. But the conclusion is valid and was accepted when it came to re-negotiating WSA. There was, and had to be, a considerable measure of participation — or the appearance of it — of which the circulation of a draft agreement was the most important part. Only when people generally felt they had a chance to influence what went into the agreement would they feel it was something of their own as happened most successfully in working out job descriptions.

This is strikingly demonstrated by the difference in the reaction to MUPS and to WSA. The agreements are substantially similar yet in many places — particularly the main opposition centres — there is still a violent reaction against the first and a quite different feeling about the second. MUPS was 'a load of rubbish', 'a try-on' and 'We weren't going to fall for that . . .' But a number of times phrases in WSA were pointed out which 'came from us': from the recommendations of some meeting or group. The point is not whether an individual or group did or did not influence the agreement (many could legitimately claim ownership of the same parts

of WSA and many of the suggestions were almost identical)
but that a machinery was provided which made suggestions
possible and that the negotiations were carried out relatively
openly. Against this, I have been told that initially secrecy
was essential for the agreement to be discussed at all. But I
have been told it in the same terms — it was the other side
that insisted on secrecy — by management and unions. Which
suggests that secrecy was tacitly desired by both sides:
important and difficult issues were to be decided; publicity
was not likely to be helpful.

One conclusion might be that the design process ought to
be one involving the whole community that is to be affected.
But here we come up against the political realities of the
1965 situation. Had such an idea — discussion groups stretching out to the crack of doom — been put forward in March
1965, it would certainly have been rejected. And, indeed,
protracted as the discussions were — effectively lasting for six
months — they were vastly more efficient as a way of dealing
with the issues than a more diffuse process. However, in
retrospect, given the time-scale of the total exercise from
1965 to 1972, a first phase of discussion and fact-finding was
a possible way into negotiations both as a device to gain
general ownership of the changes and, perhaps more important, as part of a learning process which was to take place
anyway.

5. Trials

It is for these reasons that the approach through trials was
chosen; what has been called the 'infected cell strategy'. To
select and isolate some limited areas for experiment had
obvious attractions both for management and the unions,
legitimately concerned about the effects of such radical
changes. They were laboratories in which a new cure for an
old, virulent disease could be tried out with safety; only
when its worth had been proven would it be tried on a larger
scale. If undesirable side effects outweighed the benefits, the
need to negotiate the whole agreement on a company basis
would provide the opportunity to deal with them. Quite
practically, it is unlikely that any other approach would have
been acceptable, either to the unions or the Main Board.

However, the trials strategy contained features that were

not foreseen at the time, dangers that were greater for management than for the unions. It may have seemed that the trials were only that, and capable of being spirited away if they didn't work. In practice, it is hard to see how the changes, once introduced, could have been reversed. It was, in fact, a risky strategy: the trial sites were unlikely to return to earlier rates of pay without considerable disruption; and if they were not returned they would act as a new set of precedents for pay claims. Secondly, the dynamics of trials made 'natural' modes of discussion difficult to achieve. People behave differently when on show. The trial sites became — although they were not intended to be — arenas of ritual combat between managers and unions, local champions jousting on behalf of their colleagues elsewhere. It happened within the company; it happened with greater intensity within a site where, as at Wilton and Billingham, no action could stand up to the jealous scrutiny of the watchful non-combatants.

What can measure up to such standards, to the passionate righteousness of people who are not engaged in the practical problems of finding some workable compromise between incompatible but internally logical systems? I once witnessed a confrontation — it was at an American university, MIT, in 1970 — between a student and a member of the MIT administration. The student was attacking the administrator for not doing anything to stop the Vietnam war. 'What have you ever done for peace?' he ended up. The older man seemed at a loss for words and then explained, with restraint, that as Scientific Adviser to President Kennedy he had played a significant part in setting up the Geneva disarmament talks. In the event, they had come to nothing — but I was left to reflect that they had probably done more for peace than liberating the MIT chairman's office. Major changes in complex systems come by the accumulation of small shifts, any of which could be discarded in advance for not eliminating the manifold faults of the system. Paradoxically, the desire for perfection prevents movement; the revolutionary becomes a force for conservatism and the enemy of change. I shall pick up this point in the next chapter, in the context of a discussion on centralised control.

PART VI

Necessity and
the Objectives of Change

So far, I have kept within the bounds of one company's agreement: a limited solution to a highly complex — but limited — problem. And there the matter could rest, except that the problems that afflicted ICI have been felt in more acute form throughout British industry. They are felt in some form in many of the institutions that make up Western society: the breakdown in authority, questioning of values, loss of faith in the effectiveness of democratic government, the willingness of powerful minorities to assert themselves against the wishes or interest of the majority — all of these arising from the erosion of the social contract. Perhaps it is the death wish of a spent society, or perhaps (as I suggested in the Introduction) the end of the road for systems of control based, at however many removes, in coercion. This is why I think WSA and agreements like it are so particularly interesting. For they represent a small step, hugely difficult to take, towards a society in which people have more ownership of the decisions that affect their lives. In affluent Western societies, they have the power and are asserting it in a thousands ways. The problem which ICI faced was one of changing the institutions to match this reality. It was not a matter of giving away power but of putting decisions where the power to take them had already gone.

16

Choice and the Balance of Power

What has happened at ICI has not been an isolated occurrence. I am not thinking here of the surge in Britain of productivity bargaining in 1967-70 but much more of the parallel attempts, mostly by large companies in the industrialised West, to bring about changes as manifold and complex as those of WSA. It is misleading to put them all together, since they are so different, but they have broad similarities. As yet they are to be numbered in dozens; many of the names will already be well-known. Most are to be found in the USA, where such companies as TRW, Polaroid, Texas Instruments, IBM and Procter and Gamble have been looking at new ways of organising work and managing people for more than a decade. (There is a characteristic US bias toward using behavioural science to fit people into organisations in which the structure and technology are accepted as 'givens' while in Europe there appears to be a greater willingness to take people as given.) In Britain the companies involved include English China Clay, British Oxygen, Shell and, in different ways, subsidiaries of foreign companies such as Philips and ITT. Other agreements of the kind that interest us are found in Northern Europe — in Sweden, where the Saab and Volvo experiments have aroused much interest; Norway where 'autonomous groups' were first tried at Norsk Hydro; in Denmark and Holland. (Why there should be so little activity in Southern Europe is an interesting question.) I have included these, in many ways dissimilar, agreements together for reasons that will become more apparent later in the chapter. Suffice it to say at this stage that IBM, Polaroid and Texas Instruments were more concerned to keep unionisation at bay; Volvo and Saab to find ways of maintaining in existence a mundane low technology activity in an advanced economy; and the British companies to find ways around a low productivity deadlock.

As we have seen with WSA, these initiatives all serve several purposes. Inasmuch as they have been management initiatives (which has not been the case in Scandinavia, where the unions have also been active), they can be rationalised in terms of the companies' well-being. But this is saying very little, for managers do not commonly take decisions that are intentionally against their company's interests. It is more useful to see them in terms of the needs which they served: economic, social and political.

1. *Economic.* This is the 'rational' surface of changes, the purpose for which Main Boards exist: minimising cost and maximising profit or revenue, securing the financial health of their companies. If the organisational changes did not offer economic benefit for the companies, they would not be made. For ICI the benefit of WSA was that it might offer a solution to problems being raised by technological change and, more generally, by the poor use of people. In Volvo, reorganised assembly lines may provide the answer to the problem of using an increasingly demanding workforce in mundane and repetitive work. In Texas Instruments the company is concerned to make unionisation unnecessary, to reduce labour turnover and improve quality of production. All of these fall into the area of traditional managerial problems, even if the solutions are not traditional.

2. *Social.* Ask a behavioural scientist — or one of the many consultants ICI used — what WSA was intended to achieve, and you will be given a very different justification. To many of the people most closely involved in the change processes, they are justified by improved group functioning and increased satisfaction for the individual. But this is to say, among other things, that people working 'at the coalface' are more likely to be sensitive to the human implications of work and the benefits for the individual of change than managers handling the abstractions of economic rationality. These normative social objectives — which, as I have pointed out, were embodied in ICI's long tradition of 'ethical' management — coexist with the economic objectives. They

would not have the force to drive through a programme of change by themselves but, once the enabling economic conditions are met, they can become important.

3. *Political.* A more sinister view has been taken by Left-wing commentators of productivity bargaining specifically, but the arguments could be extended to similar kinds of change elsewhere. In this view, the process was designed by the management to recapture control at the workplace just at the moment when the workers had acquired enough power to take control for themselves. If it is accepted that workers' control (or something like it) is desirable, anything that taps off the head of steam is hostile to that end — let alone actions designed to re-introduce management discretion into areas where management had been cribbed and confined by union power. It seems to me pointless to deny that there may be some truth in this view — at its most superficial. That is, it was one of the aims of MUPS (less explicitly for WSA) to encourage the growth of 'staff-type attitudes', implicitly replacing a commitment to union values with a commitment to the company. Moreover, there was unquestionably a group of managers who hoped that MUPS would, by providing a direct link to the shopfloor, cut through the attempts of shop stewards to control communications between workers and managers. As far as I have been able to make out, such hopes were not widely cherished; they did not last once the realities of the trials emerged from the golden fog of pre-trial expectations; and they had disappeared altogether by the time WSA was being thought of. More to the point, neither in my culling of the files nor in discussion with the people involved, have I discovered evidence to support a conspiracy theory of organisational change. Indeed, such theories can amount to very little more than assertions since they cannot be proved wrong: they depend on a disposition to believe them. But take out the conspiratorial overtones and there is a useful residue of information. For it seems to me unlikely that any individual or group will voluntarily give away their power to control events and that, where this has happened, it must have been to some extent enforced. The US companies I have earlier referred to have engaged in elaborate programmes benefiting their employees in order quite explicitly

to create conditions in which unionisation is unattractive. The benefit to the employee — an important criterion of improvement — is the same whether the company is running ahead of the unions or reluctantly trailing in their dust. Moreover, seen as responses to growing union power, the two are identical processes. Only if it is assumed that there is an absolute benefit in trade union dominance will such management initiatives be seen as sinister and resisted, whatever form they take.

At the beginning of the chapter, I lumped together a number of dissimilar programmes of change. They have some superficial similarities: they are all intended to achieve economic benefits for their companies, if only the negative benefit of not going out of business. They have all used theories drawn from behavioural science, bringing about social change within the organisation as a means for achieving their economic ends. And while the changes they have achieved have been almost bewilderingly diverse, they have been characterised by one dominating feature: the centre of gravity of decision-making has moved down into the organisation. This is my fundamental justification for including them together. For, while they have all been more or less consciously designed to achieve certain organisational ends, they can also be seen as an unconscious, enforced response to broader changes in their social environment: the institutionalisation of *de facto* shifts in the balance of power.

The power to make decisions is the essence of management. Why should this be handed down, and decisions (or pieces of decisions) which were formerly the preserve of management handed over for more general participation? Why else except that the management no longer had the power to take those decisions unchallenged? Alan Flanders has said that the only way for managers to retain power was to share it, but this implies a voluntary handing over of the reality of power which I do not consider to have been the case. Instead, an informal power reality has been formalised in order that the power should be directed toward organisationally legitimate ends — and not used disruptively, against the organisation's interest. As I have said, this process can only be objected to if disruption of the organisation is thought to be desirable, even at a heavy cost to employees.

The changes in the balance of power that I have in mind have risen from the changed relationship of the worker with the economic (employing) system. Specifically, conditions of full employment, higher pay and the effects of education, television and travel have increased the range of choice available to individuals and the diversity of their demands. A job held precariously with no alternative available — indeed, as one ICI supervisor reminisced, with a queue of men outside the factory gate waiting for it — is something like slavery, however benevolent the intentions of the company. A choice between two jobs, even if neither is altogether satisfactory, allows the individual the opportunity to make a decision in his own interest. More money gives him the means to exercise choice in the market. Broadening of his mental horizons enables him to choose between — or vainly strive after — a wider range of 'life models'. Without making any judgments on their benefits — the price of freedom is eternal vigilance: it may also be eternal discontent — the immense power of these changes, the forces they release within society, are manifest. And they affect the world within which organisations operate, introducing limitations on what is possible. I go into these changes in more detail in the first five chapters of my book, *Organisations in a Changing Environment.* Apropos the changes for management, I said:

'The difference between what managers could demand from their workers 40 years ago and what is possible now has complex roots . . . One change is straightforward: a man facing privation and a long period of unemployment as the alternative to compliance with his supervisor's orders is in quite a different position from a man who can walk down the road not only to another job but to more money . . . The "natural" style of management in hierarchical organisations is authoritarian, and it is to be expected that managers will adopt this style when conditions permit. But once the managed are in a position to make their needs felt, a more persuasive — and ultimately more participatory — style become appropriate. MacGregor's "Theory X" set of assumptions may not be evil so much as appropriate to conditions which are disappearing . . .'

An important reason why some repetitive, assembly-line industries like motor manufacture and electronics are migrating to underdeveloped countries is that these conditions are still to be found somewhere in the world and they may be the only conditions in which such technologies can be made to work.

Choice is the key. Where people have a choice, however limited, they will exercise it in their own interest. Full employment and higher wages have given important degrees of choice so that, in spite of gloomy prophecies about the loss of individual freedom, the decisions that determine the texture of our society are more widely taken than they ever have been. WSA and the programmes I have cited are moves that reflect this new reality. I am quite sure that this was not the explicit intention of anyone associated with them; the objectives were quite different, and in some cases opposed to that view. Seen in the perspective of the larger changes in their social environment, they are all small, blind, crabwise moves to accommodate other problems. This makes it easier to understand (but still not to explain) a great puzzle at the heart of WSA: Why did ICI do it? Why would any company undertake such a huge project for such uncertain results? And the answer lies somewhere between blindly purposeful Destiny and Chance, with Reason desperately holding the balance.

Organisations have often been compared with biological systems: they ingest; they excrete; they are complex, consisting of highly differentiated and specialised subsystems; their purpose is the maintenance of internal stability — or, more familiarly, survival. They adapt to changes in their environment, either that or die out. For animal populations, the process of adaptation is slow and only over time is it purposive — any of the small steps taken in this process of change is quite random. Each is a possible solution to the problem of survival in particular conditions, which must be tested. Social systems are incomparably more adaptable, since the processes of change lie within the control of its designers (managers). Commercial organisations in particular have developed an extraordinary capacity for adapting rapidly and efficiently to changes in those parts of their environment which have direct consequences for their survival: technological, commercial, financial ... the focus has shifted over time and is, in any case, different between industries. But changes in the social environment have not, on the whole, been much of a threat to the organisation's survival. Major variations were mediated, or managed away, by conditions of high unemployment and low wages which delivered a reliably homogeneous workforce (and allowed residual variations to be managed away internally). These conditions were enshrined in a sort of organisational morality and became one of the comforting aspects of the organis-ation's stability. Meanwhile, however, the environment changed, and at an increasing rate. But organisations are not equipped to see these changes accurately. This is not to say that a company like ICI, where a great deal of intelligent effort was devoted to industrial relations, did not make changes – but they were within the framework of the old assumptions.

Like scientific theories, organisations represent solutions to problems. While the solutions work, they are viable. As information accumulates which cannot be fitted into the solution – is dissonant with it – attempts are made, at first without much thought and later with increasing (sometimes dangerously obsessive) determination, to fit the dissonant information into the old solution. Eventually the dissonant information breaks the bounds of the old and a new solution has to be found: a new theory is accepted; the animal grows another head; the organisation adopts another policy. But many solutions will be tried before the new one fits the problem snugly enough. The process of generating and testing them is the process of evolutionary change. The organisation moves, amoeba-like, through an environment filled with threats and opportunities; it changes its shape and moves into areas where the food seems richer – but never smoothly, neatly, completely, without disruption or pain.

Looking at ICI's experience – which is not untypical, except in the boldness of what was attempted all at once – it is illuminating to see how necessity and chance combined to produce the particular solution that was WSA. The necessity arose from the dissonance between the organisation and its environment, emerging in forms which both defined the problem and signalled the organisation's readiness to change.

But change in which directions? The ideas in WSA, or rather MUPS, had been floating around ICI in some form for years, like spores. Like spores, they had no power for action — they could not grow — unless the conditions were favourable: there is no absolute value to ideas beyond their appropriateness to particular circumstances. Doubtless other solutions (bring in the tanks; move to Taiwan) are also floating around, perhaps doomed forever; for still more (break the company up; hand over control to the workers), their time may yet come. Even so, it is by no means obvious that the radical solutions proposed in WSA were so manifestly superior to more cautious policies (although I believe them to be so). That they were adopted is due to the accident which threw up a number of powerful and committed individuals at the crucial moment in the company's history. It was also due to the capacity of radical and potentially revolutionary ideas to assume a less threatening guise: partly a matter of design — slipping into the citadel in the Trojan horse of trials; and partly because only rare individuals, like poets, have the capacity to see the present let alone the future, except in terms of the past. I cannot believe that, had ICI's management known the effort and expense that would be involved in WSA, they would have supported even limited trials. But then what kind of politician is it who would engage his country in a war, however just, if he knew in advance how many millions would be killed?

The migration of decisions

As a demonstration of the enormous capacity of social systems to adapt themselves consciously to changed conditions or, at least, to take decisions that move them in necessary directions, as important feature of MUPS/WSA was that it started within one framework of assumptions about the power of the centre (both management and unions) to enforce its decisions and ended with quite another. In the course of the long programme, the decisions moved to a level where they were consistent with power realities. The corporate objectives of ICI and the national unions could not be enforced at the local level. It was only when they were re-interpreted in local terms that the ownership of the need and of the means for change were brought together. Let us consider the following rough scheme of the company and unions at national and local levels.

	Management	*Union*	
National	1. Main Board Head Office Division Boards	National Officers Regional Officers District Officers	4.
Local	2. Works Management Plant Management Supervision	Senior Stewards Shop Stewards Shopfloor	3.

This is a crude simplification; it is not intended to imply that the levels are equivalent, only that there are two command structures where decisions are taken that are appropriate to levels of aggregation ranging from the national to the local. Both have coherence and a unity of purpose — or rather values. But in terms of power, the management structure can command greater coherence in action than the unions. A decision agreed among top management will have force for action through the whole structure not just because of a coherent set of management (or corporate) values, but because of the reward structure, career expectations and the habit of obedience. A decision agreed in the union structure has, at best, only a moral force below the formal (national) structure; the informal organisation that exists at local level does not answer to any comparable system of rewards which can enforce national decisions.

The vertical affinities are dominating. Probably for most purposes — and certainly in a situation of conflict — people would see themselves as belonging to the management structure (if in quadrants 1 and 2) or to the union structure (if in 3 or 4) rather than having any other affiliation. But horizontal affinities also have power for action, a community whose common interests extends across sectarian boundaries. It was possible for ICI's central management and the national officers of the signatory unions to find common cause and to agree over MUPS: both groups operated within the same horizons of geography (national) and time (long-term). But such agreement did not match local perspectives, where union and management structures had more unconscious horizontal sympathies than either did vertically. Thus management and unions colluded nationally and locally in various ways that were potentially strong enough to over-come vertical affinities.

If we were to ask the question: Where was the ownership of the *need* for change, and where the ownership of the *means*? We might answer that the need lay in quadrant 1 and the means lay in quadrant 3. To get from 1 to 3 — to influence 3 with needs felt in 1 — it was necessary to go through 2 or 4 (to go across the middle seems to be impossible). And since there is a discontinuity between 4 and 3 — the split between formal and informal union organis-ation — the only route available for bringing about substan-tial management-led change lay down the management structure to the local level and across, at the local level. This is, of course, what happened. And it raises three points: concerning the national unions, shop stewards and the prospects for changing large systems. The first is the question-mark this analysis puts over the formal union structure, for it is not immediately obvious that it serves a necessary purpose in a process of this kind. Not a positive purpose anyway: it was always possible for the unions to block movement, but not to make it happen. The second point concerns shop stewards, for they emerge as having a commanding position — standing astride the channels of communication into quadrant 3, from both union and management structures. Seen in this light, it becomes less surprising that one of the unanticipated consequences of productivity bargaining has been greatly to increase the importance of shop stewards.

Most important, this framework of analysis carries the focus of attention to the local level — where, as I have several times said, the real changes occurred. And this by itself makes clearer some of the problems encountered in bringing about change from the national level: for there was no way of convincing the local groups, management and unions, of the legitimacy of the nationally-agreed objectives. We are brought back to the initial rejection of MUPS by groups of people in the works, who questioned what relevance an agreement made at the national level could have for them.

Management were able to demand the, sometimes reluctant, cooperation of their own people — moving action from quadrant 1 to 2 — but the unions could not move action from 4 to 3. It was not until, through interaction between quadrants 2 and 3, a degree of ownership had been gained where the means for change were to be found, in quadrant 3, that change became possible. This suggests that some part or perhaps a substantial part of the effort expended by ICI management to maintain the integrity of nationally agreed objectives was irrelevant. There was a gap between national and local objectives that could not be bridged. It was only when the action moved to the local level, where objectives were more closely matched, that there was progress.

There is always a balance to be struck between corporate and individual objectives. It should be clear by now that there were strong reasons for maintaining central control. But when change is agreed at the centre, it can only be enforced when there is power to enforce it from the centre: which had been the situation in the far-off days of management prerogative. MUPS was launched within a framework of such assumptions about the existence of power to enforce agreements. But the power no longer existed: people refused to concede control over the area of an individual's work until each was persuaded that he would benefit as an individual. Until then there could be no movement, only suspicion and resistance.

An end to gigantism?

All of this casts shadows, not to say question marks, over the large organisations that make up so much of society. But before we assume that they should be abolished in the interests of humanity, we ought to ask what their necessary purpose is. The dominating processes of industrial development are integrative. That is, development has been characterised, and indeed driven, by the elimination of slack within and between systems, knitting them together into bigger systems and these into the even bigger systems of government and industry. ('Slack' in all its forms is inefficiency and foregone profit; it is also human values and quality of life — but we'll leave that for the moment.) Companies will tend to grow even in the absence of obvious benefits. But there are benefits. Production economies may cut off well below the size of large companies, but financial and other economies appear to continue indefinitely; providing an economic rationale for growth. Perhaps more important, for these are the decision-makers, there are considerable inducements — psychological as well as monetary — for the people running large groups to increase their size still further. And more vaguely, scientific rationality appears to demand central management of larger and larger groups.

The prerequisites for the growth and continued existence of these groups are twofold: the technology of control and the power to command — or, its silken sister, rewards to induce — obedience to central directives. Communications systems and data processing techniques have now been developed to a pitch that provides control over units of a size, government departments and multinational companies, that would have been unthinkable before the days of jet travel and the computer. The first law of technology says: What can be done will be. And this alone provides an inducement to grow.

The second prerequisite is power. For nearly all purposes, the power still exists within companies to make decisions taken at the centre effective throughout. These decisions, commercial and economic, are the purpose for which the organisation exists. However, for other purposes it may be that organisations can no longer allow themselves the luxury of size. Their very success in solving the economic problems of industrial development has generated choice which has been used to create areas of self-determination within the organsation. And this lies at the heart of the question I asked earlier: How are decisions made in the first quadrant (where the need for change was identified) to be put into effect in the third (where the means for change are found?) That there is a problem of power is demonstrated by the fact of asking the question at all, and it suggests that the ability of management to control large units for certain purposes is strictly limited. I think that it would be more constructive to accept that, for some purposes, the organisation may have to disaggregate, to behave as if it was a number of smaller organisations and to push some decisions down to levels

which are more in tune with the power realities. It is not a
question of devolving power from the centre, for the power is
no longer there. In terms of ICI's experience, this is what
happened; but many of the problems encountered in introducing the agreements were the direct result of attempting
to manage the whole complex operation from the centre —
however good the reasons for doing so were. And in fact, the
initial failure to push MUPS trials from the centre demonstrated the ability of the shopfloor to resist and forced the
management to disaggregate. A large degree of control was
maintained from the centre, but it was at a high cost; and the
action and decision-making migrated out to the works.

This line of thought takes us into issues which are the
subject of the next chapter. It also raises questions about
logically related developments, specifically about workers'
control, industrial democracy and other ways of institutional-
ising power-sharing. This is a subject in itself and outside the
scope of this book. I do not wish to go further than I have
gone already, only to point to categories of decisions which,
in response to a redistribution of power, are being devolved
to smaller decision-making units. However, this implies the
existence of decisions which are taken centrally: the very
decisions on matters of finance, investment and the rest
which provide the arguments for large size. The arguments
for devolving all decisions, or providing some sort of
representative system for participating in them, do not seem
at this moment to be compellingly strong. What matters first
is that decisions are taken where there is the power to
enforce them; that people should be involved in decisions
that affect their lives directly. The development of work
groups in ICI seems to offer a route towards this; the next
step, towards autonomous group working, is already being
taken. The result could be a form of contract which is open
and voluntary.

That this should be in tension with the over-arching needs
of the total organisation is not a serious criticism. We are all
individuals but live in small groups: small groups in communities, communities in cities which are parts of nations.
The tension is potentially fruitful, and to eliminate it in the
interests of consistency — in favour of either complete
centralisation or of complete decentralisation — may be

intellectually attractive, but it would lose the benefits of each extreme. The state has not withered away in Communist countries, as Lenin promised; nor, I guess, would management hierarchies disappear from democratically-run companies. The situation demands something less apocalyptic, more tuned in to this moment. This is where the changes I listed at the beginning of the chapter are important. They represent an uncoordinated, but nonetheless coherent, series of moves by companies towards meeting the needs of their employees. No political programme could be half so effective, nor so constructive.

17
Politics and Reality

The problems which ICI and the other companies I have mentioned have been tackling all have a strong family resemblance to the national problem of Britain's industrial relations, because they have their roots in the same shifts of power. And indeed, the progress of the 1971 Industrial Relations Act and of WSA were strikingly parallel. Or rather, the parallel is with MUPS: the contrast with WSA shows even more illuminating divergencies. The differences are glaring and do not need to be stressed, but should be stated to leave the parallels standing clear. Most important, ICI was acting to change a situation that was, to a far greater degree than can be true for a government, within its control. (The opposite is also true, of course, in the sense that no management can pass laws that are binding on employees.) The company is limited, finite; its activities internally are answerable to the dictates of a unified management structure. ICI's problems took, initially anyway, specific forms to which there could be specific answers — for example, in terms of wages structure.

Over the years, ICI had developed close relations with the signatory unions. The company is deeply experienced in the practical matters of industrial relations. A dialogue was therefore possible on a basis of understanding and a shared perception of some problems. All of this made it possible for the company to propose a cooperative approach to designing MUPS. Governments do not customarily invite the participation of people likely to be affected by their legislation. The resulting agreement (MUPS) was, for all its faults, a practical and workable package that offered a judicious balance of inducements to both sides. The Industrial Relations Bill included a number of sweeteners designed to achieve some sort of balance: among them, the right to belong to unions;

protection against unfair dismissal; access to company information. But, in consistency with Conservative dogma, these were mainly aimed to restore individual rights. In sum they comprised a thin coating of sugar on the basic intent of the bill, which was to reintroduce the Rule of Law into an area which was traditionally exempt: mainly by proposing registration of unions and setting up a National Industrial Relations Court with the power to fine.

The proposals were different, but both were attempts to bring about changes in complex social systems and each was introduced in a framework of assumed compliance. Designed at the centre, MUPS had the legitimacy of ICI's agreement with the signatory unions and the command system of the management to administer it; the 1971 Act had the authority of a democratically elected government behind it and to introduce it the awesome machinery of the legislative process. But these assumptions were inadequate. Both sets of proposals contained threats to the people whom they were meant to affect: in ICI the shopfloor workers, or rather their representatives, saw in MUPS 'five principles' an attempt to take away protections and safeguards that had taken generations to acquire; nationally, the unions were to be brought within the grasp of the legal system, exemption from which had been crucial to their survival. Both groups had the power to bring the attempts to a halt by simply refusing to abide by, on the one hand, an agreement and, on the other, a law.

It may have been scandalous and a threat to the basis of society but there was nothing to be done about it except talk about democratic government, the national interest, mandates and disruption. It was very painful and humiliating. But moral arguments (which these were) only have the force they are conceded and, in the end, submission to them has to be voluntary. A priest might be able to persuade an armed bandit to give himself up — if he were religious enough; even an ungodly bandit might have residual worries about shooting people that would predispose him to listen.* But it would

---

* I have lost count of the films that have ended with the priest and bandit — childhood friends and rivals as young men for the entrancing Dona Pepita, daughter of immensely wealthy *haciendisto* José Miguel — shooting it out with words on the sun-bleached slopes of a distant *arroyo* while the evil Cefe closes in with his uncouth *espadrilleros*.

need powerful arguments, especially if the bandit knew he would be hanged once the law got its hand on him. In the end, the law could always drop a bomb on him, and society would applaud. But you don't drop bombs on several million trade unionists. ICI's need for MUPS was not owned where the means for putting it into effect was owned, at the shopfloor; nor was the government's (nation's?) need for the solutions proposed in the 1971 Act owned by the people who had the power to oppose it. The Catch 22 of trade union legislation runs: If the government had possessed the power to make the Act work, it wouldn't have needed the Act. We could go further and say that the need for the solution was the signal that it was too late to oppose the problem. Social changes appear in disguise, like a new hand slipping into an old glove, and it is not until they grip that they are noticed. When they do, the automatic response is to seek a return to a comfortably familiar set of rules. In fact, ICI and the unions were proposing some new solutions, although the framework of introduction was traditionally 'managerial'. But the solutions proposed by the Conservative government, in effect, amounted to a return to an earlier, lawful order. In both cases, the method of introduction assumed the existence of power to enforce the solutions. And in both cases the power did not exist.

Once the opposition was encountered ICI had the huge advantage of being able to withdraw, lick its wounds, probe the reasons for rejection and test alternative routes. Out of the early period of naive learning came a deeper understanding of the obstacles and ways round them. The company was able to build these into its approach to the new agreement. One can only speculate on the lessons learned by the government from its failure. External evidence suggests that no new ways round were thought feasible, beyond increasing the sugar coating on the pill and screwing up the level of confrontation. The lesson that the problem of change included the originators of the solutions may have been too challenging to a government that had sought to impose unilaterally a solution by a return to authority. Nor is the legislative process able to adopt a more exploratory method of proceeding. It provides discrete solutions to discrete problems, hunting down the symptoms of social problems.

Laws are monuments to the problems of the past, the
markers of social change. When change is relatively slow,
which it has been, the process is adequate. But something
more experimental may be needed in times of rapid change.
That the solution may itself be a *process of seeking a solution*
is quite outside the scope of traditional lawmaking.

There is no sign that the new (1974) Labour government
has learned this lesson. At the time of writing, it is only
possible to be sure that the 1971 Act will be repealed – an
expected but hardly a constructive move – and that the
powers of the unions will be further strengthened. (More
workings of Catch 22: If they were weaker, there would be
no need to strengthen them.) This approach, if it is a fair
statement of the government's intentions, has the advantage
over the previous attempt of at least matching power
realities; the unions are not likely to oppose it. But it has two
weaknesses so grave as to vitiate the policies altogether.

However misguidedly, the Conservative policy was an
attempt to come to grips with industrial relations so anarchic
as to have become a tourist attraction. Nothing in its
successor's statements suggests that a solution is being
offered to this that is more constructive than ignoring it.
There are advantages to leaving complicated systems alone:
they are immensely resistant to any attempts to influence
them; changes often have unpredictable effects. Moreover, a
return to *status quo ante* favours Labour's most powerful
supporters: it is delivering to them the power to make their
peace with industry on their own terms. But as we have seen,
the power is not exercised from the central union organisations; it is exercised, without restraint, at the shopfloor. The
Conservatives made an attempt to bring this power back into
the system where it might be answerable to some broader,
more socially oriented objectives, although they did so by
accepting the convenient fiction that local were subject to
national organisations. By leaving it outside the larger system,
the Labour government seems to offer the prospect of this
power continuing to be exercised disruptively. By returning
old protections and exemptions to the unions, the government is making its solution more, and not less, difficult. For
the exemptions had grown, or been conceded, to meet a real
need: to offer protection for weak groups against the

unscrupulous and legalistic attacks of powerful employers. But that is no longer the situation. The balance of power has shifted, and with that change has gone justification for exemption from the rules that govern the rest of society.

Secondly, no less than the Conservatives, the present government appears to be responding to the radical challenge from a new situation by seeking a return to the past: the 1971 Act reeked of nostalgia for the stability of an authoritarian past; the present government's policies (what are visible of them) of a nostalgia for an age of proletarian innocence. The Labour government's moves seem more to be acts of piety than of imaginative government. Indeed, nothing could more clearly demonstrate the religious functions of the unions than their (and the Labour Party's) unquestioning pursuit of goals that have become items of dogma and of which the meaning has been lost in history — a political cargo cult. The irrelevance of the goals and the potential redundancy of the unions themselves emerge from the spontaneous growth of informal organisations that would not need to exist if the unions were serving their members' needs. The Labour Party's policies toward industrial relations are to this extent no less ill-judged than those of the Conservatives. But instead of leading back to unworkable solutions they seem to be leading back to solutions to problems that no longer exist.

No less than ICI and the signatory unions were when they launched MUPS, the political parties, unions and government departments are proposing solutions that are completely at odds with the new realities of a 'voluntary' society: a society in which people have the power, given by choice, to make important decisions about their lives and in which the capacity to coerce its members of the large organisations that make up the traditional power structure has been greatly diminished. Faced with this situation, ICI was able to adapt; the decisions about change were taken down to where the power (ownership of the means for change) was found, at the shopfloor; ICI disaggregated parts of the decision process. (The 'autonomous groups' at Norsk Hydro had control over *all* the decisions in their work area.) But such changes appear not to be within the power of the larger systems; or perhaps the need is not perceived. Instead, while preaching change, the actions of the main antagonists merely serve to confirm existing relationships. By attempting to return to an authoritarian stability, the Conservatives re-confirmed the ancient role of the unions. By giving the unions power without restraint to take a larger share of society's wealth, the Labour Party has confirmed the values of a materialist, consumer society. By restricting their role to negotiation over, or demands for, more money for their members, the unions shackle their members to the wheel of consumption, and cut them off from the possibility of other satisfactions more securely than admass could ever hope to. This is not to suggest that the rival groups collude. On the contrary, the struggle for advantage is bloody and unremitting. But the rules of the game are not questioned: that the purpose of the struggle is to obtain control of society's resources in order to increase their members' material well-being; that this can only be done on a zero-sum basis; and that the outcome will finally be decided in terms of the power that the groups can mobilise. It is certainly true that this accurately describes the rules of the game that society has played in the past — and played greatly to the advantage of the possessors of economic power and privilege. But it is not obvious that the same rules must apply in the new situation. And it does not seem likely that we can afford to continue to play by these rules.

More fundamental and, in a true sense, radical solutions are required. And these can only come from questioning some of the most basic assumptions of society: how the decisions that form it are to be made; what is its purpose or, if it is the 'good' of soceity, how that is to be defined.

But to these calls for a radical adjustment of the institutional arrangements of society, the existing institutions must be deaf. For if they have anything in common it is the wish to survive. Implacably opposed they may be, but their present form is determined by the web of relationships in which they exist and the assumptions underlying them. Challenge these, and their existence is called into question. It is in this way that revolutionaries are as steadfast in upholding the existing forms of society as the reactionaries they attack. For true revolution, for truly radical change, we shall have to look elsewhere — to some surprising places.

18

Steps to a New Social Contract

To say that an event is unexpected is often to say no more
than that something else would have been more expected. We
expect politicians to generate, or at any rate to be concerned
with, certain sorts of social change; we likewise expect
companies, who are often in the target area of their
attentions, to resist. The basic assumption of this stereotype
is that profits and workers' welfare are in competition. That
political parties and other institutions which exist to promote
reform are implicitly opposing the forces of change is
unexpected; that profit-seeking organisations are both more
efficient and more radical in devising ways of improving their
workers' welfare is doubly so; and that the efforts of these
organisations should serve as a model of change for the rest
of society stretches belief. But I believe these things to be
true.

If there is a paradox, it does not lie in the events
themselves, but in the dissonance between them and our
expectations. Because the changes brought about by agreements like WSA benefit people — and implicitly, although
more diffusely, the changes in the processes of productivity
bargaining — it is tempting to think of them as in some ways
'moral'. A company's pursuit of profit, and through that of
survival, is if not immoral certainly morally neutral, unmoral
perhaps. It seems paradoxical that an act without moral
intention should have moral effects. Yet, while there was a
significant moral (ethical) element in the WSA exercise, it is
self-evident that the enormous energy for change was not
drawn from that source: morality does not change and if it
had been enough, WSA or something like it would have
appeared half a century ago. The energy for the change came
from its hoped-for value in securing the company's commer-

cial survival — and there is nothing paradoxical or unexpected in a company's acting in its own interest.

By the same reasoning we ought not to expect this sort of innovation to emerge from political institutions whose survival is not being directly threatened. (On the contrary, the devolution of power and decision-making is a threat to centralised government.) Moreover, the energy for further change is low in organisations that have comfortably achieved their aims. The unions exist to oppose the power of the employers. But when they are in a position to bring down a government, as they did in 1974, and to dictate terms to its successor it is idle to pretend — what has been the main source of energy for union action — that they are any longer the underdogs. And when a group — a political party, for example — has substantially achieved the purpose for which it exists, the driving *necessity* for further change is diminished.

Necessity is the source of energy for change, and it is in necessity that the seemingly opposed forces of evolutionary and revolutionary change meet. They appear to be opposed because one is undirected and slow and the other direct, forceful and rapid. Evolution proceeds randomly, by trial and error, like a meandering stream, while revolution is a three-lane expressway, the expression of human will and the impatience of the intellect. Evolution appears to be the ally of conservatism and the guarantor of continuity, since it always builds on the past; revolution offers the promise of a clean start and is based on the axiom that the past is irrelevant. Evolution appeals to those who benefit from the existing system; revolution to those with no investment in it. But both are ways of proposing solutions to problems that arise in society. (The philosopher Karl Popper has said that living itself is a process of solving problems.) Seen in this light, the difference between evolution and revolution is to be found in the ways in which solutions are generated. Evolution proceeds by piecemeal changes at the margin; revolution offers solutions on a grand scale for complete systems. In an animal population, for example, mutations put up a range of random changes from which viable solutions to problems posed by the environment are selected and built into the biological design; in an unchanging environment, the animal represents a more and more complete solution to the problems of survival posed in its particular ecological niche. Social change, evolutionary or revolutionary, is immensely more rapid and powerful because of the capacity of human intelligence consciously to define problems and propose solutions to them. However, processes of 'natural' or 'generational' change are, as in biological evolution, piecemeal. Any of them may individually be random, but over time they are purposive: viable solutions are selected and built into the on-going organisation design — which slowly 'tracks' the moving problems posed by a continuously changing social environment (which is itself affected by the solutions). Evolutionary social change is purposive in this sense: the stream of evolution meanders, but it is always moving towards the sea. To the revolutionary consciousness, however, the process is wasteful and slow. Revolutions are built around ideologies which contain some implicit (or explicit) ideal of society. The sea (the ideal society) lies just over *that* mountain range — of established values, privilege, corruption, brutish opposition. Why endure the hesitations, the false starts and lengthy detours of a 'natural' process of change that may not even get there? Blast a channel through! And the revolutionary sets to with grim enthusiasm to dig a new channel towards his ideal. Intellectually it is difficult not to accept the logic of revolutionary change, if only because it is an intellectual response to social problems. Throughout history there cannot have been many thoughtful people, apart from those cynically benefiting from the existing state of affairs, who were not dissatisfied with society; nowadays, to reject the need for revolutionary change is, apparently, to ally one's self with the *status quo*. But there are more practical considerations. First, the complexity of society, the difficulty of foreseeing all the consequences of political decisions, the impossibility of controlling a process of change once it has been started, all mean that the deep-cut channel of revolution, no less than the broad, wandering stream of natural change, will be deflected from its course. Moreover, no ideology can offer a complete answer to the problems of society, both because they are complex and because they change with time — whereas it is in the nature of political ideology that it does not change, a feature it shares with other systems of morality. Secondly, the social and material cost of bringing about change by revolution is high and must be weighed, if it can be foreseen, against the benefits. If the end is always shifting it is hard to see how it can, except rarely, justify the means. It may not be possible to make an omelette without breaking eggs — but you must be surer than you probably can be that it is an omelette you want, and not more chickens.

Seen from a sufficiently Olympian viewpoint it is possible to make some sense of this paradox of revolution. Or rather, seen from the Popperian perspective — that change and growth, living itself, is a process of problem-solving — we can put revolution in place not in opposition to but in the context of evolution. If social evolution is distinguished from biological evolution in the way solutions to the problem of survival are generated, revolution stands at the farthest extreme of man's capacity consciously to generate his own solutions. But the need to test and select remains and, from a far enough distance, revolutions merge into the evolutionary process. The stream moves in wider sweeps towards a sea that is not, after all, just over the next range of mountains — or that perhaps recedes in a continually changing landscape.

It is for this reason that Karl Popper suggests* that the most successful societies will be those that are most efficient at solving their problems. Magee comments:

'. . . it has been widely believed . . . that rationality, logic, the scientific approach, call for a society which is centrally organised and planned and ordered as a whole. Popper has shown that this, besides being authoritarian, rests on a mistaken and superseded conception of science. Rationality, logic and the scientific approach all point to a society which is "open" and pluralistic, within which incompatible views are expressed and conflicting aims pursued; a society in which everyone is free to investigate problem-situations and to propose solutions; a society in which everyone is free to criticise the proposed solutions of others, most importantly those of the government . . . and above all a

---

* In *The Open Society and Its Enemies* (Routledge 1962). Bryan Magee's *Karl Popper* (Fontana 1973) is a helpful introduction to Popper's thought.

society in which the government's policies are changed in
the light of criticism . . .'

It is a society geared to means rather than ends, to the
process of problem-solving rather than to particular solutions,
to travelling rather than arriving. And this throws into
sharper relief the place in social change of ideologies and, the
corollary, the limitations on the effectiveness of political
parties that are committed to particular solutions. The
ideology becomes institutionalised, the institutions acquire a
commitment to it and to their own survival in ways that may
have nothing to do with the problem to which the ideology
originally provided a solution. The important insights of
Marx and Freud have long been absorbed into our thinking
— the evolutionary process of testing and selection has
ensured the survival of what is valuable in their work — but
the Marxists and Freudians still struggle manfully to fit
dissonant new information into systems of thought that
were, in their specific details, a response to particular
circumstances. For this reason, it is almost more important to
reject the old solutions when they cease to fit the circumstances than it is to accept the new (which can become no
more than an undiscriminating appetite for sensation). Yet an
organisation built around an ideology can hardly do this
without threatening its own existence. 'People in organisations tend, on the contrary, to turn a blind eye to evidence
that what they want is not happening, in spite of the fact
that such evidence is precisely what they ought to be looking
for. And of course the perpetual search for, and admission of,
error at even the organisational level is hardest of all in
authoritarian structures' (Magee). No less than the 'open
society', organisations should be built around problem-solving.

It is for this reason that the ends can never justify the
means — because the means *are* the ends. This has a deeper
meaning even than in terms of Popper's open society. It is
difficult — except, it seems, to the passionate revolutionary
— not to be aware of the arbitrariness of ends, the great
causes whose passing has left us no more enduring monument
than the suffering wrought in their names. (Which moves us
more, the aims of the Inquisition or the suffering of those
tortured to death to achieve them?) The ends pass, to be

replaced by other ends, and an indefinite commitment to suspend the rules of civilised society in order to secure them. But the means *are* ends, because society exists whatever the ends it is pursuing. What determines the nature of a society, therefore, is the nature not of its ends but of its means, the way in which its business is transacted between the organisations and the individuals that comprise it. Inhumanity, exploitation and injustice only become possible when there is a willingness to subordinate the means, the fine web of transactions that go to make up a society, to ends — any of which is, of course, rational and even moral within its own terms. It is the reverse of this, the willingness to subordinate sectional ends to the overriding morality of the means appropriate in a just (open) society, that comprises the new social contract.

This may be overstepping the bounds of Popper's open society — which he sees as not so much moral as efficient — but it is not (although it may appear to be) far removed from WSA, neither in the agreement itself nor in the way it arose. In Chapter 16 I said that the behavioural science-based programmes of change all have different, some of them highly manipulative, motives; but they all have in common a dispersion of decision-making in the organisation. It is a step towards a Popperian ideal, an organisation built around the process of problem-solving. Indeed, WSA was explicitly set up as a process rather than an end-product: the purpose of the agreement was to be a different way of dealing with organisation problems; the 'content' aspects, of re-organising work, were no more than a starting-point. The result, ideally, would be an organisation in which there would be a far greater freedom in proposing trial solutions, discussing and criticising them and, following this process, a greater possibility of change than there could have been in the traditionally authoritarian 'managerial' organisation. As will be apparent from the account of WSA, the result has been extremely gritty and uneven. The works are strung along a line between the extremes of failure and success. Moreover, at the time of writing (early 1974), the mood of cooperation even at the 'better' works is evaporating: the fragility of the 'spirit of WSA' and its dependence on the creation and maintenance of artificial conditions in the relatively enclosed world of the works is being demonstrated. The works are not enclosed. They exist in a social environment whose values and objectives have not been changed by WSA. And to maintain WSA working against the pressure of unchanged expectations will require constant vigilance.

But if one were looking for the first signs of major social change, it seems to me that this is precisely the way in which it would appear: spontaneous, widely scattered but broadly consistent attempts to adapt to some new but unacknowledged social reality; lights flickering in a darkened landscape. At first the innovations appear in disguise, usurping existing forms, and are received as responses made within the framework of existing assumptions to problems that are perceived and analysed in familiar terms: ICI's commercial crisis and the focus on the use of people within the company; IBM's need to keep ahead of, and render unattractive, unionisation; the problem posed by the assembly line in an advanced society like Sweden. The problems are felt in some form throughout industry in the developed world. For the most part the response has been traditional, and still is: to work within the bounds of the traditional wage/work bargain. Here and there, as in the companies I have mentioned, there has been a sharper and more imaginative response. But even this is seen in terms of existing forms: specifically, the behavioural science approach is deplored as 'soft' but reluctantly accepted by management (and eagerly watched for signs of failure) within a framework of values that may be paternalistic and manipulative; for the unions, it offers another way of increasing their members' wages, more managerial initiatives to bargain over. Meanwhile, the solution to the problem posed by the re-distributions of power within society gathers strength. As the relevance of the solution is seen, however it is misunderstood, it will be tried by more companies. The ideas of participation and devolution of power have already been picked up, experimentally and in a garbled form, by some politicians. They will not stop short of transforming society.

The millennium is not here, yet. Nor may it even be around the corner. But when it (or, more modestly, major social change) comes, this is how it will appear: not with a flash, a puff of smoke and a blast of trumpets; not by revolution but by small steps, small changes that go unrecognised when they occur. This book has been a celebration of one of those small steps. The old social contract based, *pace* Thomas Hobbes, on many kinds of coercion is breaking down as the balance of power in society is changing. A new social contract must emerge from this period of transition or society will be torn apart by the competing demands of powerful, uncontrollable minorities. WSA is a small step in the direction of that new social contract, a contract in which coercion will be replaced by ownership.

Appendices

Appendix Ia Chronology of Main Events in the Introduction of MUPS and WSA

1964	Oct	Rutherford Panel set up.
1965	Feb	Approval given by Main Board for approach to unions.
	May	Discussions started with union representatives.
	Oct	Signature and launch of MUPS; resistance develops at trial sites (Wilton, Billingham, Hillhouse) in next two weeks.
	Nov	Effective moratorium on trials; informal talks at Hillhouse; anti-MUPS resolution by AEU ICI Committee; Boilermakers withdraw; Warren House conferences start.
1966	Jan	Joint ICI/ETU meeting for Wilton stewards at Esher — other meetings refused; MUPS ideas begin to float around other works, notably around Gloucester.
	Mar	Visit of Tallon (AEU) to Hillhouse; local officers agree to enter talks.
	Summer	Deadlock at Wilton; discussions at Billingham.
	Sept	Need for new sites accepted at centre; Gloucester starts informally; AEU participates in joint discussions at Hillhouse.
	End year	Hillhouse programme under way; small progress at Billingham; deadlock at Wilton.
1967	May	New sites officially nominated; AEU reject agreement at Hillhouse.
	Oct	"Reds under bed" row at Wilton.
	Dec	Wilton productivity talks start.
1968	Jan	MUPS starts at Hillhouse, Gloucester, Stowmarket; other "new sites" under way; Northeast put on shelf.
	Apr	Ariel meeting.
	May	Productivity talks peter out at Wilton.
	June	First of management workshops.
	July	Chairman visits Wilton, sets up Callard Committee on return.
	Sept	Unions officially apply for renegotiation; consultation procedure starts.

	Dec	5% of workforce covered by MUPS. Discussions proceeding in 12 works.
1969	Apr	Draft WSA circulated for discussion.
	May	WSA agreed; introduction gets under way throughout Company.
	Sept	11,700 covered, ex-MUPS trials.
1970	Feb	Wilton management weathers strike, hope revives.
	Mar	14,600 covered by WSA.
	May	19,200 covered by WSA.
	July	O&M plans circulated at Wilton.
	Sept	T&G strike at Billingham against AEU obstruction; management agrees to go piecemeal. 24,900 workers covered.
	Dec	First general workers covered by agreement at Wilton; 49,000 workers (90%) covered by WSA.
1971	Apr	AEU District Committee agrees to take part in discussions at Wilton.

Appendix Ib (overleaf)
Defining Characteristics of Trial Sites

Site (and year in which introduction started)	No. of Works on Site [1]	No. of plants on Site [2]	Monthly Staff	Male Weekly Staff	Region	Year in which ICI opened factory	Technology and Main Products	Local Factors
Wilton (1965)	10	38	3,960	9,494	NE	1947	Mixed: predominantly large, continuous process units. Making bulk petro-chemicals. Anomaly of large, labour-intensive Terylene Works.	Wilton and Billingham are within 13 miles of each other, across Tees River. One of the oldest industrial areas in Britain. Mainly heavy industry — steel, mining, ship-building etc — much of it in decline. Long history of high, cyclical unemployment. Well-organised and powerful craft unions.
Billingham (1965)	11	68	3,719	10,546	NE	1926[3]	Large continuous process units; some anomalies (eg anhydrite mine). Main products fertilisers and petrochemicals.	
Hillhouse (1965)	2	17	696	2,402	NW	1945	Continuous processes in Mond Works: chlorine-based chemicals. Batch processes in Plastics Works.	Old-established region of mainly light industry. Relatively isolated Works. ICI locally dominant employer.

	1	4	593	2,190	SW	1960 (as BNS)	Assembly-line, mass production type of operation. Nylon fibres.	Centre of aircraft industry established during War which subsequently declined. No strong union tradition. Isolated from other main industrial centres.
Gloucester (1966)								
Castner-Kellner (1969)	1	32	567	2,285	NW	1926[3]	Wide range of activities and products, mainly in continuous process units.	Old industrial area. Draws manpower from Merseyside (docks: high unemployment) and Cheshire (salt and chemicals: stable employment). Unions active but not militant.

1. Works are relatively self-contained factories making a related group of products.
2. Each works contains several plants, which were the operational units of MUPS/WSA introduction. These figures are not comparable since the works – whose numbers they are – have used different criteria for calculating them. However, they are broadly indicative.
3. Taken over from precursor companies at ICI's formation.
4. Not organised into plants. Because of nature of process, divided into three large production sections, in which the jobs are broadly the same.

Appendix II
Salary Scales and Earnings Comparisons

Grades and annual basic salaries on the MUPS and WSA scales are given in Table 2 for 1965 to end 1973. Two figures are given for each grade, the first being the starting rate and the second the full rate applicable when working to MUPS/WSA standards — which is to say, allowing for a period of training and running-in on the job. The Grade 8 on the MUPS scale was changed to 'Specialist and Technical' Grade (S&T) with WSA.

Some idea of how Weekly Staff are distributed between grades can be gained from Table 1 (also, in more detail, from Figure 11, p.261). There are two peaks, at Grades 4 and 5 and Grade 7, corresponding to the main groups of general and crafts workers respectively. More interesting, the Table shows how earnings — for convenience, only for adult males — are built up on the basic salary rates. Apart from the obvious difference between general workers, a significant part of whose earnings comes from shift allowances, and craftsmen, mainly on day work, the table shows how much of the workers' earnings are still — nominally anyway — subject to fluctuation. ('Nominally' because, as with the bonus incentives the new salary scheme replaced, a large part of the fluctuating element is *de facto* consolidated.)

It is important to bear this structure of earnings in mind when considering the Table 3. This is intended to give some idea of the relationships between MUPS/WSA *rates* for Grades 4, 5 and 7) and *earnings* of general and crafts workers at Gloucester, Hillhouse and Billingham. The basic rates for the grades do not, of course, include overtime or shift and other allowances; nor do they correspond with any precision to the categories of general and crafts workers. No strict comparison is intended, or indeed possible. But the differences between general workers' earnings and the rates for Grades 4 and 5 (where three-quarters are assessed) and craft workers' earnings and the rates for Grade 7 (where nearly four-fifths are) provide information about a number of issues: the importance, and variability, of overtime; the effects of technology, for example in the high overtime of general workers at Gloucester; the systematic differences between different parts of the country, reflecting local pressures and management control (the predicament of the North-east would have emerged more clearly in data from Wilton, which was not available; at the time of introduction Billingham was in decline); and, lastly, some measure of the attractiveness of the MUPS and WSA offers. This last point is controversial and probably not very strong, since comparing rates with earnings is not — to say the least — comparing like with like. But it is probably right to say that the workers initially took a simple view of the offer, rather than a more complex view in which the place of overtime and other allowances was considered. It is more to the point still that the true relationship between earnings and rates is not to be discovered at the level of aggregation showed below — not in a Works and certainly not in a large site like Billingham. For it was only to a relatively small part of the population, particularly among crafts workers, the MUPS appeared to offer a substantial drop in earnings and this could only emerge in the sort of detailed job-by-job analysis described in the section on the Callard Committee. However, this perhaps underlines the importance of explicitness of making any such offer.

Table 1. Average weekly earnings 4th Qtr. 1973

			Included in Total				
WSA Grade	% of "Graded staff"	Standard Basic sal. June 73	Overtime pay	(% of total)	Shift & conditions allowance	(% of total)	Adult male total earnings
		£ p.w.			£ p.w.		
Basic	—	24.97	2.50	(9)	1.40	(5.3)	27.80
2	2	27.16	3.70	(10.9)	3.90	(11.4)	34.10
3	9	29.36	4.70	(12.7)	4.10	(11.1)	37.10
4	28	31.55	6.00	(14.6)	4.80	(11.6)	41.20
5	29	33.75	5.70	(12.5)	7.60	(16.6)	45.70
6	7	36.36	7.50	(15.4)	6.20	(12.7)	48.80
7	20	38.97	6.90	(14.7)	2.30	(4.9)	47.00
Set	5	41.58	6.60	(13.2)	2.70	(5.4)	49.90

Table 2. MUPS and WSA grades and salaries from 1965 (initial/full salary)

MUPS	BASIC	2	3	4	5	6	7	8
October 1965	650/ 720	695/ 770	745/ 825	790/ 880	840/ 935	890/ 990	940/1045	990/1100
June 1966	685/ 760	745/ 830	810/ 900	875/ 970	935/1040	1000/1110	1060/1180	1125/1250
September 1967	715/ 795	785/ 870	850/ 945	915/1015	980/1090	1050/1165	1115/1240	1170/1310
November 1968	765/ 850	835/ 930	910/1010	975/1085	1050/1165	1120/1245	1190/1325	1260/1400

WSA	BASIC	2	3	4	5	6	7	8
July 1969	800/ 850	900/ 950	1000/1050	1100/1150	1200/1250	1300/1350	1400/1450	1500/1550
March 1970	880/ 935	990/1045	1100/1155	1210/1265	1320/1375	1430/1485	1540/1595	1650/1705
May 1971	1073	1122/1183	1232/1293	1342/1403	1452/1513	1573/1634	1694/1755	1815/1876
June 1972	1202	1257/1312	1367/1422	1477/1532	1587/1642	1708/1773	1839/1904	1970/2035
June 11 1973	1302	1359/1416	1474/1531	1588/1645	1702/1760	1828/1896	1965/2032	2101/2168

Table 3

	Pay Rates[1] Grades 4	5	Earnings General Workers Gloucester	Hillhouse	Billingham[3] (Day)	(Shift)
(p/hr)			(Not in ICI)			
1965	42.3	45.0		44.9	37.9	45.0
1967	48.8	52.4	54.7	49.7	43.8	50.4
1969	55.3	60.1	71.2[2]	65.6[2]	52.9	61.3
1971	67.3	72.9	89.7	82.7	73.8[4]	88.9[4]
1972	73.5	78.7	96.0	91.6	82.8	97.8
1973	78.9	84.4	102.1	102.5	92.0	105.0

	Grade 7		Craft Workers Gloucester	Hillhouse	Billingham[5] (Day)	(Shift)
1965	50.2		(Not in ICI)	51.4	45.0	52.9
1967	59.6	54.1	55.0	50.4	57.9	
1969	69.7		70.4[2]	72.0[2]	64.6	77.9
1971	84.5		85.6	89.7	88.7[4]	105.0[4]
1972	91.3		93.7	98.1	97.4	112.0
1973	97.4		100.7	111.4	104.0	124.0

1. For a sample week in October of each year. This inevitably introduces a random element since the fluctuating element in earnings, mainly overtime, is not entirely seasonal and represents, particularly for crafts workers, the load of work commissioning new plant, crisis conditions, breakdowns and so on.
2. MUPS working fully introduced.
3. The Billingham earnings figures cover a much larger community than the other two, with a wide range of conditions.
4. WSA working substantially introduced.

Appendix III Text of MUPS

*Agreement for Trials of Proposals of Manpower Utilisation and
Payment Structure between Imperial Chemical Industries Limited and
The Trades Unions concerned.*
Sections B (*Employment Conditions*) and C (*Implementation of Trials*)
have been omitted.

INTRODUCTION

The Company and the Signatory Unions have a common aim in
achieving and maintaining the maximum efficiency in the Company's
operations and in ensuring that the payment structure and conditions
of employment are appropriate to the present day industrial situation.
In pursuance of these aims, it is common ground:-

1. That an employee must be employed to the best of his ability for
   as much of his time as possible
2. That an employee must be given the status and remuneration
   which will recognise the importance of his contribution to the
   Company and his acceptance of further responsibility.

The Company and the Signatory Unions have agreed that trials
should take place at certain works to verify their joint views on how
these aims may be achieved. Given the successful conclusion of these
trials, it is the intention to make a further agreement on the basis of
these proposals for implementation works by works throughout the
Company. It is recognised that any conditions of employment including
those which are unaffected for the trials may be reviewed when the
final agreement is under consideration.

The basis of the trials shall be as follows:-

UTILISATION OF MANPOWER
It is agreed that to achieve the optimum utilisation of manpower, the
following will be implemented:-

(a) Production operators with suitable training can use tools to carry
    out the less skilled craft tasks which form only a subsidiary part of
    their work.
(b) In appropriate circumstances tradesmen will be expected to
    operate plants.
(c) Tradesmen and general workers can be given general supervision by
    men of any background.

(*d*) Tradesmen can do work of other trades which forms a subsidiary part of the main job of their own trade, according to their availability at the time.

(*e*) Support work for tradesmen can be done by tradesmen, semi-skilled or general workers as is appropriate in the circumstances.

In implementing the above, the following must be taken into consideration:-

i.   A job should be looked at in its totality and if it is largely craft work then it will come within the craft sphere. Similarly if predominantly general work it will come within the general worker sphere.

ii.   That when manning jobs the aim must be to get the right man in the right job bearing in mind that men of high skill should carry out as little mundane work as is consistent with maximum efficiency.

iii.   Much retraining will be essential. To achieve this it will be necessary for all employees to cooperate with the Company in giving and receiving training.

iv.   That in order to achieve the maximum efficiency in the use of manpower, management will continue to use method study and work measurement and all other relevant techniques to establish and maintain correct manning levels at standard performance (in Work Study terms) or as near to it as the requirements of the job will allow.

v.   That working practices, however modified as a result of this agreement, can continue to change as other relevant circumstances change.

The method of implementing the principles *will be the subject of local discussions and agreements on each works or site*. After local agreement has been reached on changes in manning and practice, these must be established to the satisfaction of the Company and the Signatory Unions before the employment conditions in Section B of this agreement are applied.

Appendix IV Text of WSA

Weekly Staff Agreement 1969
Sections 4 (*Implementation*), 5 (*Disputes*) and 6 (*Variation or Termination*) have been omitted.

1. Aims
The purpose of this Agreement is to establish a means by which the Company and the Signatory Unions can achieve common aims. These are to develop and maintain maximum efficiency in the Company's operations by more effective use of people, plant and materials, and to improve the rewards, status, security and job satisfaction of employees.

Greater effectiveness and job satisfaction will be achieved by employing each person to the full extent of his time and capabilities and by eliminating unnecessary and wasteful practices, in production, maintenance, services or management activities. This state cannot be reached without the co-operation and involvement of all employees working with management and making their contribution towards decisions affecting working arrangements. For this reason improved security of employment, status and remuneration are needed to encourage employees to make their fullest contribution and to accept further personal responsibility and involvement.

In the future a continuous programme of examination and change will be required because technological and social change will continue. The benefits of such change carried out in the spirit of this Agreement will be that the Company will be able to provide a more secure and more rewarding future for its employees and be better able to maintain its competitive position in world markets.

2. Means of achieving the Aims
To achieve the above aims the following are of key importance.

Relationships in the Workplace
Management should accept that employees have knowledge and skills which can contribute to the knowledge and skills which can contribute to the solution of workplace problems. Employees should understand the management point of view, the needs of the business and also have regard to the interests of other groups of employees. Where alterations to working or manning practices seem necessary to improve plant

efficiency there should be joint discussion and agreement between those directly concerned.

Organisation of Work
Work should be organised so that each employee's time, skills and capacity to accept responsibility can be fully and effectively employed. The joint cooperation of employees and Management will be needed to achieve this. The outcome should be more interesting, more responsible and therefore more highly rewarded jobs. All re-arrangement of work will be consistent with the Company's policy of safe working.

ICI and the Signatory Trade Unions
The working links between the Company and the Signatory Unions and between the individual Signatory Unions should be strong and constructive at all levels.

Payment and other Conditions of Employment
The payment structure and other conditions of employment should be such as will encourage employees to accept further personal responsibility in their jobs and make their maximum contribution to the success of the business.

3. *Agreement*

The Company and the Signatory Unions agree to take steps to achieve their aims.

Accordingly the Company agrees.

(i) To provide improved status and conditions for employees covered by this Agreement. These are fully detailed in the booklet 'Salaries and Payment Conditions for Weekly Staff' which constitutes part of this Agreement.

The main provisions relate to

Annual salaries paid weekly (or as otherwise agreed) and based on a job assessment scheme for weekly staff jobs.
Stability of earnings when working and when absent sick.
Shift disturbance payments.
Overtime payments.
Special payments for certain circumstances, e.g. for call-out and working conditions.
(ii) To accept the principle that weekly staff employees should undertake to join an appropriate Signatory Union. Therefore from the date of implementation of the Agreement in a particular workplace, membership of an appropriate Signatory Union will be a condition of employment for all newly engaged adult weekly staff employees, which membership shall not be unreasonably

withheld by the Signatory Unions nationally or locally. The question of the extension of this practice to existing employees will involve consideration of Union spheres of influence and an Appeals procedure to safeguard the position of Unions and individuals. These will be matters for further discussion between the Company and the Signatory Unions.

(iii) That there will be no enforced redundancy at any location as a direct result of this Agreement and any necessary reductions in numbers of people will be achieved by normal turnover or other locally agreed means.

(iv) To provide training necessary to equip employees to cope with any changes which have been agreed.

(v) To ensure that its managers and supervisors are fully aware of the spirit behind the Agreement and are committed to achieving its aims.

In consideration of the above the Signatory Unions agree.

(i) That as a result of discussions between management, supervisors, employees and Union representatives it will be possible to identify, agree and implement more effective ways of carrying out work so that each employee can use his time, knowledge and skills to the best advantage.

Proposals for changes of this kind could lead to anxieties among employees. It is therefore emphasised that the underlying intention is not to make substantial changes in the general allocation of work between craft and non-craft employees but to eliminate wasteful practices wherever they occur and provide for sensible flexibilities in operations which will lead to improved productivity.

The Company and the Unions cannot in Company-level discussions state in detail the ways of improving productivity on a particular plant. It is an essential feature of the Agreement that proposals be worked out between the management and employees directly involved and agreed in discussion at each location.

To achieve the aims of the Agreement some flexibility will be required in existing working arrangements, viz: Some flexibility between craft employees to enable a craftsman in the course of his job to undertake some part of the work within his capacity, which hitherto had required other craftsmen of different crafts.

Some flexibility between craft and non-craft employees, for example to assist in the continuous working of plants and equipment. Such flexibilities will be introduced by agreement between local management and workplace representatives of the Signatory Unions concerned. They will not involve the more highly skilled part of the craftsman's job or the use of tools other than those necessary for simple operations.

Supervisory arrangements in which craft and non-craft employees can be given general, but not technical, supervision by men of any background.

The employment of craftsmen on plant operation should the requirement be indicated by the nature of the plant.

The undertaking of maintenance support work by craft or non-craft employees.

It is accepted that flexibility will take place only when mutual agreement has been reached between the local management and Signatory Unions concerned.

This means that
(a) Only the Signatory Unions in possession of the work can agree to any other trade or grade performing any of that work.

(b) Each Signatory Union reserves the right as to whether or not to accept any particular work from any other trade or grade.

(c) The flexibilities agreed in each workplace will be recorded in the Job Descriptions, jointly-signed copies of which will be given to Shop Stewards and Local Officials concerned.

(ii) That the results of work measurement and method study techniques appropriate for establishing and maintaining correct manning levels at standard performance (in work study terms) or as near to it as the requirements of the job will allow, need to be openly used and applied in each situation. This will ensure an unbiased, mutually agreed and systematic approach towards sharing responsibility, enlarging jobs, introducing flexibilities and making work more effective.

(iii) To devise methods of dealing locally with inter-union problems and to use their best endeavours to reach agreement on Signatory Unions spheres of influence.

(iv) That employees should co-operate with each other and with the Company in giving and receiving any necessary training.

(v) To develop that participation on the part of their full-time officials, shop stewards and members which will bring about successful implementation of the Agreement throughout the company.

Appendix V 'Stages of Introduction'

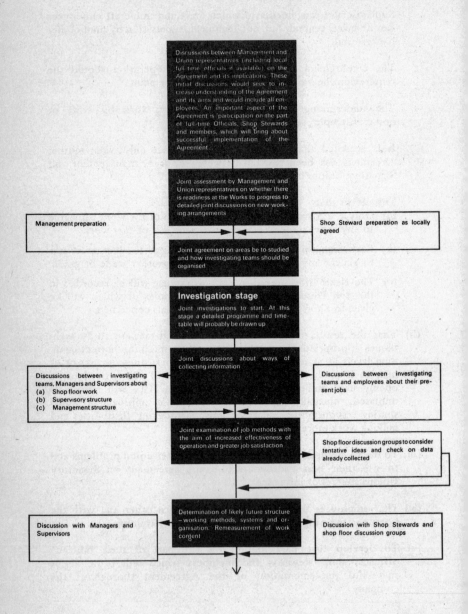

Discussions between Management and Union representatives (including local full-time officials if available) on the Agreement and its implications. These initial discussions would seek to increase understanding of the Agreement and its aims and would include all employees. An important aspect of the Agreement is participation on the part of full-time Officials, Shop Stewards and members, which will bring about successful implementation of the Agreement.

Joint assessment by Management and Union representatives on whether there is readiness at the Works to progress to detailed joint discussions on new working arrangements

Management preparation

Shop Steward preparation as locally agreed

Joint agreement on areas be to studied and how investigating teams should be organised

Investigation stage

Joint investigations to start. At this stage a detailed programme and time-table will probably be drawn up

Joint discussions about ways of collecting information

Discussions between investigating teams, Managers and Supervisors about
(a) Shop floor work
(b) Supervisory structure
(c) Management structure

Discussions between investigating teams and employees about their present jobs

Joint examination of job methods with the aim of increased effectiveness of operation and greater job satisfaction

Shop floor discussion groups to consider tentative ideas and check on data already collected

Determination of likely future structure – working methods, systems and organisation. Remeasurement of work content

Discussion with Managers and Supervisors

Discussion with Shop Stewards and shop floor discussion groups

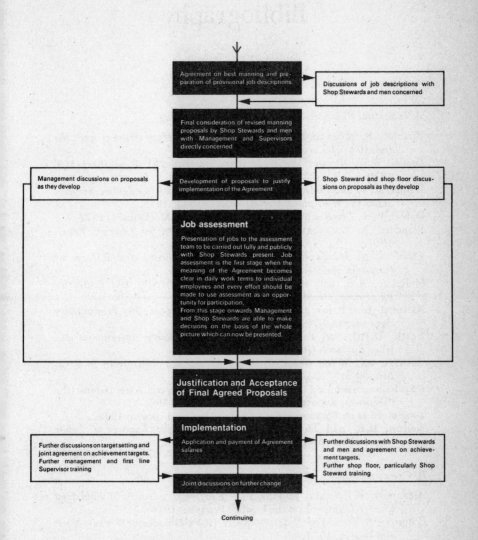

Agreement on best manning and preparation of provisional job descriptions

Discussions of job descriptions with Shop Stewards and men concerned

Final consideration of revised manning proposals by Shop Stewards and men with Management and Supervisors directly concerned

Management discussions on proposals as they develop

Development of proposals to justify implementation of the Agreement

Shop Steward and shop floor discussions on proposals as they develop

Job assessment

Presentation of jobs to the assessment team to be carried out fully and publicly with Shop Stewards present. Job assessment is the first stage when the meaning of the Agreement becomes clear in daily work terms to individual employees and every effort should be made to use assessment as an opportunity for participation.
From this stage onwards Management and Shop Stewards are able to make decisions on the basis of the whole picture which can now be presented.

Justification and Acceptance of Final Agreed Proposals

Implementation

Application and payment of Agreement salaries

Further discussions on target setting and joint agreement on achievement targets. Further management and first line Supervisor training

Further discussions with Shop Stewards and men and agreement on achievement targets.
Further shop floor, particularly Shop Steward training

Joint discussions on further change

Continuing

Bibliography

A. Industrial Relations and Productivity Bargaining

Blauner, R. *Alienation and Freedom: the Factory Worker and His Industry*. Chicago University, Press, 1964.

Daniel, W.W. *Beyond the Wage Work Bargain*. PEP Broadsheet 519, 1970.

Daniel, W.W. and McIntosh, N. *Incomes Policy and Collective Bargaining at the Workplace*. PEP Broadsheet 541, 1973.

Daniel, W.W. *The Right to Manage?* PEP Report, MacDonald, 1972.

Flanders, A. *Collective Bargaining: Prescription for Change*. Faber, 1967.

Flanders, A. *Management and Unions: the Theory and Reform of Industrial Relations*. Faber, 1970.

McKersie, R.B. and Hunter, L.C. *Pay, Productivity and Collective Bargaining*. MacMillan, 1973.

National Board for Prices and Incomes. Report 36, *Productivity Agreements*. HMSO, Cmnd. 3311, 1967.

North, D.T.B. and Buckingham, G.L. *Productivity Agreements and Wage Systems*. Gower Press, 1969.

Roberts, B.C. *Trade Union Government and Administration in Great Britain*. Bell, 1956.

Royal Commission on Trade Unions and Employers' Associations (the "Donovan Report"), HMSO Cmnd. 3623, 1968.

Towers, B. et al, *Bargaining for Change*. Allen and Unwin, 1973.

Walton, R.E. and McKersie, R.B. *A Behavioral Theory of Labor Negotiations*. McGraw-Hill, New York, 1965.

B. Cases and Studies of Organisational Change

Alexander, K.J.W. and Jenkins, C.L. *Fairfields: a Study of Industrial Change* (shipyard on the Clyde). Penguin, 1970.

Cotgrove, S. et al. *The Nylon Spinners* (ICI's Gloucester Works), Allen and Unwin, 1971.

Edwards, Sir R. and Roberts, R.D.V. *Status, Productivity and Fay: A Major Experiment* (Central Electricity Generating Board). MacMillan, 1971.

Flanders, A. *The Fawley Agreements: A Case Study of Management and Collective Bargaining* (Esso's Refinery). Faber, 1964.

Hill, P. *Towards a New Philosophy of Management* (Shell Refining UK). Gower, 1971.

Owen Smith, E. *Productivity Bargaining: A Case Study in the Steel Industry* (Steel Company of Wales). Pan, 1971.

Paul, W.J. and Robertson, K.B. *Job Enrichment and Employee Motivation* (experiments in ICI). Gower, 1971.

Philips, N.V. *Work Structuring: a Summary of Experiments at Philips 1963-68*. Philips, Eindhoven, 1969.

Roberts, C. and Wedderburn, D.E. *ICI and the Unions: the Place of Job Enrichment in the Weekly Staff Agreement*. Unpublished report for the TUC Social Sciences Working Party, Imperial College, 1973.

Thorsrud, E. 'A strategy for research and social change in industry: a report on the industrial democracy project in Norway, (the Norsk Hydro autonomous groups experiments). *Social Sciences information* 9(5), Social Sciences Council, Paris.

Wedderburn, D.E. and Crompton, R. *Workers' Attitudes and Technology* (studies in plants within one large site). Cambridge University Press, 1972.

C. Some new ideas about organising work (behavioural science, organisational development, job enrichment, participation, worker control . . .)

Argyle, M. *The Social Psychology of Work*. Penguin, 1972.

Argyris, C. *Integrating the Individual and the Organisation*. Wiley, New York, 1964.

Beckhard, R. *Organisation Development: Strategies and Models*. Addison Wesley, Reading, Mass, 1970.

Bennis, W. *Changing Organisations*. Wiley, New York, 1958.

Blumberg, P. *Industrial Democracy*: the Sociology of Participation. Constable, 1968.

Clegg, H.A. *A New Approach to Industrial Democracy*. Blackwell, 1960.

Emery, F.E. and Thorsrud, E. *Form and Content in Industrial Democracy*. Tavistock. 1969.

Fox, A. *A Sociology of Work in Industry*. Collier-Macmillan, 1971. *Man Mismanagement*. Hutchinson, 1974.

Goldthorpe, J.N. et al. *The Affluent Worker*. Three studies, Cambridge University Press, 1969, 1970 and 1971.

Guest, D. and Fatchett, D. *Worker Participation: Individual Control and Performance*. Institute of Personnel Management, London, 1974.

Herzberg, F. et al. *The Motivation to Work*. Wiley, New York, 1959.

Likert, R. *New Patterns of Management*. McGraw-Hill, New York, 1961.

Lippitt, R. et al. *The Dynamics of Planned Change*. Harcourt, Brace and World, 1958.

MacGregor, D. *The Human Side of Enterprise*, McGraw-Hill, New York, 1960.

Maslow, A. H. *Motivation and Personality*. Harper and Row, New York, 1970 (2nd end.).

Roberts, B.C. *Worker Participation and Management in Britain*. London School of Economics, 1972.

Roeber, R.J.C. *The Organisation in a Changing Environment*, Addison Wesley, Reading, Mass., 1973.

Roethlisberger, F. and Dixon, W.J. *Management and the Worker*. Wiley, New York, 1964.

Schein, E. *Process Consultation: Its Role in Organisation Development*. Addison Wesley, Reading, Mass., 1970.

Topham, A. and Coates, K. *Worker Control*. Panther, 1970.

Index

Numbers in italics refer to illustrations.